The Rise of *Homo sapiens*

dedication

To my wife, Patricia, who patiently listened to me read every chapter aloud on our walks.

Frederick L. Coolidge

To my wife Elizabeth and my children, Donald, Emily, and Rachel.

Thomas Wynn

The Rise of *Homo sapiens*

The Evolution of Modern Thinking

Frederick L. Coolidge and
Thomas Wynn

A John Wiley & Sons, Ltd., Publication

This edition first published 2009

© 2009 Frederick L. Coolidge and Thomas Wynn

Blackwell Publishing was acquired by John Wiley & Sons in February 2007. Blackwell's publishing program has been merged with Wiley's global Scientific, Technical, and Medical business to form Wiley-Blackwell.

Registered Office
John Wiley & Sons Ltd, The Atrium, Southern Gate, Chichester, West Sussex, PO19 8SQ, United Kingdom

Editorial Offices
350 Main Street, Malden, MA 02148-5020, USA
9600 Garsington Road, Oxford, OX4 2DQ, UK
The Atrium, Southern Gate, Chichester, West Sussex, PO19 8SQ, UK

For details of our global editorial offices, for customer services, and for information about how to apply for permission to reuse the copyright material in this book please see our website at www.wiley.com/wiley-blackwell.

The right of Frederick L. Coolidge and Thomas Wynn to be identified as the author of this work has been asserted in accordance with the Copyright, Designs and Patents Act 1988.

Wiley also publishes its books in a variety of electronic formats. Some content that appears in print may not be available in electronic books.

Designations used by companies to distinguish their products are often claimed as trademarks. All brand names and product names used in this book are trade names, service marks, trademarks or registered trademarks of their respective owners. The publisher is not associated with any product or vendor mentioned in this book. This publication is designed to provide accurate and authoritative information in regard to the subject matter covered. It is sold on the understanding that the publisher is not engaged in rendering professional services. If professional advice or other expert assistance is required, the services of a competent professional should be sought.

Library of Congress Cataloging-in-Publication Data
Coolidge, Frederick L. (Frederick Lawrence), 1948–
  The rise of homo sapiens : the evolution of modern thinking / Frederick L. Coolidge and Thomas Wynn.
       p. cm.
  Includes bibliographical references and index.
  ISBN 978–1–4051–52532 (hardcover : alk. paper) – ISBN 978–1–4051–52549 (pbk. : alk. paper)
  1. Human beings—Origin. 2. Human evolution. 3. Human evolution—Psychological aspects. 4. Human beings—Psychology. I. Wynn, Thomas, 1975– II. Title.
  GN281.C589 2009
  569.9′8—dc22

                                                         2008048192

A catalogue record for this book is available from the British Library.

Set in 10.5/13pt Minion by Graphicraft Limited, Hong Kong
Printed in Singapore by Fabulous Printers Pte Ltd

1   2009

Contents

Figures

1

Introduction

Sometime about 25,000 years ago the last true Neandertal died, and with him or her a way of life that had successfully coped with the European world for over 200,000 years. True, the climate was changing, slowly deteriorating into full glacial conditions so that by 20,000 years ago Europe was colder than it had been in over 100,000 years. And the animals were changing; woolly rhinoceros and mammoth were fewer and harder to find. But Neandertals had adapted to environmental changes before, including a long, harsh glacial period between 180,000 and 130,000 years ago. They were tough, and well adapted to the vagaries of their European habitat. Something else had changed. A new and different kind of people had moved into Europe, beginning about 40,000 years ago. From our Neandertal's perspective they would have appeared odd – tall and skinny with child-like, bulbous heads, small noses, and ridiculous pointy chins. They were comparatively weak compared to Neandertals but, like Neandertals, they were effective killers of animals, large and small. However, unlike Neandertals, they preferred to kill from afar rather than get in close to spear their prey from short range. There were other differences that would have puzzled Neandertals: these people wore ornaments on their clothes and bodies and probably sat around their fires late into the night talking. They also crawled down into dark caverns and painted the walls with images of real and imagined creatures. For several thousand years these people shared the European continent with Neandertals, but eventually the Neandertals disappeared. This fate was shared by other humans when they, too, encountered these new people, who were, as the reader has no doubt deduced, modern humans.

Modern humans evolved in Africa, and beginning sometime after 70,000 years ago they began to leave their natal continent to colonize the habitable world. By 40,000 years ago, perhaps even earlier, they had colonized the island continent of Australia, a feat that required that they sail over the horizon, in boats, to a place that they could not directly see, accompanied by their mates, children, and dogs. By 15,000 years ago they had achieved an equally remarkable journey: they had sailed across the Pacific Arctic to colonize the continents of North and South America. No previous human had ever migrated so far, so fast. Whenever they encountered more archaic humans, in Asia and in Europe, the more archaic forms eventually disappeared, leaving *Homo sapiens* in sole possession of the planet.

What powered the success of these first modern humans? It was not technology; their stone tools were little different from those of Neandertals and other archaic humans. It was not a more powerful physique (they were actually rather weak), or a larger size, or a more efficient digestion, or indeed anything about their bodies. It was something about their minds, an ability that they possessed but that their cousins did not.

Executive Functions of the Frontal Lobes: A New Perspective on an Old Story

On September 13, 1848, an apparently responsible, capable, and virile 25-year-old foreman of a railroad construction crew, named Phineas Gage, accidentally dropped a $13^1/_4$-pound iron tamping rod on a dynamite charge. The resulting explosion drove the rod through the left side of his face and out the top of the frontal portion of his cranium. He was taken to his nearby hotel, which was to serve as his hospital room until 32 days later, when he was able to leave his bed. At this point, people noted that Phineas was eating well, sleeping well, and his long-term memories appeared to be intact. Seventy-four days after the accident, Phineas was able to return to his home 30 miles away. But there were discernible differences in Phineas's behavior, not related to his health, general intelligence, or memory. The original contractors who had hired him considered the "change in his mind" so great that they refused to rehire him. Phineas told his attending physician, J. M. Harlow (1868), that he could not decide whether to work or to travel. There were reports that Phineas was roaming the streets, purchasing items without his usual concern about price. About this same time, Harlow noted that Phineas's mind seemed "childish" and that he would make plans, change them capriciously, and then abandon them quickly. More importantly, Harlow wrote:

Previous to his injury, though untrained in the schools, he possessed a well-balanced mind, and was looked upon by those who knew him as a shrewd, smart business man, very energetic and persistent in executing all his plans of operation. In this regard his mind was so radically changed, so decidedly that his friends and acquaintances said he was "no longer Gage." (p. 340)

In the psychological literature, the quote "no longer Gage" has more often become associated with Phineas's personality changes: his postmorbid use of profanity as well as depression, irritability, and capriciousness. Clearly, though, it seems that Harlow was associating Phineas's most important change to the loss of his once shrewd business acumen and his former ability in "executing all of his plans of operation." It must have been these latter abilities that originally made him valuable as a foreman. Significantly, Harlow's description may have been the first in the written literature for the frontal lobe metaphor: that the frontal lobes serve as a kind of executive that makes decisions, forms goals, devises strategies for attaining these goals, plans, organizes, and changes and devises new strategies when initial plans fail.

This executive functions model has been developed by a scientific discipline known as neuropsychology. This field provides explanations for brain and behavior relationships based on studies of brain-damaged patients, clinical populations with suspected brain dysfunction, and healthy people. Tests and measurements on the latter group help to define what normal or average functioning is so that behavior that deviates from standard functioning can be better defined. Neuropsychology is also broadly concerned with how the brain and its parts function and in identifying the symptoms of dysfunction.

One of the most prominent neuropsychologists of modern times was Russian Alexander Luria (1966), who wrote extensively about these executive functions of the frontal lobes. Luria noted that patients with frontal lobe damage frequently had their speech, motor abilities, and sensations intact, yet their complex psychological activities were tremendously impaired. He observed that they were often unable to carry out complex, purposive, and goal-directed actions. Furthermore, he found that they could not accurately evaluate the success or failure of their behaviors, especially in terms of using the information to change their future behavior. Luria found that these patients were unconcerned with their failures, and were hesitant, indecisive, and indifferent to the loss of their critical awareness of their own behaviors. Lezak (1982), a contemporary

American neuropsychologist, wrote that the executive functions of the frontal lobes were:

> the heart of all socially useful, personally enhancing, constructive, and creative abilities. Impairment or loss of these functions compromises a person's capacity to maintain an independent, constructively self-serving, and socially productive life no matter how well he can see and hear, walk and talk, and perform tests. (p. 281)

Welsh and Pennington (1988) defined executive functions in a neuropsychological perspective as the ability to maintain an appropriate problem-solving set for the attainment of a future goal. Pennington and Ozonoff (1996) view the domain of executive functions as distinct from cognitive domains such as sensation, perception, language, working memory, and long-term memory. Also, they see it as overlapping with such domains as attention, reasoning, and problem-solving "but not perfectly." (p. 54). They also add interference control, inhibition, and integration across space and time as other aspects of executive function. Their central view of executive function is a:

> context-specific action selection, especially in the face of strongly competing, but context-inappropriate, responses. Another central idea is maximal constraint satisfaction in action selection, which requires the integration of constraints from a variety of other domains, such as perception, memory, affect, and motivation. Hence, much complex behavior requires executive function, especially much human social behavior. (p. 54)

The ability to integrate across space and time or sequential memory function, is, no doubt, another salient feature of the executive functions. Successful planning for goal attainment would require the ability to sequence a series of activities in their proper order. Current neuropsychological assessment of executive functions invariably includes measures of planning, sequential memory, and temporal order memory (e.g., Lezak, 1995). It is also important to note that the frontal lobes have greater interconnectivity to subcortical regions of the brain than any other lobes of the cortex. The frontal lobes have extensive and reciprocal connections to the thalamus, basal ganglia, limbic system, and also posterior portions of the cortex (e.g., Bechara, Damasio, Damasio, and Lee, 1999; Furster, 1979; Luria, 1973; Gazzaniga, Ivry, and Mangun, 2002).

More recently, Goldberg (2002), who trained with Luria, claimed the development of the frontal lobes and its executive functions were the hallmark feature of the development of modern civilized behavior. In fact, he viewed the frontal lobes as the most "human" aspect of the brain. Not only, in Goldberg's opinion, do the frontal lobes conduct complex mental processes but they also appear to make our social and ethical judgments as well. Goldberg offered numerous pieces of evidence demonstrating how damage to the frontal lobe and its executive functions often results in chaotic, criminal, and antisocial behaviors.

Two Leaps in Cognition

Human cognitive abilities undoubtedly have a very long evolutionary history covering tens of millions of years. For most of this development, our ancestors were unremarkable in their cognitive abilities; as we shall see, they were just a group of bipedal African apes. But somewhere along the line they acquired cognitive abilities that set them clearly apart from their primate cousins. The fossil and archeological evidence suggests that there were two periods marked by especially significant cognitive developments, the first about 1.5 million years ago, and the second only about 100,000 years ago. We believe that the first major leap in cognition accompanied the evolution of an early member of our genus, *Homo erectus*, who developed a very different way of life that included movement away from the relative safety of wooded habitats, and expansion into a variety of new habitats. Within a relatively short evolutionary period (given the complete primate evolutionary history of over 50 million years) of less than half a million years, *Homo erectus* developed a dramatically new adaptation that included developments in spatial cognition and perhaps social cognition linked to changes in social life and landscape use. We think that this first leap in cognition may have been facilitated by physiological changes in sleep patterns tied to ground sleep.

Our second proposed leap in cognition led to completely modern thinking and occurred sometime between 100,000 and 40,000 years ago. In the archeological record this leap is even more dramatic than the first, and includes evidence for personal ornaments, art, elaborate ritual burials, complex multi-component technologies, and scheduled hunting and gathering organized months and years in advance. To explain this leap, we propose that a neural mutation occurred that led to a reorganization of the brain that enabled modern executive functions; specifically, we suggest an enhancement of working memory capacity, a cognitive ability originally defined by experimental psychologist Alan Baddeley (Baddeley and Hitch, 1974; Baddeley, 2001), and which has received voluminous experimental support over the past quarter-century.

This Book

And thus we return to the purpose of this book: an explication of the origins and evolution of modern thinking. We are not the first to tackle this problem; 17 years ago cognitive neuroscientist Merlin Donald (1991) wrote a provocative, neuropsychologically informed discussion in his *Origins of the Modern Mind*, and 10 years ago the archeologist Steven Mithen (1996) published a similarly provocative account in his *Prehistory of the Mind*. Also in 1996, psychologist William Noble and archeologist Iain Davidson published *Human Evolution, Language and Mind: A Psychological and Archeological Enquiry*. These books covered much the same ground that we intend to cover (and they took the best titles!), so it is reasonable to ask what justification there is for yet another book. First, there have been 10 to 20 years of additional research providing a wealth of new information. This is especially true in the area of neuropsychology and neuroanatomy; neuroscientists are finally beginning to understand how the brain works. The paleoanthropological picture is also clearer, enhanced by evidence from modern genetics, and new fossil and archeological finds. Second, our approach is rather different from earlier approaches in that it does not focus on language as the key to the modern mind, although we will address its role. Instead, our book focuses on a different component that we feel is equally important – the executive reasoning ability lost by Phineas Gage in such a spectacular fashion. Third, our book is co-authored by a psychologist and an archeologist. We have first-hand experience with trying to understand the peculiarities of one another's disciplines. We have found that what may seem obvious to one of us, may be a mystery to the other. This has sobered us to the task of writing a book on cognitive evolution that is both empirically based and accessible.

The book will begin with an introduction to the brain; we are both reductionists in agreeing that the brain is the source of an individual's thinking, and the logical starting place for any discussion of cognitive evolution. We will follow this with a brief discussion of brain evolution, and the methods of scientific investigation upon which the remainder of the book rests. Our actual documentation of human cognitive evolution will begin with non-human primates, after which we trace cognitive developments from early hominins through the final emergence of the modern mind.

2

The Brain

The purpose of this chapter will be to give the reader a solid understanding of the evolution and development of the brain and its functions. The study of the brain has ancient roots. Strong physical evidence of brain-behavior investigations comes from the process of trepanation, the intentional boring of a hole in the skull of a living person. Trepanned European skulls have been found dating back over 10,000 years and some 3,000-year-old trepanned South American skulls have also been discovered. The margins of the holes in many trepanned skulls indicate that the individual survived the ordeal, suggesting that trepanation was a carefully performed procedure. Because the first written records in many of the great early civilizations attached spiritual or demonic associations to abnormal behavior and the brain, it has been suggested that trepanation may have allowed the demons or evil spirits to escape. It is also possible that trepanation may have been used to treat headaches, epilepsy, or closed head injuries.

The earliest written evidence of investigations into the relationship between the brain and behavior comes from ancient Egyptians through hieroglyphics written on papyric paper as far back as 3,000 BC. These writings are amazingly advanced for their time. Some of the most valuable early Egyptian knowledge about the brain comes from the Edwin Smith surgical papyrus. The origins of the papyrus itself are largely a mystery. It was apparently buried with its last owner in about 1650 BC and plundered by nineteenth-century grave robbers. It was not fully translated until 1930 by University of Chicago Professor James Henry Breasted, who determined that it was a copy of a much earlier document that dated back another thousand years (about 2700 BC) to the age of the great pyramids. The translations of discoveries in the manuscript are breathtaking; the word "brain" was used for the first time in known human writings, the convolutions of the cortex (upper part of the brain) are likened to corrugations on metal slag, the meninges (thin, but tough, membranes covering the brain and enclosing the cerebro-spinal fluid that nourishes the brain) are described, and the behavioral results of brain injuries are given, with reference to the side of the head that was injured and its effects upon the limbs. The papyrus showed that the Egyptians were well advanced in the science of medicine and surgery, even in the oldest kingdoms of Egypt.

The manuscript reports a series of medical cases. In one vivid description, the attending physician describes the first recorded case of what would come to be known as Broca's (a famous neurologist of the 1800s) aphasia. Aphasia is a speech or language disorder. In this particular case, the patient appears to be able to understand the physician, because the physician deemed it appropriate to inquire about the patient's malady. But the papyrus reads that the patient was speechless or voiceless yet he cried and wiped his tears during the questioning. Although there are now known to be many types of aphasia, Broca's aphasia is diagnosed when a patient has lost the ability to speak, although understanding and comprehension are spared. Frequently, Broca's aphasic patients become depressed, perhaps because speech comprehension allows them a fuller understanding of their disability. It is also curious that the physician noted that the patient wiped away his tears like a child might, and the physician noted that the patient "knows not that he does so." This addition does cast some doubt on the previous diagnosis. Were the patient's tears in response to the disability or were they random? Was the hand movement an automatic gesture? Did the physician inquire about the hand movements and, because the patient could not explain, did the physician conclude that there was limited awareness, like that of a child?

In another case within the manuscript, the physician noted that the patient's brain injury affected his body and limbs. In this case, the patient's skull had been shattered like an egg shell, although there was no specific external wound. The physician noted: "swelling protruding on the outside of that smash which is in his skull, while his eye is askew because of it; (and) he walks shuffling with his sole on the side of him having that injury which is in his skull."

This physician had begun to detect the phenomenon of localization, that is, linking specific parts of the brain to particular functions. In this case, however, the surgeon had probably been misled by the *contra coup effect*, where a blow to one side of the head propels the brain inside the skull to hit the opposite side of the skull (away from the injury site) with great force and, many times, the *contra coup* site exhibits greater dysfunction than the actual site where the skull was initially injured. Because it is now known that the right side of the body is controlled by the left hemisphere of the brain, and vice versa, the surgeon may have erroneously concluded same-side brain injuries resulted in same-side of the body paralysis.

Despite some very obvious mistakes by these ancient surgeons, the Edwin Smith papyrus stands as a monument to the beginnings of brain-behavior relationships no less than do the great pyramids or the Sphinx for archeologists. All of the previously noted contributions were remarkably sophisticated, particularly in light of how much was lost, forgotten, or misunderstood over the next 5,000 years.

Ontogeny of the Brain

The human brain develops rapidly and is visible within only three weeks of an egg's fertilization. There are four guiding principles in the brain's development: cell proliferation, cell migration, cell differentiation, and cell death (apoptosis – pronounced *a-poe-toe-sis*). As the fertilized egg divides itself repeatedly (cell proliferation), it begins to form a shape like a very small fried egg. This thickening in the center is called the embryonic disk. By the third week, a groove begins to develop along the length of the disk, and it forms the neural groove, which is the beginning of the spinal cord and brain. As the cells proliferate, they are genetically programmed to migrate to specific locations and subsequently develop specific forms (cytoarchitecture) and specific functions (cell differentiation). After the third week, the neural groove begins to close up and form the neural tube with holes that will eventually form the ventricles (spaces) of the brain. By the seventh week, the neural cells have proliferated, migrated, and differentiated enough to be clearly recognized as a brain (cerebrum or cortex), subcortex (below the cerebrum), and spinal cord structures.

Cell proliferation is mostly complete by about the twentieth week. Neural migration continues until about the twenty-ninth week. Cell differentiation and maturation (growth of axons and dendrites) continues until after birth. Surprisingly, however, both the neurons (brain cells) and its synapses begin a very precipitous decline after about one year of age and continue until about 10 years of age! This process is called apoptosis or programmed cell death. It is estimated that as many as 50 percent of the brain's neurons will die during this period and up to 66 percent of the established synapses will be eliminated. Thus, the final form of the brain is created much more like a sculpture than the creation of a building, with unnecessary pieces progressively removed over time.

The cerebral hemispheres

The most obvious visual landmark in a human brain is its two cerebral hemispheres, which together are also referred to as the cortex. The left hemisphere is actually slightly bigger than the right, both in humans and great apes (like chimpanzees and gorillas), and in humans the potential for each hemisphere is different: the left hemisphere in humans will be devoted to the processing of language and the right hemisphere will be concerned with non-verbal and visual-spatial functions, although the two hemispheres interact on nearly all of these functions. After puberty, the two hemispheres will lose much of the plasticity (ability to handle different functions) that enabled them to take over each other's functions. Thus, if a left hemispherectomy (*-ectomy* means *removal*) was performed on a post-pubertal human, that person would be essentially mute with very limited language abilities. Before puberty the right hemisphere could learn some but not all language functions, but after puberty this plasticity would be lost.

The two hemispheres are separated by a major fissure running from anterior (front) to posterior (back). They communicate rapidly by means of a commissure (communicative connective tissue) called the corpus callosum. The corpus callosum lies beneath the dorsal (top) surface of the cortex. Because of this location, the corpus callosum is considered a subcortical structure.

The interior of the brain is separated by four major ventricles, which are filled with cerebrospinal fluid that nourishes the brain with nutrients like oxygen. The cerebrospinal fluid is created by the brain surfaces forming the ventricles, and it flows like a river over the interior surfaces and then is reabsorbed. Its flow is aided by tiny cilia lining the ventricles. If the flow is blocked, the resulting syndrome is hydrocephalus (*hydro* meaning *water*, and *cephalus* meaning *brain*), which causes brain malformation and growth failure if it occurs in infants. The shunting or siphoning of this fluid reduces the cerebrospinal fluid pressure and ameliorates the hydrocephalic condition.

The cortical surface of a living brain is actually reddish-brown in color. Its surface is gray in a laboratory or dead brain, hence, the name *gray matter*. Beneath the surface of the cortex, it is substantially white because the myelin sheath lining the axons of brain neurons is made up of fatty matter, hence, the name *white matter*. The fat speeds up the transmission of nerve impulses. Thus, demyelinating diseases, such as multiple sclerosis, interfere with motor activity, and motor slowing is its major initial symptom.

Lobes of the cortex

The frontal lobes: motor cortex

The frontal lobes are the largest most clearly demarcated of all of the lobes of the brain. Their inferior (lower) convolutions are bordered by the lateral or Sylvian fissure (a deep indentation). Their posterior convolutions, which border the parietal lobes, are formed by the central sulcus (a less deep indentation than a fissure). See figure 2.1 for more details.

One of the first models of brain function was developed by two German physiologists, Fritsch and Hitzig, in 1870. This model, based upon their work with dogs, is still roughly used today. It noted that the area just anterior to the central sulcus appeared devoted to motor movements, and thus was labeled motor cortex. The area posterior to the central sulcus (thus, in the parietal lobes) was called sensory or somatosensory cortex. When stimulated, the other areas were "quiet," so they became known as

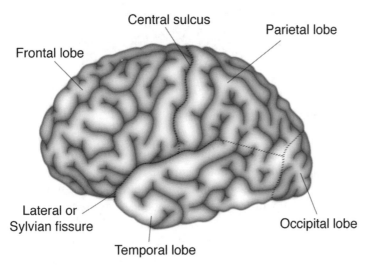

Figure 2.1   Lobes of the cerebral cortex (lateral view)

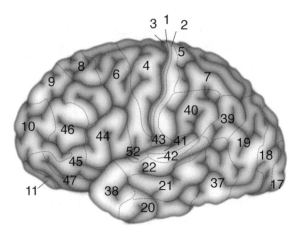

Figure 2.2a   Brodmann's areas (lateral view)

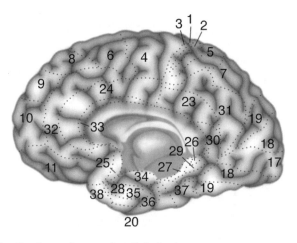

Figure 2.2b   Brodmann's areas (medial view)

association cortex and were assumed to support the motor and sensory cortex. In 1909, another German neuroanatomist, Korbinian Brodmann, classified the brain into 52 regions, roughly based on presumed cell type and function. Brodmann's system is also still in use today, although his numbering system proceeds mostly on what region he chose next to study, rather than related functions. See figure 2.2 for Brodmann's areas.

One of the most recent provocative and influential brain-function models was proposed by Canadian neurologist MacLean in 1971. Although now thought to be of limited usefulness, he proposed a triune evolutionary development of the brain: (1) a reptilian brain which humans share with all reptiles, which includes the brain stem (whose function is the control of basic life systems such as heart rate, respiration, and blood pressure), and the cerebellum (controlling fine motor coordination and also playing some role in cognitive processes); (2) a mammalian brain, which includes the limbic system (controlling memory and emotions); and (3) the neo-mammalian brain with its elaborate neocortex.

The regions of the brain are now currently referred to by multiple systems: Brodmann's areas (e.g., Brodmann's area 44 or BA 44), presumed function (e.g., primary visual cortex), cortical location (e.g., dorsolateral prefrontal cortex), convolution location (e.g., superior temporal gyrus), or even the gross anatomical name (e.g., cingulate cortex or lunate sulcus).

Interestingly, because only the posterior portions of the frontal lobes were clearly shown to have a demonstrated function, the frontal lobes were often referred to as the "silent lobes." In chapter 3, we shall show that the evolution of the frontal lobes may have played a major role in the overall initial beginning of modern thinking, especially in the early ascendancy of mammals versus reptiles.

In the 1860s, Paul Broca, a French neurologist, identified the left hemi-sphere as important to language. At that time, his claim went against the current wisdom, which was that there were no specific locations of the brain with specific functions. That thinking persisted from the early 1800s onwards because Franz Gall, an Austrian neurologist, had mistakenly promoted *phrenology*, the idea that bumps on the surface of the skull had very specific functions like a love of God and psychopathic tendencies. Broca, based on his observations of many left-hemisphere-damaged patients, pro-posed that the ability to speak was a left-hemisphere function. Today, an area of the left hemisphere (BA 44 and 45) is labeled *Broca's area*, and it is thought that damage to this area results in a specific neuropsycho-logical syndrome known as *Broca's aphasia*, as noted earlier, which refers to a condition where a patient has retained the ability to understand spoken language but cannot speak. The motor cortex itself is associated with BA 4. BA 6 is considered premotor cortex.

Frontal lobes: prefrontal cortex
Research for the past four decades has demonstrated the importance of the area anterior to the motor cortex, and it has demonstrated as well how not only is this area far from silent but it may indeed be the most important

area of the brain for the overall control and direction of behavior. The general area is known as the prefrontal cortex, and it is commonly divided up into the dorsolateral prefrontal cortex (BA 6, 8, 9, 10, 46), orbitofrontal prefrontal cortex (BA 11, 45, 47 and inferior portions of 24 and 32), and ventromedial prefrontal cortex (BA 44). It is now known that the prefrontal cortex is critical to forming both short- and long-term goals and forming plans and strategies for attaining these goals. Interestingly, nearly four centuries ago, the French philosopher, mathematician, and scientist Descartes searched for a "center" of the brain. Ironically, he decided on the pineal gland because it did not appear bilaterally (on both sides) in the two hemispheres. Although he was wrong, modern brain researchers such as Goldman-Rakic (personal communication, 2002) have pondered whether the prefrontal cortex could be considered the center of the brain for its role in attention and choice in human and animal behavior. The dorsolateral prefrontal circuit is generally associated with classic executive functions such as selective attention in spite of interference, organizing tasks in space and time, selective inhibition, response preparation, goal-attainment, planning, and flexibility. The orbitofrontal prefrontal region is more closely connected to the limbic system and has been shown to be connected with the processing of emotions and the regulation and decision-making associated with social behavior and social interactions. The more central part of the orbitofrontal cortex is called the ventrolateral prefrontal cortex (and towards the middle of the brain, this region is called the ventromedial prefrontal cortex), and we will discuss its functions again in chapter 3. See figure 2.3.

With regard to social and emotional behavior, it has been recognized for over 150 years that damage to the frontal lobes can result in profound changes to one's personality. Beginning with the tragic story of Phineas Gage in 1848, which was recounted in chapter 1, it became an intentional brain operation in the mid-twentieth century, a frontal lobotomy (*-otomy* means severing connections). Frontal lobotomies actually involved severing connections within each frontal lobe (i.e., left and right frontal lobes) rather than severing the connections between the two frontal lobes. Frontal lobotomies were performed (and are still performed) mostly on violent or highly anxious patients whose behavior could not be controlled by medications. The result of a frontal lobotomy leaves the patient much less violent, much less anxious, and profoundly apathetic. Such patients have no change in their IQ or memory functions, but they become much less spontaneous, humorless, and blasé. The operation became almost faddish

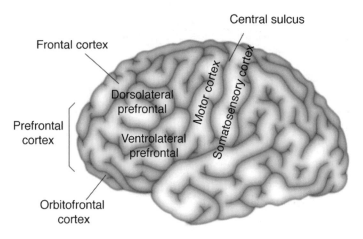

Figure 2.3 Frontal and prefrontal, motor and somatosensory cortices (lateral view)

in mental hospitals in the 1950s and early 1960s. However, as soon as the serious consequences of the operation became well known and as major new antipsychotic drugs became available, it was reserved for only the most difficult cases (with permission, of course, from the patients and their families).

In the movie *One Flew over the Cuckoo's Nest*, after his frontal lobotomy, Randle McMurphy was smothered to death by Chief Bromden. The Chief knew that McMurphy's boisterous, playful, and highly spontaneous personality would be forever lost because of the lobotomy.

However, there are some dramatically different responses than apathy to frontal lobe damage (not necessarily frontal lobotomies). One of these syndromes is known as the *pseudopsychopathic syndrome*. In these cases, the patients act in antisocial ways such as unbridled impulsiveness, hypersexuality, excessive and harmful gambling, and social inappropriateness such as cursing and exposing one's self.

Frontal lobes: cingulate cortex
Inferior to the prefrontal cortex and running anterior to posterior in the medial (middle) portions of the inferior cortex is the cingulate cortex or cingulate gyrus (BA 23, 24, and also 26, 29, 30, 31, 32). The anterior portion of the cingulate cortex (BA 24) is known to be important to attention and selection of appropriate stimuli. It appears to be responsible for one's choice

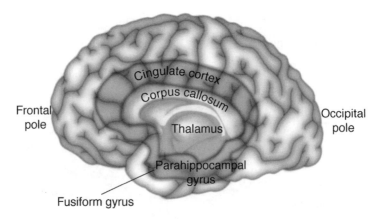

Figure 2.4   Cingulate gyrus and adjacent areas (medial view); the cingulate cortex and parahippocampal gyrus form part of the limbic system

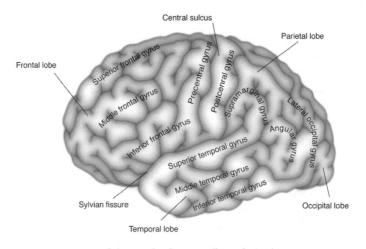

Figure 2.5   Major gyri of the cerebral cortex (lateral view)

of what to attend to in the external and internal environments. In other words, this area is important in our attention, especially regarding our chosen goals both short- and long-term. See figures 2.4 and 2.5.

Parietal lobes
The parietal lobes (BA 3, 5, 7, 39, 40) have a relatively clear demarcation as they begin posterior to the central sulcus. This area includes the

somatosensory cortex (BA 1, 2, 3), known to control and integrate our senses, especially touch, including the senses of feeling, pain, temperature, movement, pressure, texture, shape, vibration, etc. The parietal lobes are critical in the manipulation of objects in visual space (visuospatial processing). Damage to the parietal lobes results in the classic symptom of *apraxia*, an inability to conduct intentional motor movements.

There are two important subregions in the inferior portions of the parietal lobes, the supramarginal gyrus (BA 40) and the angular gyrus (BA 39). The supramarginal gyrus appears to control sensory discriminations, particularly tactile interpretations, learning, and memory. The angular gyrus, which is posterior and inferior to the supramarginal gyrus, appears to have the important function of phonological storage, that is, the ability to take speech sounds or written words and turn them into internal speech (subvocal articulatory processing). Phonological storage capacity will play a central role in our theory of cognition in chapter 3.

Although the expansion of the frontal lobes appears to have played the major role in the early evolution of the brain 100 million years to 2 million years ago, it may be that expansion of the parietal lobes has played the major role in our more recent evolutionary development, including our cerebral differentiation from Neandertals. We shall address this issue later.

Temporal lobes
The temporal lobes (BA 20, 21, 22, 36, 37, 38, 41, 42) are clearly demarcated by the lateral fissure. Their location is inferior to the parietal lobes, and they lie anterior to the occipital lobes. They also enclose the hippocampus and the amygdala, important limbic system structures, which will be discussed shortly. The temporal lobes appear to be specifically programmed to handle language and sound interpretation functions, and as such they are also referred to as auditory cortex. The temporal lobes also appear to provide meaning to speech and written words, help form memories, and interpret visual stimuli and faces. The temporal lobes thus play a major role in thinking, speech, visual processing, and memory.

The temporal lobes can be further divided into three gyri and other areas. The superior temporal gyrus (BA 22) is also called Wernicke's a rea (a student of Broca in the 1800s), and this region is responsible for the understanding of speech. Damage to this area results in Wernicke's aphasia where the understanding of speech is impaired but some ability to speak is retained. Another region within the posterior part of the superior temporal gyrus is the planum temporale. It is typically larger in the left hemisphere than in the right hemisphere, and this asymmetry has been claimed to be more predominant in chimpanzees (Gannon, Holloway, Broadfield, and Braun, 1998). In humans, symmetry in the left and right hemispheres in this region has been found to be associated with some learning and reading disabilities. The planum temporale has been shown to have a role in music, particularly the perception of pitch and harmony. The superior temporal gyrus also contains an area (BA 41, 42) known as the transverse temporal gyrus, which is responsible for hearing and basic sound processing, and it receives input nearly directly from the cochlea (inner ear). Thus, this area is considered primary auditory cortex.

The inferior temporal gyrus also processes language, particularly word and number recognition. One specific area, the fusiform gyrus (BA 36, 37), appears to be responsible for facial recognition, and this appears to be true for humans and other primates.

Damage to the temporal lobes, particularly the left temporal lobe, can result in Wernicke's aphasia. Another disorder with its possible cause rooted in the temporal lobes is epilepsy. Epilepsy is a seizure disorder, which results in temporary losses of attention, motor control, and consciousness. Epilepsy is commonly associated with damage at birth to the temporal lobes, primarily because of a brief loss of oxygen (anoxia). However, most epilepsy is said to be *idiopathic*, which means of unknown origin, and temporal lobe epilepsy (TLE) and epilepsy are nearly synonymous terms. The temporal lobes are also associated with dream-like states, altered states of consciousness, and dissociative states (e.g., out-of-body experiences, feeling robotic, etc.). If the site of the seizures can be localized through EEG evaluation or other neurological measures or procedures, then this site is called a localized, or the focal, *epileptogenic* area.

Occipital lobes
The occipital lobes (BA 17, 18, 19) sit posteriorly to the parietal lobes and temporal lobes, and their chief function appears to be primary visual recognition and processing. The occipital lobes are much more clearly demarcated from parietal and temporal lobes by the lunate sulcus in great apes and monkeys. In humans, this differentiation is not as clear. It does appear in the evolution of the cortex of humans that the lunate sulcus has moved posteriorly, suggesting a diminished role of the primary visual cortex in modern human evolution compared to other primates.

Damage to the occipital lobes, if diffuse enough, can result in blindness because of the *contra coup* effect. Pugilistic blindness, most often in boxers, results from being hit in the front of the head so often or so severely that the occipital lobes are damaged. Interestingly, in some of these cases patients may deny being blind, and they provide poorly masked excuses for not being able to see such as it being too dark to see. Providing imaginative excuses to mask errors is labeled *confabulation*. It is not known to what extent confusion plays a role in the mixing of imagination and memory or what other motivations may be involved.

Limbic system

The limbic system, originally conceived of as the emotional processing center of the brain, consists of a number of brain structures or regions, to some extent identified as a system arbitrarily because of their general functions and/or location. In general, the limbic system in involved in the processing of emotions and the formation of memories; however, it is generally accepted that the processing of emotions is a highly complex function, and unlikely to have a single brain circuitry or simple neuronal basis. That these two major functions, emotional and memory formation, are entwined in a common neural substrate also suggests an intimate relationship between the two, and empirical research strongly supports the role emotions play in memory formation. As noted earlier, the limbic structures are housed ventrally and medially within the cortex and temporal lobes. The limbic system most often includes the hippocampus, amygdala, cingulate cortex, hypothalamus, mammilary bodies, nucleus accumbens, parahippocampal gyrus, orbitofrontal cortex, and parts of the basal ganglia, including the striatum, globus pallidus, and substantia nigra. They are all bilateral structures (appearing in both hemispheres). Although in MacLean's triune brain model the limbic system was considered mammalian brain, limbic structures are phylogenetically older than the neocortex, and they are far more prominent in nonmammalian brains. This chapter will address in some detail only three of these structures, the hippocampus, amygdala, and basal ganglia. See figure 2.6.

Hippocampus

The hippocampus is a bilateral horseshoe-shaped structure whose first known purpose was the memorization of spatial locations in both humans and animals. On September 1, 1953, a 27-year-old man, known even today only by his initials, H. M., underwent a bilateral hippocampectomy

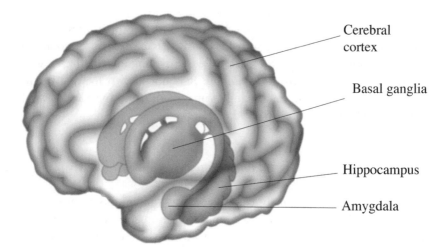

Figure 2.6   Basal ganglia (considered to be subcortical structures) and the hippocampus and amygdala (the latter two are considered limbic system structures)

(the removal of the hippocampus in both hemispheres) and a bilateral amygdalectomy (two almond-shaped structures that sit adjacent to and in front of the hippocampus, one in each hemisphere). H. M. was suffering from uncontrollable seizures (epilepsy) which disrupted his consciousness. He would also bite his tongue, become incontinent, and fall into a deep sleep afterwards (this group of symptoms is labeled *grand mal epilepsy*). EEG studies of the surface of his cortex did not consistently show any single area as an epileptogenic site, but falling deeply asleep after a seizure does suggest the temporal lobes as an epileptogenic area.

At this time, his neurosurgeon William Scoville had performed numerous psychosurgeries, including frontal lobotomies, primarily to try to improve the psychological functioning of seriously disturbed schizophrenic patients. The lobotomies were performed without much positive success in changing their personalities, although one serious side effect was to become well known – apathy – and the popularity of the operation declined. However, with the exception of severe apathy, it was noted that the schizophrenics rarely got worse in terms of their psychotic thought processes and the procedure rarely interfered with intellectual reasoning or IQ.

Scoville began experimenting with resectioning the medial and posterior regions of the frontal lobes and portions of the temporal lobes. He did this because he wanted to see if there were any therapeutic effects to be gained from moving from the frontal lobes to the temporal lobes. At this time, it was also an accepted medical procedure to partially resection or remove parts of the temporal lobes in order to reduce the severity of epileptic seizures or to stop them completely, if the cause of the seizures could be identified as a single epileptogenic area. Because the worst that might be expected might have been difficulty with memorizing spatial locations, it seemed a fair risk given the quality of his life with weekly *grand mal* seizures.

After the operation, H. M. appeared to be a normally functioning adult with understanding, speech, reasoning, and old memories fully intact. There were no apparent neurological deficits like paralysis, or any apparent visual or perceptual problems. However, H. M. no longer recognized the names or faces of the hospital staff as he had done so readily before the operation. He could not find his way to the bathroom. In fact, he could not seem to remember events from the operation back in time to about three years earlier (this is labeled *retrograde amnesia*). For example, he did not remember the death of a favorite uncle three years before the operation. Interestingly, his earlier life memories remained intact. H. M., unfortunately, still had seizures, but his major convulsive seizures were down to one every two or three years where before his operation he had a major one weekly. Before the operation he had minor seizures as often as every ten minutes throughout the day. After the operation, his minor seizures were down to one or two daily.

Neuropsychological testing revealed that his learning of new verbal material (also called *declarative* memory) was severely interrupted (labeled *anterograde amnesia*). He could not learn any difficult words and had severe trouble with learning even easy words, and his performance did not improve with practice. He could eventually learn a new word, but it took hundreds or even a thousand trials. Because H. M. also had difficulty recalling events up to about two or three years before the operation (called *retrograde amnesia*), it was concluded that that newly acquired memories are vulnerable to disruption far longer than was previously thought. Interestingly, his procedural memory, defined as a memory for nonverbal performance tasks, like learning to juggle, learning to ride a bicycle, or making a stone tool, was completely intact. H. M. was able to learn a new procedural task, perform normally, and retain this knowledge upon subsequent testing. However, he could not recognize the task the next day, but he did demonstrate that he remembered the task by his performance. Current speculation as to this behavior is that it may be that procedural memories are not processed through the hippocampus for long-term storage, while declarative memories (memories for facts, events, and names) appear to depend heavily on the hippocampus for placement in long-term storage.

Amygdala

These bilateral almond-shaped structures on the anterior tips of the hippocampus play a well-researched role in emotional processing, particularly fear and rage responses (LeDoux, 1996). As noted earlier, because emotions play a key role in memory formation, the amygdala plays an important role in memory as well. The amygdala and other limbic structures are phylogenetically much older than the surrounding cortex. In fact, the cortex is often referred to as the neocortex or new cortex for this reason. Thus, the amygdala and other limbic structures are much more prominent features in the brains of reptiles.

In studies of mammals, amygdalectomies result in a "taming effect" and electrical stimulation of the amygdala can instill rage reactions. Rage reactions have even been demonstrated in mice against much larger natural predators. Amygdalectomized humans become apathetic (as was the case in H. M.) and show little spontaneity, creativity, or affective expression. On August 1, 1966, former Marine and University of Texas student Charles Whitman climbed into the university's 307-ft tower and killed 14 people by rifle fire. He was shot and killed by the police within a few hours. Upon autopsy, which he ironically requested in a note that he left because he suspected something was wrong with his brain, pathologists found a small tumor pressing into one of his amygdala, although no one could conclude that it was necessarily the cause of Whitman's horrific violence.

Basal ganglia

The basal ganglia (a plural form, ganglion is the singular) is a collection of subcortical neurons whose most clear function appears to be the control of movements. A section of these ganglia, the substantia nigra (adjacent to the amygdala), is responsible for the manufacture of dopamine, a chemical neurotransmitter responsible for motor instigation and control and novelty-seeking. In the initial phase of Parkinson's disease, there is the destruction of the neurons in the substantia nigra, which results in a disruption of dopamine production. Parkinson's disease usually results in tremors of a finger, hand, or foot on one side of the body. Muscles often become rigid and stiff, especially facial muscles, resulting in a mask-like face. The ability to walk becomes impaired, and the patient may move with a shuffling gait. A Parkinson's patient often moves slower (called bradykinesia), or they may even "freeze" in their movements, often reporting they are "stuck to the ground." Later in Parkinson's disease there is a loss of the surrounding tissue and other brain neurons, which will eventually result in dementia (memory problems and a loss of intellect). The initial dopamine production problem can often be ameliorated by levodopa (L-dopa), a drug that mimics dopamine. However, the effectiveness of L-dopa generally diminishes over time, and its long-term use can cause dyskinesia (involuntary movements). Interestingly, the actor Michael J. Fox, who had early onset Parkinson's (before the age of 40), opted for a pallidotomy, which is an intentional lesioning of the globus pallidus. The surgery appears to reduce neuronal activity in the globus pallidus. It is usually performed unilaterally but can be performed bilaterally. This procedure appears to be effective for treating tremors and bradykinesia. Recently, deep brain stimulation has become a more popular surgical treatment of Parkinson's disease, where electrodes are implanted to electrically block abnormal nerve impulses causing the symptoms. Other syndromes and diseases attributed to the basal ganglia are obsessive-compulsive disorders (obsessive thoughts and/or the compulsion to perform specific acts hundreds of times a day, e.g., handwashing) and Tourette's syndrome, which has the symptom of the irrepressible production of non-meaningful sounds, e.g., barks or cries, motor tics (involuntary jerking, especially of facial muscles) and often coprolalia (irrepressible cursing).

Recently, Hazy, Frank, and O'Reilly (2006) investigated the important role of the basal ganglia in controlling actively maintained task-relevant information in the prefrontal cortex. We will present their tripartite model of information-processing involving the basal ganglia, hippocampus, and the prefrontal cortex in chapter 3.

Other Subcortical Brain Structures

Cerebellum

Like the basal ganglia, the cerebellum (meaning "little brain") has one of the oldest evolutionary lineages, and the circuits in the cerebellum are relatively similar in all classes of vertebrates. The cerebellum, in particular, is visually distinctive in the brains of reptiles. In the nearly 50 million-year-old history of primates, it becomes less obvious visually as the neocortex becomes a much more prominent feature. Recent research (Weaver, 2005) has shown that Neandertals were distinct from modern humans in having smaller cerebella. In fact, Weaver has concluded that there was a rapid expansion of the cerebellum in modern humans. And, as is true of the neo-cortex, there appear to be areas of the cerebellum that have evolved more recently, i.e., the neocerebellum. The cerebellum is positioned inferior to the occipital lobes.

The most prominent behavioral role of the cerebellum is the integration of sensory perception and motor output. The cerebellum has extensive con-nections to the motor cortex, and it appears to control fine motor movements as well. Although the cerebellum has been implicated in some cognitive processes such as attention and some language functions, it may be fair to say it plays some role but no central or *sine qua non* role in cognition. Lesions or damage to the cerebellum tend to cause difficulties in fine motor move-ments, equilibrium, balance, and correct positioning and posture. Although the cerebellum accounts for only about 10 percent of the total brain volume, it is thought to account for about 50 percent of all brain neurons. It is also divided into two hemispheres, just like the cerebral cortex. The cerebellum does not instigate walking and posture per se, but it coordinates these activ-ities into well-timed, smooth, integrated movement. See figure 2.7.

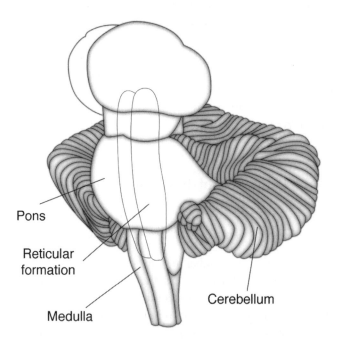

Figure 2.7   Mid-brain, brainstem structures and the cerebellum

Brain stem

The spinal cord is contiguous with the brain stem, and thus it forms the upper part of the spinal cord but is considered a lower brain structure. The upper part of the brain stem, the pons, receives sensory and motor input from the body and sends it to both halves of the cerebellum. The pons is also the site where the information from the body crosses over to be processed by the opposite side of the brain, i.e., information from the left half of the body is sent to the right side of the brain for processing and vice versa. The reticular formation is housed at a similar level as the pons in the brain stem, and it is one of the oldest phylogenetic areas of the brain. It has connections to the thalamus, hypothalamus, cortex, and cerebellum. As one of the older areas of the brain, it appears to regulate many basic automatic functions such as sleep, eating, and sex, and also alertness, attention, and motivation. Below the pons is the medulla oblongata, which processes the flow of information between the body and the brain. The medulla also controls most involuntary muscle movements and activities of the glands, and it controls vital functions such as heart rate, breathing, and blood pressure. Any major damage to this area results in death.

Thalamus

This egg-shaped structure (thalamus means "inner room" in Greek) at the top of the spinal cord serves as a gateway to the cortex for sensory systems, and it has reciprocal loops with all regions of the cortex. Brain stem structures also innervate thalamic functions, and the brain stem has reciprocal loops with these structures as well. Specific sections of the thalamus also have more specific functions, and one of these most important functions is attention, regulated by the pulvinar nucleus in the posterior part of the thalamus.

Hypothalamus

This structure sits below the thalamus, and it has projections to the prefrontal cortex, amygdala, and spinal cord. It also connects to the pituitary gland beneath it. As such, the hypothalamus is important to the regulation of the autonomic nervous system, the endocrine and hormonal systems, and the regulation of the body's general homeostasis. The hypothalamus is also reciprocally affected by hormones circulating in the blood, and, thus, there is a high degree of reciprocal interaction between the hypothalamus, the pituitary gland, endocrine glands, and the hormones they regulate and produce.

Handedness

Each hand has ipsilateral (same-side) and contralateral (opposite-side) connections to the two cerebral hemispheres. However, the contralateral connections between hands and hemispheres are much stronger than the ipsilateral connections; thus, the right hand is an instrument of the left hemisphere, and the left hand is an instrument of the right hemisphere. For example, after a major right hemisphere stroke (a disruption of the blood supply to an area of the brain), a patient will generally be paralyzed on the left side of the body and will be unable to gain control of a hand through the ipsilateral connections from the brain.

Approximately 90–95 percent of people favor their right hand, either by their stated preference or by their performance. For the other 5–10 percent of people, they most often claim they are left-handed or ambidextrous. In neuropsychological testing, handedness is most often assessed by the speed at which a person can tap their index finger on each hand. Interestingly, nearly half of those who claim to be left-handed will finger-tap faster with their right index finger than their left, whereas nearly all people who claim to be right-handed tap faster with their right finger. Because people who claim to be left-handed have such variable neuropsychological testing results, they are sometimes referred to as non-right-handed people.

It is interesting to note that right-hand preference appears to be largely a human trait. Only in chimpanzees has a weak right-hand preference been demonstrated, and typically only in captivity, which may be indicative that the chimps are emulating their human caretakers (e.g., McGrew and Marchant, 1997). It is also interesting to note that nearly all right-handed people have speech located in their left hemisphere, and about 70 percent of non-right-handed people also have speech in their left hemisphere. It is thought that less than about 10 percent of non-right-handed people are "mirror" left-handed people, that is, they have speech in the right hemisphere and favor their left hands.

Although right-handedness appears to be a human trait and most major language functions are predominately located in the left hemisphere in humans, there is left hemisphere localization for vocalizations in a wide variety of animals including birds, amphibians, and mammals. Broca's area in the left hemisphere, noted for its role in speech production in modern humans, appears to be enlarged in *Homo habilis* about 2 million years ago but not in the earlier australopithecines, who lived about 3 million years ago (Holloway, 1983). However, this is somewhat difficult to determine given that cranial morphology must be estimated strictly from internal fossil skull features, as the brains themselves rarely if ever fossilize. But anthropologists tend to be in some agreement that *Homo habilis* may have relied more on vocalizations than the australopithecines.

The causal relationship of language location and hand preference is debatable. Corballis (2002) has argued that because vocalization appears to have a very early, left hemisphere localization (100 million years ago or more), handedness emerged about 2 million years ago as manual gestures were incorporated into the prototypic language of *Homo habilis*. He also speculated that, as manual gestures were removed as a requirement of language, rapid advances in technology may have occurred in *Homo sapiens*. Corballis also noted that Broca's areas in chimpanzees have been found to possess mirror neurons, which produce excitation when a chimpanzee witnesses another chimpanzee manually gesturing. Thus, if vocalization had a very early evolutionary left hemisphere localization, and manual gestures served as a basis for language, then mirror neurons may have aided the acquisition of manual gestures and reinforced a right-hand bias for gesturing. Corballis offers further evidence by Toth (1985), who examined the stone tools from 1.4 million years to 1.9 million years ago (more than likely associated with *Homo erectus*). He found that they were produced by right-handers more than left-handers at a ratio of about 1.3 to 1 as opposed to the modern ratio of right-hand preference to non-right-handed preference of about 9 to 1. Curiously, Uomini (2006) recently found a near absence of left-handed knappers in more recent hominins such as *Homo heidelbergensis*, Neandertals, and Upper Paleolithic *Homo sapiens*. The latter finding may suggest that there was an increasing preference for right-handedness across our evolutionary past, although whether this bias occurred through vocalization's ancient left hemisphere localization, genetic drift, cultural biases, or a combination of factors appears uncertain.

Ears and Hearing

The connections of the ears to the cerebral hemispheres follow the same pattern as the hands. Each ear has ipsilateral and contralateral connections to the hemispheres. However, the contralateral connections between ears and hemispheres are much stronger than the ipsilateral connections; thus, the right ear is an instrument of the left hemisphere, and the left ear is an instrument of the right hemisphere. In neuropsychological research and assessment, a dichotic listening paradigm has been employed, where different words or short lists of words are played simultaneously to each ear. Each ear and hemisphere hears the words distinctly, as they are not jumbled together; however, the participant or patient can only reply with a single word at a time. Right-handed people show a strong preference for first reporting words from their right ears, because a word played in the right ear goes directly to the left hemisphere where speech resides (because the contralateral connections are stronger than the ipsilateral connections). A word played to the left ear goes directly to the right hemisphere; however, in order to be spoken, the word has to be transferred to the left hemisphere via the corpus callosum. This small delay thus favors words played to the right ear.

Eyes and Vision

Each eye is connected to both hemispheres. Contralateral and ipsilateral connections are of equal strength. The left half of the left eye has an ipsilateral connection to the left hemisphere and the right half of the left eye has a contralateral connection to the right hemisphere. The same is true of the right eye: The right half of the right eye has an ipsilateral connection to the right hemisphere and the left half of the right eye has a contralateral connection to the left hemisphere. The only tricky part is that the left half of each eye views the right field of vision (right visual half-field), and the right half of each eye views the left field of vision (left visual half-field). Primates appear to be unusual in this arrangement, and it seems to support the hypothesis that there was a reorganization of the visual system in primates.

Given this system of organization, if a participant or patient is focusing straight ahead (in neuropsychological assessment, patients focus on a star

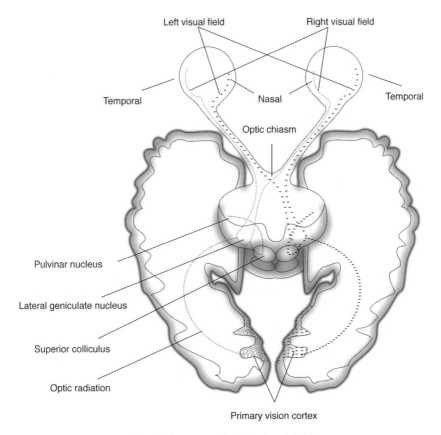

Left visual field

Right visual field

Temporal

Nasal

Temporal

Optic chiasm

Pulvinar nucleus

Lateral geniculate nucleus

Superior colliculus

Optic radiation

Primary vision cortex

Figure 2.8 Organization of the eyes and their visual fields

or circle directly in the middle of their field of vision) and a picture of a key is shown in their left field of view and a picture of a ball is shown in their right field of view (but very briefly), right-handed participants will predominantly report "ball, key" rather than "key, ball." This occurs because what is shown in the right field of vision will appear in the left half of each eye, and the left halves of the eyes are connected directly to the left hemisphere where speech resides. The picture of the key (in the left field of vision) will be perceived in the right half of each eye which are both connected to the right hemisphere. The knowledge of the key must then be transferred from the right hemisphere over the corpus callosum to the left hemisphere in order to be spoken. See figure 2.8.

Split-Brain Studies

Neurosurgeon Roger Sperry received the Nobel Prize for Medicine in 1981 for his work on split-brain patients. Sperry worked with intractable epileptic patients, that is, those whose seizures could not be controlled by medication. Sperry had noticed that seizures would often begin in one hemisphere (the eliptogenic focus) and spread to the other hemisphere, and because the two hemispheres are so synchronous in their various functions, they would mimic the seizure activity of the other hemisphere. Often, the non-damaged hemisphere will become damaged by long-term mimicry of the seizure activity of the damaged hemisphere. Sperry then found that severing the corpus callosum in these patients reduced their seizure activity significantly. He also found that accompanying behavioral repercussions of this commissurotomy appeared to be minimal. However, subsequent testing of these split-brain patients offered great insight into each hemisphere's varying roles in perception, understanding, and speech. Sperry and his students found the left brain hemisphere, for example, was better at analytical, sequential, and linguistic tasks, and the right was better at some nonverbal and spatial tasks. Of course, this appeared to set the stage for the popularization of left and right hemisphere differences, and overlooked in the subsequent media hype was the extent that the two hemispheres work synchronously to some extent on virtually all tasks.

Dichotic listening in split-brain patients

Severing the corpus callosum does not affect the neural connections from the ears to the hemispheres. But whatever is played to the left ear ends up primarily perceived by the right hemisphere, although speech resides in the left hemisphere. A commissurotomy, therefore, does leave the knowledge of the word played in the left ear, in the right hemisphere, and that knowledge cannot be spoken except by the left hemisphere. Thus, if the word DOG is played in the left ear, and the word TREE is played in the right ear, a right-handed person would say the word TREE, and then say DOG. They would say the word TREE first because it goes immediately from the right ear into the left hemisphere where speech resides. The word DOG goes from the left ear directly into the right hemisphere but the knowledge of that word (or the idea of that word) must pass over the corpus callosum in order to be spoken by the left hemisphere. This delay gives the word TREE its ability to be spoken first. However, a split-brain patient would only say the word TREE. A non-right-handed person (not a split-brain patient) would still more likely say TREE-DOG than the reverse.

Visual half-field experiments in split-brain patients

A commissurotomy also does not affect the connection of the eyes and the hemispheres. In right-handed (not split-brain) people, if a picture of a tree was displayed in the right visual field and a picture of a dog was displayed in the left visual field (very briefly and the participant was forced to focus straight ahead and asked to report what they saw), the person would say TREE then DOG. Remember, what appears in the right visual field is perceived by the left half of each eye. The left halves of each eye are connected to the left hemisphere, and speech resides in the left hemisphere, thus giving TREE the advantage over DOG to be spoken first. The word DOG shown in the left visual field is relayed to the right hemisphere. In order to be spoken, it must pass over the corpus callosum to the left hemisphere. In this same paradigm with a split-brain patient, the patient would say only TREE (shown in the right visual field). The knowledge or idea of TREE is stuck in the right hemisphere and cannot pass over the corpus callosum to be spoken by the left hemisphere. See again figure 2.8.

Hand and eye task functioning in split-brain patients

Let us use the same paradigm as previously, except that the patient must now choose either a plastic tree or a small plastic dog from behind a screen (so that the patient could feel the items but not see the items). First, let us review: a split-brain patient is shown a picture of a tree in the right visual field, and a picture of a dog is shown in the left visual field. They are asked to place their left hand under a screen and select which item they saw. Remember, the left hand is largely an instrument of the right hemisphere. What did the right hemisphere see? The right hemisphere is connected to the right half of each eye and views the left visual field. Thus, a split-brain patient will pick out the tree with his or her left hand. The patient would have picked out the plastic dog with his or her right hand.

Brain Myths

Now that we have reviewed just some of the essential areas and functions of the brain, it may be useful to discuss a few of the prevailing myths about the brain.

Myth #1: We only use 10 percent of our brains.

I (FLC) always say in class, if this is true, I sure hope it's the 10 percent that controls breathing, blood pressure, and heart rate. Actually, this is a complete myth, and no one is quite sure of its origin. First, what does that statement mean? What is the other 90 percent of the brain doing? Are the other brain neurons absolutely inert? Second, how would a scientist measure the 10 percent of the active neurons? You cannot conduct neuroimaging while a person is walking about or even sitting. To conduct neuroimaging, a person typically must lie down in a scanner. In a recent study (Vincent et al., 2007) that has implications for human brains, it was found that the anaesthetized monkey brains had widely distributed cortical activation despite their profound lack of consciousness. This cortical activation appeared in areas well known to be critical to and to be highly active in various cognitive tasks. In other words, areas of the brain operate without concomitant behavior activation, and behaviors are often performed without concomitant brain activation. Thus, the very definition of "we use only" can be severely called into question. However, more importantly, besides the highly inexact definition of "We *use* only . . ." and the measurement problems, the myth is probably a good example of a benign false hypothesis. Many psychologists think the underlying intention of the myth is to encourage people or motivate people to think more or to do more. For example, "Gosh, I use only 10 percent of my brain! I should be doing a lot more with my brain!" Thus, the consequences of this false hypothesis are generally benign. Unless one is a terrorist or serial killer, thinking more or doing more is generally harmless at worst and helpful at best.

Myth #2: Alcohol destroys brain cells.

This myth is often propagated by those who rail against the evils of alcohol. However, there is little or no sound evidence that it is true for those who drink moderately and have adequate diets. Perhaps this myth got its start in Korsakoff's psychosis (Korsakoff's syndrome). Korsakoff's is a neurodegenerative brain disease that has severe memory problems as its symptoms, including severe anterograde and retrograde amnesia, confabulation, apathy, and lack of insight. It most often accompanies severe and long-term cases of alcoholism. However, it appears to be exclusively caused by a lack of thiamine (vitamin B_1), and thus poor nutrition is the cause, and not alcohol abuse per se. Certainly, early alcohol use and heavy alcohol abuse, coupled with long-term (decades) of abuse may have adverse consequences for the brain. And, certainly, alcohol can damage the brain of a fetus in a pregnant woman. However, it is doubtful whether scientists will ever be able to document irreversible brain damage in adults specifically from moderate alcohol use coupled with good nutrition (at least the authors hope not).

Myth #3A: The brain cannot regenerate its neurons.
Myth #3B: The brain can regenerate its neurons!

Believe it or not, each of these disparate claims has some grain of truth. The philosophical position you adopt will probably fall into one of these two categories: minimalism and maximalism. The minimalist position is that the limited evidence for brain neuron regeneration has been vastly exaggerated. On the whole, people with massive brain damage from gunshot wounds, car wrecks, major cerebral strokes, and dementing illnesses do not get dramatically or miraculously better, and many get progressively worse. Whatever neuronal brain regeneration occurs after injury is more often than not limited, and not dramatic. To date, there is only evidence that adult neurogenesis occurs in the olfactory bulb and the hippocampus. Cases of dramatic recovery are the exception rather than the rule in neuropsychology. The maximalist position is that there is evidence for neuronal brain regeneration, but sometimes these claims are based on a case of dramatic recovery. One methodological problem with such claims is that a case of dramatic recovery does not necessarily imply that neurogenesis has occurred. We (your authors) have already stated the apparently limited neuronal and behavioral significance of this regeneration, so you can probably tell we favor the minimalist position.

Myth #4: Gay men's and lesbians' brains are different from heterosexuals' brains.

The minimalism/maximalism position is also true of the search for brain differences between gays/lesbians and heterosexuals. There is some evidence for neuronal organization differences in the hippocampus of gay men. Yet, again, no cognitive consequence of this purported difference has been demonstrated whatsoever. Also, it appears, just as in the research with sex differences, these results are used for political purposes on both sides, and, as such, it makes this research hard to evaluate, given its social and political consequences. Perhaps one moral of the previous two myths and other myths like them is that there are generally these two philosophical positions, and it may be useful in your evaluation of any research to see if you can identify whether the authors are initially in one camp or the other.

3

Working Memory

In this chapter we address directly the hypothesis we set out in chapter 1 – that an enhancement in working memory capacity powered the appearance of the modern mind. By the 1950s, psychologists had come to a more or less general agreement that people relied on two distinct kinds of memory, short term and long term. But by the early 1970s, experimental psychologists, including Alan Baddeley, recognized limitations in this two-component model of memory. At that time, short-term memory research was largely devoted to the study of an acoustic, temporary, limited capacity verbal store. It was typically measured by a simple digit span task, where subjects were asked to repeat varying series of numbers. If prevented from rehearsal (usually by another task) short-term memories vanished in a matter of seconds, either because the electrical "trace" of the memory simply faded, or because later perceptions interfered with them, or so the competing models claimed. Yet both the "trace" model and the "interference" model failed to account for significant experimental results; for example, it was unable to explain why some simultaneous tasks interfered with one another (e.g., memorizing a list of words while reciting a list of numbers) but others did not (e.g., remembering the colors of presented objects while reciting a list of numbers). In 1974, Baddeley and his colleague Graham Hitch proposed a more comprehensive cognitive theory that accounted not only for the standard operations of short-term memory, but also how memory is enjoined and directed, and how it related to long-term memory. The resulting model had a profound effect on the field of brain and memory research. Over the past two decades, it has been arguably the single most provocative and intensely researched model in the field of cognition.

The initial Baddeley and Hitch model included an attentional, panmodal controller or central executive, and two subsystems, the phonological loop and the visuospatial sketchpad. Recently, Baddeley (2001) expanded the central executive's functions by adding a new component, the episodic buffer, which serves as the memory component of the central executive and integrates and temporarily stores information from the other two subsystems. The phonological loop contains two elements, a short-term phonological store of speech and other sounds, and an articulatory loop that maintains and rehearses information either vocally or subvocally. Baddeley viewed its primary purpose as evolving for language acquisition and comprehension. The visuospatial store was hypothesized to involve the maintenance and integration of visual ("what" information like objects) and spatial ("where" information like location in space) elements and a means of refreshing it by rehearsal.

The Central Executive

With some modifications, Baddeley and others (e.g., Baddeley and Logie, 1999; Miyake and Shah, 1999) currently view the central executive either as a unitary system or multiple systems of varying functions including attention, active-inhibition, decision-making, planning, sequencing, temporal tagging, and the updating, maintenance, and integration of information from the two subsystems. Some brain function models present working memory as simply one subcomponent of the various functions of the prefrontal cortex. However, with a raft of new evidence from empirical studies (for a review of contemporary working memory models and empirical evidence, see Miyake and Shah, 1999; Osaka et al., 2007), it is more parsimonious to view Baddeley's working memory model as having subsumed the traditionally defined aspects of executive functions. In most current models, working memory not only serves to focus attention and make decisions but also serves as the chief liaison to long-term memory systems, and to language comprehension and production. Indeed, Baddeley (1993) has noted that had he approached these systems from the perspective of attention instead of memory, it might have been equally appropriate to label them "working attention."

One provocative part of the tripartite working memory model is the concept of the central processor or executive. Baddeley adopted an attentional control system called the Supervisory Attentional System (SAS), originally proposed by Norman and Shallice (1980), as the basis for his central executive. Gazzaniga et al. (2002) recently attributed its attentional functions primarily to the anterior cingulate gyrus. The SAS takes control when novel tasks are introduced, when pre-existing habits have to be overridden, or when danger threatens and task-relevant decisions must be made.

More recently, Kane and Engle (2002) have also given Baddeley's central executive a neural basis (primarily the prefrontal cortex), based on a wide variety of evidence including single-cell firing, brain-imaging, and neuropsychological studies. Through the general framework of individual differences, they proposed "executive-attention" as the critical component of working memory, whose chief function is the active maintenance of appropriate stimulus representations relevant to goal attainment in the face of interference-rich contexts. Collette and Van der Linden (2002) have also postulated, based on empirical brain-imaging studies, that the central executive component of working memory recruits not only frontal areas but also parietal areas. They conclude its operation must be understood as an interaction of a network of cerebral and subcortical regions.

The theoretical status of Baddeley's central executive as a single unit is not without criticism. He admits that multiple segregated information-processing modules may ultimately replace his notion of a single central executive controlling system. Interestingly, Goldman-Rakic (1995) noted that while current evidence favored multiple working memory domains, the idea of a central panmodal executive processor could not be completely dismissed. She stated that the human brain may have a genuine cortical center, oblivious to informational domains. She speculated that future studies may reveal the location of this area (or network) but noted that they have not thus far. Some (e.g., Miyake and Shah, 1999) have also suggested that the notion of a central executive begs the question of a homunculus (Baddeley freely admits the problem of the homunculus in his model (Baddeley, 2001; 2007)), and until recently it has been an unaddressed question in most current working memory models. However, Hazy, Frank, and O'Reilly (2006) have proposed a complex model, called PBWM (prefrontal cortex, basal ganglia working memory model), which purports to account for the mechanistic basis of working memory, the central executive, and its executive functions. As its name suggests, they view the prefrontal cortex as critical in maintaining representations of an individual's perceptions in the broadest sense, which are dynamically updated and regulated by reinforcement learning systems that themselves are based on chemical neurotransmitters (primarily dopamine) activated by the basal ganglia and the amygdala. They further propose that these learning systems can be modified, and so can learn to control themselves and related brain areas in order to act in a task-appropriate manner. They also offered some empirical support for their hypotheses, and thus feel that they have rendered moot the issue of a homunculus.

In a search for the core nature of the executive functions, Oberauer, Suss, Wilhelm, and Wittman (2003) proposed that working memory could be differentiated into two facets: one, the content domains (akin to Baddeley's phonological loop and visuospatial sketchpad), and the other related to its cognitive functions (executive functions as appearing in the neuropsychological literature). Oberauer et al., in a statistical factor analysis of 30 working memory tasks, claimed there were three meta-working memory functions: simultaneous storage and processing, supervision, and coordination of elements into structures. Earlier, Miyake et al. (2000), also through factor analysis, identified three factors in executive functions: mental set shifting, inhibition of prepotent (predispositional) responses, and information updating. None of Oberauer et al.'s working memory functions appear to be completely identical to Miyake et al.'s functions. One problem may be methodological: all factor analytic studies' outcomes are completely dependent on the initial set of variables. The previous studies' differing conclusions show the highly complex yet interrelated nature of working memory and its executive functions.

Whether the central executive is a unitary or non-unitary concept, we may still ask where, how, and why does it make its decisions? Miyake and Shah (1999) have proposed that the attention and decision-making qualities of the central executive may be an emergent property that arises as a function of the dynamic interplay of the multiple and interrelated systems associated with working memory, including the two subsystems, the multiple long-term memory systems and their cortical and subcortical connections. Barkley (2001) also favored an evolutionary perspective to explain executive functions. He viewed them as a biological adaptation resulting from interpersonal competition in groups. He saw executive functions as a useful social self-defense against resource theft (including spouse) and against interpersonal manipulation. He also saw them as advantageous in social exchanges (like reciprocal altruism or selfish cooperation) and useful in imitating and learning from others without the dangers inherent in trial and error. Barkley also proposed executive functions evolved in gradual stages over a period of at least a million years. Certainly, the ability to attend to relevant stimuli, filter out irrelevant stimuli, and to make quick and efficient decisions would have been favored over static processes. Support for the decision-making nature of the central executive also comes from

Frankish (1998a, 1998b), who has speculated that it is an innate predisposition of human consciousness to accept, reject, or act on propositions. He postulates a "super mind" constituted by higher-order decision-making (as cited in Carruthers, 2002). These propositions are framed by language, most often through inner speech or subvocalization, which are aspects of the phonological loop.

Can the central executive be linked to any specific neural structure? Gazzaniga, Ivry, and Mangun (2002) have emphasized that its functions do not reside in a single structure but appear to result from the interplay of diverse cortical and subcortical neural systems. There are a number of models for the neurocircuitry and functionality of executive functions. Alexander, DeLong, and Strick (1986) proposed five parallel but segregated frontal-subcortical circuits: two of these circuits are thought to be related to motor functions and to influence oculomotor and skeletal motor areas of the cortex. The three remaining circuits were the dorsolateral prefrontal cortex, the orbitofrontal prefrontal cortex (also known as the ventromedial prefrontal cortex), and the anterior cingulate cortex. Recently, Middleton and Strick (2001) presented evidence for two additional frontal-subcortical circuits and emphasized their interrelationships to subcortical structures, particularly the basal ganglia and the cerebellum. Much neuropsychological research has focused on the three frontal-subcortical circuits that are associated with the greatest neurological and behavioral repercussions from damage or dysfunction; the dorsolateral, ventromedial, and anterior cingulate cortices (e.g., Chow and Cummings, 1999).

As we noted in chapter 2, the dorsolateral circuit is generally associated with the classic executive functions, i.e., complex problem-solving, decision-making, verbal fluency, and some of the operations of working memory. The orbitofrontal prefrontal region is more closely connected to the limbic system and is associated with the regulation of emotions and social behavior. Both systems are closely connected, and the prefrontal cortex has extensive projections to the temporal and parietal lobes, some projections to the occipital lobe, and to subcortical structures such as the basal ganglia (especially the amygdala), the cerebellum, and the brain stem. Again, it appears that the prefrontal cortex, and thus the central executive in the working memory model, coordinates the processing of broad regions of the central nervous system. And, as noted earlier, Hazy, Frank, and O'Reilly (2006) stated that there is also a critical interaction of the prefrontal cortex with the basal ganglia in explaining the neural substrate of Baddeley's working memory model.

Phonological Loop

The phonological loop is intimately involved in language use. Baddeley hypothesized that the phonological loop has two components, a brief sound-based storage that fades within a few seconds and an articulatory processor. The latter maintains material in the phonological store by vocal or subvocal rehearsal. Spoken information appears to have automatic and obligatory access to phonological storage, and Baddeley therefore hypothesized that the phonological store evolved principally for the demands and acquisition of language. Baddeley and Logie (1999) also wrote that "the phonological loop might reasonably be considered to form a major bottleneck in the process of spoken language comprehension" (p. 41).

Repetition of sounds held in the phonological store, usually by means of the vocal or subvocal articulatory processor, will relegate those sounds into long-term declarative memory, if there is sufficient motivation or emotional salience. A strong motivation to memorize, or an elevated emotional meaning (e.g., someone to whom you are attracted has an unusual first name), will increase the likelihood that that sound will be successfully transferred into long-term memory. Sounds can be relegated to long-term memory even if they have no initial meaning. For example, repeating "won-due, era-due, muru" over and over, either vocally or subvocally, will eventually transfer them to long-term memory without any meaning attached to them whatsoever (they are the phonetic sounds of "1, 2, 3" in a south Indian Dravidian language, Kannada). Baddeley, Gathercole, and Papagno (1998) have, thus, noted the important role that the phonological loop plays in adult second-language learning, and also its important role in the acquisition of native language learning in children. The process of vocal and subvocal articulation also appears to play an important role in memorizing stimuli in the visuospatial sketchpad, for example, thinking or saying, "Ah, a small blue chair!" The phonological loop processes also help to explain why brain-damaged patients who have lost their ability to repeat sounds vocally can still memorize them. However, those patients (Caplan and Waters, 1995), who cannot create a sound or speech motor form through the phonological loop, cannot memorize new material.

Recently, Aboitiz, Garcia, Bosman, and Brunetti (2006) have noted that phonological storage capacity represents a short-term memory ensemble that can be phylogenetically tracked to earlier homologues in hominin evolution and to current primate brain systems. Further, they postulated that language has evolved primarily through the expansion of short-term memory capacity, "which has allowed the processing of sounds, conveying elaborate meanings and eventually participating in syntactic processes." (p. 41). They believed that an expanding memory system allowed more complex memories, representing multiple items to be manipulated combinatorially. However, they thought these manipulations demanded significant working memory resources (demands on functions of the central executive). They situate the neurological epicenter for this expanded working memory capacity, and generation of the phonological loop, in the posterior superior temporal lobe gyrus and the inferior parietal lobes areas. They also agreed with Fuster (1997), who noted that the dorsolateral prefrontal cortex plays an important role with reconciling short-term past and short-term future and cross-temporal contingencies. Thus, keeping track of what was said a few moments ago, minutes ago, and insuring that one's present speech is in accord with previous utterances is a function of the complex interactions of the prefrontal cortex, temporal, and parietal areas as well as their interconnectivity with other cortical area and subcortical structures. Becker, MacAndrew, and Fiez (1999) have also identified the neural location of the phonological store as the inferior parietal lobe of the speech-dominant hemisphere, particularly the supramarginal and angular gyri. MacAndrew, Klatzky, Fiez, McClelland, and Becker (2002) have additionally implicated Broca's area with phonological tasks that present the items visually.

Visuospatial Sketchpad

In Baddeley's model, the visuospatial sketchpad is a temporary store for the maintenance and manipulation of visuospatial information. It also has an important role in spatial orientation and solving visuospatial problems. Studies with brain-damaged patients, and with healthy adults, appear to demonstrate that the visual and spatial processes may comprise separate memory systems, although the visuospatial sketchpad is assumed to form an interface between the two systems (Logie, 1995). Visual information can also be integrated with sensory information such as touch and perhaps smell; however, not much is known about the latter aspects as there are far fewer empirical studies of the visuospatial sketchpad compared to the phonological loop.

Neuroimaging and other neuropsychological studies with a variety of brain-damaged patients and other people indicate significant involvement of the primary visual cortex (occipitals lobes), the parietal lobes, and the frontal lobes. See Shah and Miyake (2005) for a more complete review of theories regarding visuospatial thinking.

Episodic buffer

As noted earlier, Baddeley initially described the central executive as largely attentional in nature without its own storage capacity, but eventually realized that it also must have some way to store information independent of the subsystems (else how could phonological, visuospatial, and long-term memory information be integrated?). He thus proposed the episodic buffer as the storage component of the central executive. He endowed the episodic buffer with the ability to bind and integrate the two subsystems, the phonological loop and the visuospatial sketchpad, and also traces from long-term memory, via a multimodal code. By attending to multiple sources of information simultaneously, the central executive is able to create models of the environment that themselves can be manipulated to solve problems and even plan future behaviors and alternative strategies, so that if a plan fails, another may be chosen or generated. See figure 3.1 for our slight modification of Baddeley's working memory model.

A Memory Primer

Cognitive psychologists have long distinguished between declarative memories like facts, details, strings of sounds and words, and procedural memories for learned motor movements like stone-knapping and visuospatial tasks like memorizing directions for locations. Both types appear to use relatively independent neural pathways; selective types of brain damage may affect one type of memory but not the other. There are varieties of declarative memory. An episodic memory is a coherent, story-like reminiscence for an event, often associated with a specific time and place, and a feeling signature. Episodic memory is sometimes labeled *personal memory* or *autobiographical memory*. The other major type of declarative memory is semantic, the

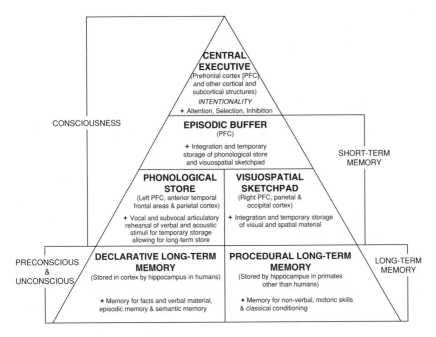

Figure 3.1   A Modification of Baddeley's Working Memory Model

memory for general facts. A reminiscence, of course, will include semantic details but its recall and subjective experience will be psychologically and neurologically different from the recall of the semantic components alone (e.g., Tulving, 2002).

As the reader is well aware, human memory is far from perfect. If people are asked to recall a list of thematically related words previously read to them, they will often identify words that are related thematically to words on the list, but were not in fact on the original list (false recognition). They will also correctly identify words as not on the list that are not thematically related to the original list (true recognition). Neuroimaging studies have shown that both true and false recognition require hippocampal and parietal lobe functioning (e.g., Schacter, 2001; Schacter and Addis, 2007; Tulving, 2002). People with hippocampal damage or an absence of a hippocampus, such as H. M. (in chapter 2), have a complete inability to form long-term declarative memories. They can form and transmit procedural memories; although they cannot remember learning them verbally, they can demonstrate the knowledge through performance (e.g., Gazzaniga, Ivry, and Mangun, 2002). There are also examples of amnesiac patients, such as a patient K. C., who could not remember his own past very well (episodic memories) because it must be recalled like a personal story, and such memories must have a time, place, and feeling associated with them, an ability that seems lost to amnesiac patients. Importantly, such patients as K. C. often have problems imagining their future (Schacter, Tulving). The confluence of memory and neuroimaging studies of healthy adults and brain-damaged patients suggests that the human memory system is actually a constructive and adaptive system that can recall the essential gist, essence, or pattern of an experience at the apparent cost of unerring accuracy. However, there is another powerful advantage of this system, namely, that people use their episodic memories to simulate future scenarios (e.g., Dudai and Carruthers, 2005; Schacter and Addis, 2007; Tulving, 2002). This ability to simulate future scenarios has been labeled *constructive episodic simulation* by Schacter and Addis.

Tulving (2002) has proposed that the ability to simulate and contemplate future scenarios has been the driving force in the evolution of episodic memory. He proposed the term "autonoesis" to refer to the ability, unique to humans, to form a special kind of consciousness in which individuals become aware of the subjective time in which past events happened. It is also this ability that allows humans to travel mentally in time. He (2002) also offered one other provocative speculation on the nature of episodic memories. Mental time travel, by way of episodic processes, allows awareness of not only the past but of what may happen in the future. "This awareness allows autonoetic creatures to reflect on, worry about, and make plans for their own and their progeny's future in a way that those without this capability possibly could not. *Homo sapiens*, taking full advantage of its awareness of its continued existence in time, has transformed the natural world into one of culture and civilization that our distant ancestors, let alone members of other species, possibly could not imagine." (p. 20). Interestingly, Baddeley (2001) viewed his own proposed episodic buffer in working memory as intimately tied to Tulving's concept of episodic memory, although Baddeley sees the episodic buffer as strictly a temporary storage buffer, whereas he views Tulving's episodic memory is primarily a system concerned with long-term storage. However, despite Baddeley's differentiation, it appears obvious that Tulving's concept of episodic memory has an important short-term component. Thus, Tulving's concept of episodic memory is one of the key features of Baddeley's episodic buffer.

Baddeley (2000, 2001) also proposed that greater working memory capacity would allow for the reflection and comparison of multiple past experiences. This might allow an individual to actively choose a future action or create an alternative action, rather than simply choosing the highest path of probable success. Although an individual would still be better off (compared to one without benefit of past experience) choosing alternatives simply based on the past (an example of an inflexible anticipatory process), Baddeley proposed that greater working memory capacity would allow for the formulation of mental models more likely to be successful as future behaviors.

Shepard (1997) postulated that natural selection favored a perceptual and representational system able to provide implicit knowledge (long-term memory) of the pervasive and enduring properties of the environment, and that natural selection also favored a heightened degree of voluntary access to this representational system (created by working memory). This access, he proposed, facilitated the accurate mental simulation of varying actions, allowing the evaluation of the success or failure of these actions without taking a physical risk. Shepard thought that the mere accumulation of facts would not result in advances in scientific human knowledge; these require "thought experiments." He also postulated that every real experiment might have been preceded by thought experiments that increased the probability of the success of the real experiment.

Recent neuroimaging studies now link the prefrontal cortex to episodic memory recall. When normal adults are asked to form episodic memories (through experimental manipulation), the left prefrontal cortices are differentially more involved than the right prefrontal cortices, whereas when they are asked to recall them, this pattern is reversed and right prefrontal cortices are more heavily involved (see Tulving, 2002, for a review of these studies). It is important to note, however, that these episodic memory tests did not necessarily involve future episodic memories or mental time travel. Thus, mental time travel and episodic memory are not completely synonymous terms, and, in our opinion, simulation and the formation of alternative future plans in all likelihood calls upon many other cortical regions.

Working Memory Capacity

Because working memory appears to involve simultaneous attention to task-relevant information, as well as its manipulation, processing, and storage, experimental psychologists researching individual differences developed the concept of a *working memory span* (e.g., Daneman and Carpenter, 1980, 1983), and more recently *working memory capacity* (Engle and Kane, 2004; Kane and Engle, 2002). These two concepts are mostly synonymous, although their measurement varies according to the experimental task. One operational definition of working memory capacity is simply how many items can be recalled during a task. Engle and Kane have importantly noted that there is probably no pure measure of working memory capacity, as a task must be designed in a domain, such as verbal, visual, acoustic, spatial, etc. Thus, whereas there may exist a domain-free working memory span, it may not be directly measurable. As Baddeley (2001) has also noted, there is the possibility that working memory span or capacity has a number of subcomponents, rather than a "single pool of processing or inhibitory capacity" (p. 92). Nonetheless, a variety of measures have been developed to assess working memory capacity. And these measures do have practical applications; working memory capacity correlates with a number of important, practical abilities, including reading comprehension (Daneman and Carpenter, 1980, 1983), vocabulary learning (Daneman and Green, 1986), language comprehension (King and Just, 1991), reasoning (Kyllonen and Crystal, 1990; Halford, Cowan, and Andrews, 2007), suppression of a designated event (Feldman Barrett, Tugade, and Engle, 2004), language acquisition and second-language learning (Baddeley, Gathercole, and Papagno, 1998), many neuropsychological measures (Engle and Kane, 2004), fluid intelligence (gF; Engle and Kane), and general intelligence (Spearman's g; Kyllonen, 1996). In a review of cognitive measures related to working memory capacity, Feldman Barrett, Tugade, and Engle (2004) found 37 processing outcomes, in six broad categories, that were moderately to strongly correlated with individual differences in working memory capacity. It is also important to note the strong relationship of fluid intelligence to working memory capacity is an important one because fluid intelligence is thought to measure one's ability to solve novel problems, and it appears less influenced by learning and culture and more influenced by some feral or inherent ability to figure out solutions to problems.

Heritability of Working Memory

No complex human behavior is without a genetic influence (e.g., Turkheimer, 2000), and it is clear that the bulk of modern human nature and behavior, including predilections, predispositions, fears, personality, psychopathology, and motivations have evolved via natural selection upon genetic mutations over millions of years. In 2001, and there has been much additional research since that time, Morley and Montgomery compiled a list of over 150 possible genes that appear to influence cognition. Thus, it should come as no surprise that there is currently good empirical evidence that working memory, its executive functions, and its subsystems have a strong genetic basis. In the first study of its kind, Coolidge et al. (2000), in an analysis of child and adolescent twins as rated by their parents, found that a core of executive functions, consisting of planning, organizing, and goal attainment, was highly heritable (77 percent), and due to an additive (see chapter 4 for an explanation) genetic influence. Ando, Ono, and Wright (2001) also found a strong additive genetic influence (43–49 percent) upon working memory storage and executive functions, in both phonological and visuospatial tasks. Rijsdijk, Vernon, and Boomsma (2002) found a 61 percent additive heritability (with an 80 percent confidence interval of 52–67 percent) in young adult Dutch twin pairs on the digit span task of the Wechsler Adult Intelligence Scale, which is one measure of phonological storage capacity. Hansell et al. (2001), using event-related potential slow-wave measure of working memory in a visuospatial task, showed solid heritability (35–52 percent) in a sample of 391 adolescent twin pairs.

Summary

Working memory is a highly heritable trait that has received considerable attention in the cognitive literature. Although it may ultimately be difficult to prove, it appears that there may be some pure (domain-free) working memory capacity that varies across individuals. It undoubtedly evolved in primates and in hominin evolution. The nature of this capacity has something to do with attention to task-relevant stimuli and the ability to maintain this information in active memory. Its nature probably also includes an equally important ability to maintain these relevant memories in the presence of external interference (irrelevant stimuli) and internal interference (inappropriate natural responses or prepotent responses). It is also probably easier to name the parts of the brain that have *not* been implicated as critical to working memory, but the neural substrate of working memory, its executive functions and subsystems, appears to be the frontal and prefrontal cortex, parietal and temporal cortices, and the basal ganglia (among other cortical and subcortical regions).

4

Brain Evolution

How Brains Evolve

The role of genes

In high-school biology we were taught that genes, which are sequences of DNA, are the blueprints controlling the morphology and physiology of organisms. A segment of DNA on a chromosome codes for the production of an amino acid, amino acids combine into proteins, and proteins are the building blocks of organisms, including their brains. Sometimes, as in the ABO blood type, a single gene controls the expression of a trait. But more often many genes work together to control expression. From this perspective, a structure as large and complex as the brain must be under the control of thousands, perhaps tens of thousands of genes, and any significant change in brain anatomy or function must require changes in many genes. As it turns out, this picture is far from complete.

One of the more surprising results of the "human genome project" was the small number of total genes found – somewhere between 20,000 and 25,000. We had been taught (university this time) that the human genome must consist of hundreds of thousands of individual genes. How else could such a complex organism be determined? The answer is that genes are far subtler in their operation than science initially thought. Yes, there are genes that code for specific amino acids, but there are also genes that "re-edit" the sequence of base pairs in the gene so that it comes to code for a different amino acid, in much the same way that a single set of letters can be recombined into many words, or a set of words into many sentences. There are also genes that control the order and timing in which other genes are activated or deactivated in development. These are the regulatory genes, and they have a profound influence on the anatomy and physiology of organisms. For example, there is a gene (*BF-1*) that regulates the number of cell divisions in the development of cortical neurons. In mice this gene allows 11 cycles of cell division; in monkeys it allows 28 (Allman, 2000). If each stage of cell division doubles the number of neurons . . . well, you can do the math. In other words, a difference in a single regulatory gene can produce a huge difference in anatomy.

Other genome projects, such as those devoted to understanding the chimpanzee genome, have also revealed fascinating insights. Research over the past five years has been devoted to the sequencing of the complete chimpanzee genome and, depending on the methods of analysis, has revealed either a genetic similarity of about 99 percent or one of 95 percent. With such a high degree of DNA similarity comes a puzzle: if humans and chimpanzees are so alike in their DNA, why are the two phenotypically so different, in both anatomy and behavior? Something other than just DNA similarity, as it is currently measured, must be at the root of these phenotypic differences, including the differences in brain and cognition. Some of these differences undoubtedly reflect changes in regulatory genes, such as those controlling neural cell division, but humans also appear to have far more of their genes coding for neuronal development (the brain) than do chimpanzees, thus rendering the high genomic similarity figures a bit misleading. This mismatch in genetic and phenotypic variability has given rise to a whole new field of epigenetics, which deals with inheritance from a non-DNA perspective (we will discuss epigenetics later in this chapter).

The role of experience

Environment also plays a role in the development of brains and cognition. Many important neural developments take place *in utero,* and the sequence and rate of these developments can be affected by changes in uterine environment. For example, male and female brains develop similarly until about the seventh week of gestation. At this point males develop testes, which flood the fetus with androgens, which are the hormones that channel the development of the fetus toward a male anatomy (Wynn, Tierson, and Palmer, 1996). But they also inhibit the growth of neurons and axons, including the development of inter-hemisphere connections. One result of this is that male brains are slightly more lateralized than female brains. Perhaps, as a consequence, males are more likely to suffer from chronic hemisphere-related deficits such as dyslexia. In a sense this difference is genetic – a gene controls the timing of fetal androgens – but this is not a gene *for* lateralization. Lateralization results from a change in uterine environment that is a by-product of the gene's primary effect. The uterine environment is sensitive to changes in the mother's diet (e.g. intake of toxic chemicals), levels of stress, and personal experience. Birth itself is a traumatic event for the neonate that very often includes several minutes of oxygen deprivation ("blue babies"), and oxygen deprivation causes the death of neurons.

As noted in chapter 2, the brain continues to develop after birth, including the addition of neurons, formation of axons, dendrites and synapses, and myelination of axons. And, as we noted earlier, one of the most significant processes of this development is apoptosis – programmed cell death. After producing over 2×10^{10} neurons, the body starts to kill them off. It is not entirely clear why, though the metabolic cost of excess neurons may be one reason. This process has also been called synaptic pruning, where the number of overproduced or weak neuronal connections are reduced. Experience plays a role in determining which neurons are culled. It is a "use it or lose it" scenario in which unused neurons die, and used neurons survive, so that the experiences of a neonate have an important effect on the pattern of apoptosis. But experience does not stop here. If a child, and to a lesser degree an adult, "exercises" a portion of the brain heavily and consistently, the number of neurons and axons devoted to this activity expand. Braille readers and string musicians, for example, have a larger portion of their motor cortex devoted to the tips of the fingers than is typical. The brain is a plastic organ that responds to experience, and this plasticity is an important component of learning.

But there are limits. Even though environment and experience influence the development of the brain, they can only do so within limits set by genes. No matter how long and diligently researchers have tried to teach a symbolic-syntactical language to an ape, the results have been limited. Yes, when exposed to human language as an infant, the bonobo Kanzi developed an ability to understand humans. This success was partly the result of the plasticity inherent in all mammalian, and especially primate, neural development (Savage-Rumbaugh et al., 1998). But, even when pressed, Kanzi cannot produce a syntactical construction of more than four symbols, and the vast majority of his productions are much shorter. He simply does not have the neurological "stuff" to do it, and this is a limit imposed by his genes.

The role of natural selection

Individuals who reproduce successfully pass more genes on to the next generation than those who do not. This "differential reproduction" is natural selection, and it is the primary mechanism of evolutionary change, including the evolution of brains and cognition. The realization and description of natural selection was Darwin's brilliant contribution to the biological sciences and, fittingly, when scholars discuss the role of differential reproduction they often refer to it as Darwinian evolution, or Darwinism. Note that Darwinism is not a synonym for evolution. Instead, it is shorthand for an evolutionary mechanism, the first realistic one to be described, and the most important for producing long-term directional changes in populations of living organisms. Evolutionary scientists often remark that natural selection is a "creative" force in evolution. But how can differential reproduction "create" anything new? The truth is that natural selection can only create change if the raw material for change already exists. Differential reproduction does not itself create new genes. Instead, it selects genes that already exist and increases their frequency (or decreases, in the case of less successful genes). If the individuals in a population of organisms were all genetically identical, natural selection could not change it (though due to plasticity some might well reproduce more, it just would not affect the gene pool). So there must be a process that produces new genes. This process is mutation. Mutation is said to occur whenever the chemical make-up of a gene, i.e. the DNA, changes. There are many causes of mutation – toxins, natural and artificial radiation, and simple errors that can occur when genes duplicate themselves during normal cell division. There is still considerable debate in the biological sciences about whether most mutations are bad or just neutral. This need not concern us. What is universally agreed is that mutations are only rarely "good" in the sense of changing a gene in a way that produces an immediate reproductive advantage for its owner. However, mutation is such a common occurrence that just by chance good results occur often enough to provide raw material for natural selection. Mutations produce small effects on anatomy and physiology, but even small advantages can yield long-term evolutionary effects. The geneticist J. B. S. Haldane (1927) devised the following example: if a new gene gave the individuals who had it only a 1 percent advantage in reproduction (101 offspring to 100 for everyone else), it would increase in frequency from .1 percent to 99.9 percent in only 4,000 generations. For humans, 4,000 generations is only 100,000 years – a very brief moment in the evolutionary time scale.

If natural selection worked only via the one gene = one amino acid route, it would be slow, but ultimately effective. What happens when natural selection works on regulatory genes? If a mutation occurred that changed, say, the number of cycles of neuronal cell division, the result would be a dramatic change in the number of total neurons. Even though the mutation itself is small, the change in anatomy would be dramatic, and if this yielded a reproductive advantage (and keep in mind that brains are metabolically expensive, so an advantage is by no means guaranteed), it would increase rapidly in frequency.

One form of mutation has been very important in the evolution of brains – gene duplication. Occasionally an error occurs during gene replication (in cell division) in which a segment of DNA doubles in length by duplicating the sequence of base pairs. There are now two copies of the gene. If this occurs in one of the structural genes that control the basic organization of anatomy, the result will be a duplicated structure. This has happened on several occasions over the 500 million or so years of vertebrate evolution. The original structure continues to perform its original function, but the new one is free to vary, which means that mutations to it will not be under severe selection against new forms. And, because it is a structural gene, beneficial mutations can yield profound changes in anatomy. This has been one of the most important avenues of evolutionary change in the vertebrate brain. Significant changes have resulted from changes in single regulatory genes.

Heritability revisited: epigenetics

Until very recently, the field of behavior genetics has been dominated by "DNA-thinking"; models of inheritance have been restricted to single genes, single regulatory genes, or additive genetic patterns (multiple genes or polygenic effects). In the past few years, thousands of research articles have been devoted to non-DNA methods of heritability, termed *epigenetics*. This field is so new there is still no generally accepted definition of epigenetics. One recent attempt by Bird (2007) defined it thusly: the structural adaptation of chromosomal regions so as to register, signal, or perpetuate altered activity states. The field of epigenetics recognizes that not all methods of genetic transmission involve traditional DNA models of dominant, recessive, and additive patterns. Epigenetics implicitly recognizes that RNA, chromatin, "junk" DNA, interactions among DNA strands, and still as yet unrecognized methods of heritability, can also be responsible for changes in phenotypes across generations. At least one reason for the rise of the field had always been the "problem" that identical twins (monozygotic) do not always have identical vulnerability to genetic illnesses, despite their theoretical identicalness in regard to their genetic make-up. One recent example of epigenetic inheritance comes from Pembrey et al. (2006) who observed that the paternal (but not maternal) grandsons of Swedish boys who were exposed to famine in the nineteenth century were less likely to die of cardiovascular disease; if food was plentiful then diabetes mortality in the grandchildren increased. This pattern is strongly suggestive, not of traditional DNA mutational genetics, but of transgenerational epigenetic heritability.

We mention the role of epigenetics at this point in our book because we proposed earlier in chapter 1 that a neural mutation may have occurred that led to a reorganization of the brain that enabled modern executive functions. More specifically, we suggested there was an enhancement in working memory capacity which came relatively late in human evolution, and in chapter 11 we will address many of the details and implications of enhanced working memory capacity. However, we will intentionally remain vague about the nature of the genetic tranmission that led to enhanced working memory. We initially assumed it might be an additive genetic neural mutation, which we still think is a reasonable assumption. Given this very new field of epigenetics, which proposes non-traditional means of passing traits across generations, we have become more conservative. We now hypothesize that some neural mutation *or epigenetic event* led to a reorganization of the brain that enabled modern thinking.

Evolutionary Psychology

We can also investigate the role of natural selection in the evolution of cognition. Ultimately, significant cognitive changes must have a neural basis, but the scientific understanding of the links between cognition and neural architecture is in its infancy. But we can ask how a cognitive feature could affect reproductive success. This basic question is the foundation for the field of evolutionary psychology.

Evolutionary psychology is not, as the name might imply, any psychological study informed by evolutionary thinking, nor is it any evolutionary study informed by psychology. Instead, it is a fairly circumscribed research emphasis that focuses on the role that natural selection played in determining specific features of human cognition. It takes a number of explicit theoretical and methodological stances in regard to the nature of cognition, and the role of natural selection. It sees human cognition as being "massively modular," consisting of a large number of specific abilities that have evolved to solve specific evolutionary problems. Irwin Silverman and colleagues (2000), for example, have studied features of human spatial cognition and, through numerous experiments, have isolated an ability they term "space constancy," which is the ability to hold an image of an object or scene constant through changes in the observer's point of view or orientation. It is the ability behind performance in "mental rotation" tests. They go on to argue that this ability evolved in "the environment of evolutionary adaptedness" to solve problems in wayfinding. If prehistoric hunters conceived of space as invariant, and were able to imagine how landmarks would appear from the viewpoint of a return journey, they would be more successful, not just in hunting but in providing for mates and offspring. More of their genes for advanced wayfinding would make it into the next generation. In addition, because space constancy was more important for males (the presumed hunters), selection would favor males with these abilities more than females. This in turn explains the significant and reliable differences between modern men and women in tests of spatial cognition. This example underlines several features of evolutionary psychology. First, the targeted ability is narrowly circumscribed; space constancy is a specific ability within the general domain of spatial thinking. Second, natural selection via differential reproductive success is the only mechanism invoked. Third, the evolutionary reasoning is based on "reverse engineering." Space constancy is a real ability; therefore it must have evolved. But how? Evolutionary psychologists answer this question by asking what the feature is "designed" to do, that is, they argue backward from form to function. This is reverse engineering. In this case, space constancy seems to be "designed" as an aid to wayfinding; therefore, wayfinding selected for space constancy. Note that Silverman and colleagues make no reference to the traditional bodies of evidence used in evolutionary science – fossils, comparative psychology, or archeology. Evidence that a cognitive ability is well designed is considered sufficient. Reverse engineering does the rest (more on this later).

Evolutionary psychology has provided a framework for making sense of experimental results that might otherwise be puzzling. The sex difference in spatial cognition is robust and reliable (Halpern, 1992). There seems nothing in the daily lives of modern people that requires it. So why is it there? Silverman's evolutionary psychological hypothesis gives an answer based in evolution and the daily lives not of modern people, but of our ancestors. One of the most important insights of evolutionary psychology is that our minds evolved long ago in conditions very different from those of the modern world. Where evolutionary psychology comes up short is in specifying when ("long ago" is pretty vague), and in what circumstances. For those pieces we need the paleoanthropological record.

The Role of Constraint

Though the creative potential of natural selection is impressive, it is not limitless. It can only work on pre-existing variation, and this variation by its very nature consists of small deviations in extant structures and behaviors. Darwin himself described variation as copious, non-directional, and small in extent. Because of this, the extant structures of an organism constrain the possible solutions to an adaptive problem, creating a biological leash. It is a bit like the engineering problem posed by the need for energy efficient, non-polluting, personal vehicles. The ideal solution would not be an internal combustion engine burning fossil fuels. However, this has been the extant technology for over a century, and it is far easier, and more cost-effective, to tweak the extant system than to start from scratch. Nature rarely, if ever, starts from scratch. When vertebrates began to develop land-based adaptive niches, legs did not miraculously appear as monstrous mutations. Instead, the extant locomotor structure, in this case lobed fins, were modified into terrestrial legs. Some of the constraints on possible anatomy and function are much older than this. The basic sequence of genes controlling the structure of the vertebrate body, including the major structures of the brain (hind, mid, and fore brain), evolved over 500 million years ago, and some of them are even shared with other major phyla of animals such as the arthropods (Allman, 2000; Gould, 2002). These structural genes are so fundamental to the organization of an individual that a mutation here probably would not be able to produce a viable offspring.

Because evolution must work with the material at hand, a very common solution to adaptive problems is change in function. Feathers are a famous example. They evolved initially in a group of dinosaurs for the purpose of thermal regulation (they are ultimately modified skin cells). They helped maintain body heat. But in one group of descendants, the birds, feathers took on the additional function of aiding flight. Gould and Vrba (Gould and Vrba, 1982) proposed the term "exaptation" for such a functional shift, and the term is now in general use.

The human brain and cognition present many examples of exaptation. The hippocampus, for example, plays a crucial role in the formulation of long-term declarative memories. In other mammals, however, its primary role lies in spatial orientation and navigation. The declarative memory formation function is an exaptation, a functional shift in a pre-existing brain structure. A specifically cognitive example involves primate facial recognition. As we shall see in chapter 5, primates, including humans, are very sensitive to minute changes in the facial expressions of others. This evolved as a response to the need for communicating subtle messages between individuals in complex social groups. But it did not miraculously appear. Instead, it built on a prior cognitive ability – shape recognition, symmetry in particular. Shape recognition had evolved much earlier as a component of mammalian mate recognition and assessment (Gangestad, 1997). Other solutions to the communication problem are easy to imagine (odor assessment, acute hearing, formal language, even telepathy), but the one available to early primates was linked to an ability already in place – shape recognition.

The Metabolic Trade-off

In addition to structural constraints on brain evolution, there are also metabolic constraints. Neural tissue is very "expensive," in the sense that it requires large numbers of calories to maintain. Every increase in the quantity of neurons will have a metabolic cost. In order for the brain to evolve in size, the organism must either evolve a way to acquire calories more efficiently, or decrease the caloric demands of some other tissue. Mammals, for example, have brains that are eight to ten times larger than reptile brains, and they "pay" for the bigger brains by having a much more efficient digestive system that includes mastication of food before it is even swallowed. Vertebrate bodies have other expensive tissues, such as the heart, the liver, and the digestive tract. From the perspective of survival and reproductive success, some of these expensive tissues are not amenable to reduction – evolving a smaller heart, for example, would have tremendous risk. So there tends to be an evolutionary trade-off between brain size and the digestive tract. Leaf-eating monkeys, who have long, specialized digestive tracts, have smaller brains than more omnivorous monkeys (Allman, 2000). The "bottom line" here is that brains are expensive, and because they are expensive they must provide some very marked selective advantage, or they will not evolve beyond the minimum size and organization necessary for the organism's continued success.

Summary

The story of brain and cognitive evolution within the vertebrates (we will not worry about cephalopods) is a story of natural selection and structural constraint. Over the last half billion years natural selection has shaped the vertebrate brain into a remarkably complex organ for acquiring, analyzing, and responding to information from the physical and social environment. We now know that brain and cognitive evolution need not have been long, slow, gradual processes, as envisioned by Darwin. Natural selection is still the primary agent of change, but the complex interrelationship between structural and regulatory genes yields long-term patterns that are anything but simple.

Methods of Study

Evolutionary science has traditionally emphasized two methods of enquiry – the comparative method and paleontology. Scientists interested in the evolution of the human brain and cognition supplement these approaches with two additional methods – archeology and reverse engineering.

The comparative method

Evolution is a story of branching and divergence, and a large-scale chart of the results of evolution would resemble a vast tree or bush. The comparative method uses similarities and differences between living organisms to reconstruct the sequences of branching, or divergence. A simple thought experiment (powered by the readers' working memory!) can illustrate the basic principles. Think of the anatomies of a dog, a bear, a horse, and a crow. Which two are most similar? We hope you answered "the dog and the bear." What is the next most similar? The horse is more similar to the dog and the bear than to the crow because it, too, has hair, a variety of teeth, and "live" birth. From these similarities and differences it is possible to hypothesize a sequence of evolutionary branching. In our simple example the first divergence was between the dog/bear/horse ancestor and the crow ancestor, followed by dog/bear and horse, and finally dog and bear. In other words, just by examining living organisms we can generate a hypothesis about the sequence of evolutionary divergence. Of course, actual comparative anatomy is more sophisticated than our simplistic example, but the basic principles are the same.

Organisms can resemble one another for two very different reasons. They can resemble one another because they are related, in which case they have inherited their similarities from a common ancestor. If we examine the teeth of dogs and bears, we find that they resemble one another in number and variety because they inherited this pattern from a common ancestor. Such similarities are termed homologies. Alternatively, two organisms can be similar because they have adapted over time to doing similar things. Dolphins resemble fish because both are vertebrates with streamlined anatomies adapted to swimming. We term such similarities analogies (a more accurate term is "homoplasies," but as the spelling of this term is perilously close to homology we opt for using the less confusing analogy). In general, analogies tend to be found in more superficial anatomies because they reflect recent adaptations through which the organism interfaces with its environment. It is usually possible to identify underlying differences in basic anatomy that prevent us from mistaking analogies for homologies. The basic functional anatomy of a fish is different from that of a dolphin (gills vs. lungs, for example). The most basic structure of all is DNA, and comparative DNA has become the most important tool for identifying homologous relationships. It is especially useful when trying to sort out relationships between closely related organisms that all share the same basic body plans (e.g., primates).

When evolutionary scientists reconstruct long sequences of divergence, our simple distinction between homology and analogy rapidly becomes inadequate. Some homologies are older than others, in the sense that they are similarities inherited from a much earlier common ancestor. All primates have a neocortex, for example, but sharing this trait does not tell us much about primates – all mammals have a neocortex. If we ask "why do primates have a neocortex?", the appropriate answer is "because they are mammals." This does not help us much with understanding primates, or the neocortex. If we want to understand the evolutionary reasons for the neocortex, we must first identify the ancestral group that first evolved this neural feature. Comparative evidence tells us that all mammals have a neocortex, which means that the common ancestor to all mammals must have had one. We say that possession of a neocortex is an "ancestral" characteristic for mammals. It is now possible to ask why; that is, to ask what conditions of the first mammals selected for an expansion of the external layers of the brain. It is also possible to ask if there is anything about primate brains that is different from the brains of other mammals. If there are, such features are "derived." Visual half-fields and an expanded visual cortex are derived features for primates. Now for the tricky bit: "ancestral" and "derived" are relative terms, and their reference varies according to the level of specificity of the question. If we ask "why do humans have an expanded visual cortex?", the answer is "because we are primates." Expanded visual cortex is now an ancestral characteristic for primates, because we are comparing members of the group to one another. Do human brains have derived features? The answer is yes. The role of the hippocampus in transferring declarative memory traces to long-term memory is a derived feature for humans; no other primate has a hippocampus that does this. Interestingly, this derived feature has no obvious expression in gross anatomy. Other primates all have a hippocampus (indeed it is ancestral for vertebrates) but it does not function in quite the same way. When neuroscientists compare the brains of closely related forms, there are usually few obvious differences in gross anatomy but there are often differences in neural functioning due to much less visible neuroanatomical differences.

The same principles apply to cognitive traits identified through experiment or observation. Humans can follow the gaze of another individual and use that information to identify an object or individual of interest. Why, in an evolutionary sense, can we do this? Is it a derived characteristic unique to humans? If it is, then we need to explain its evolution in terms of circumstances that our ancestors encountered after the split from apes. If it is ancestral, we need to identify which common ancestor first evolved the ability. When we look around at other primates we find that all anthropoids (monkeys, apes, and humans) can follow gaze. It is an ancestral ability for anthropoids. We can now ask why. It appears to have evolved as an aid to solving complex social problems (more on this later).

It is almost impossible to answer an evolutionary question without reference to the comparative evidence because it allows us to frame the question correctly. If all anthropoid primates have neural cells dedicated to recognizing faces, we cannot simply ask why humans are good at facial recognition. We must ask for all primates. In turn, comparative evidence identifies those features, such as the ability to pass a false belief test, that are derived for humans, and which make us unique. To understand how and why these unique, derived features evolved, we must turn to other evidence.

Fossils

A fossil is a rock in the shape of a once-living organism or, more often, *part* of a once-living organism. A fossil forms when minerals in the soil replace chemicals in the organism. Fossilization can only occur if an organism is buried, and the sequence of events from a living organism to a buried organism is often very destructive. This is why the fossil record is rich in mollusks, which often live on the beds of oceans and lakes where they are easily buried, and poor in primates, who live in tree tops and whose bodies rarely get buried intact after death. Hard body parts are more likely to fossilize than soft parts, which have usually been consumed, or decayed long before burial. The fossil record presents an abundance of teeth, whose enamel makes them the hardest parts of most vertebrates.

Paleontologists, the scientists who study fossils, rely on their knowledge of anatomy, and their familiarity with the comparative evidence, to identify and interpret fossils. But knowledge of comparative anatomy is only the beginning. Paleontologists also strive to reconstruct the environment in which an organism lived through analysis of the sediment, and identification of other fossil animals and plants. If a paleontologist knows what the environment was like, and has a good idea of an organism's anatomy, he or she can reconstruct how the organism lived – its adaptive niche – including diet (teeth) and locomotion (limbs).

Brains do not fossilize very often, but skulls and crania do (the cranium is the part of the skull that contains the brain). Sometimes fine-grained sediment will fill the space left behind by the brain and produce a natural cast of the external shape of the brain. Far more often, the cranium is fragmented prior to fossilization, and the paleontologist must reconstruct the cranium from pieces. If most of the pieces still exist, the reconstruction is generally reliable, assuming that the paleontologist has a good knowledge of cranial anatomy. By filling the reconstructed cranium with small seeds, or similar material, the paleontologist can measure the cranial capacity, which is a measure of brain size (cranial capacity is slightly larger than the brain itself; if one requires true brain size there is a well-established formula that can be used to convert cranial capacity to brain weight, but in practice most paleontologists are satisfied with cranial capacity). From a reconstructed cranium it is also possible to make an artificial cast of the brain, usually by pouring in liquid latex. The resulting "endocast" also preserves the external shape of the brain, because the internal surface of the cranium preserves features of the gross anatomy of the brain (Holloway et al., 2004). More recently, 3-D pictures of endocranial shapes taken by neuroimaging techniques such as CAT scans provide much more sophisticated measurements and allow statistical analyses that were previously unavailable with other techniques (see Bruner, 2003).

Brain size

Size has been the most commonly used measure of brain difference in the evolutionary sciences. There are two reasons for this. First, the animal kingdom presents a huge range of brain sizes and, more to the point, animals with large brains exhibit more complex behaviors than those with small brains. It is reasonable to suppose that larger brains, with more neurons, axons, dendrites, and synapses are simply more powerful computers than small brains. This is an especially persuasive argument in our current computer age, where raw power is measured in gigabytes or terabytes. The second reason for the emphasis on brain size is that it is easy to measure. Comparative anatomists can simply weigh brains of different animals to get a measure of size, or even compute size and shape using brain-imaging techniques, a method that has the advantage of not killing the subject. Paleontologists can measure the endocranial volume of a skull with relative ease and the internal shape with greater effort. Reliability of a fossil's cranial capacity depends on how complete a cranium is, and whether or not it has been distorted in fossilization. Complete, undistorted fossil crania are ideal, but not necessary. It is possible to estimate cranial capacity from relatively small sections of the cranial vault if one applies appropriate arcs and chords. This method works reasonably well for established taxa, but becomes problematic for a newly recognized taxon. With fossil primates, and especially with fossil hominins, it is *de rigeur* to measure and publish cranial capacity, if at all possible.

Brain size is not, however, a simple measure. The brain of a sperm whale weighs about 7,500 gm, compared to about 1,350 gm for a human. Is a sperm whale five times more intelligent than a human? Of course not (though we confess that we did not pose this question to a sperm whale). Brain size in vertebrates is correlated to body size. Large animals have larger brains than small animals. The reasons for this are partly neurological; large animals have a larger surface area, and a larger surface area in their major organs, and all of this requires nerve innervation peripherally, and neurons centrally. In other words, just running a larger body will require a larger brain. So, if we want to compare the brain sizes of two vertebrates, we must also know their body sizes. With extant animals one can simply weigh the body and compare it to brain weight. The tricky bit comes with fossils. Complete skeletons of terrestrial vertebrates (the group we are most interested in) are rare, and even for those few examples the estimation of body weight – including muscles, organs, etc. – is not a simple task. Far more often the post-cranial (below the head) skeleton is either entirely missing or represented by only a few fragmentary bones. From these the paleontologist must calculate body size using size relationships established for related living organisms. The desire for a reliable and available measure of body size has led some human paleontologists to argue that the diameter of the eye orbit correlates with body size and can be used as a reliable surrogate when post-cranial bones are missing (Kappelman, 1996)!

If these practical problems of measuring relative brain size were not enough of a hindrance, relative brain size is itself not a simple measure. If we calculate the relative brain size of a shrew, we find that its brain weight is almost 10 percent of its total body weight. For humans this figure is about 2 percent. So, are shrews five times more intelligent than humans? Again, we do not think so. Within any group of related vertebrates (mammals, say), brain size increases as body size increases, but not at the same rate. Body size increases faster than brain size, so that smaller organisms (shrews) have larger relative brain sizes than larger organisms. Evolutionary scientists use the term "allometric" to describe this kind of relationship. Allometric relationships are regular, and it is possible to graph them, and describe them mathematically. The equation for brain size is:

$$Y = kX^a$$

Where Y is brain weight, X is body weight, k is a constant (the "scaling" constant), and ^{a} is an exponent that describes the slope of a regression line

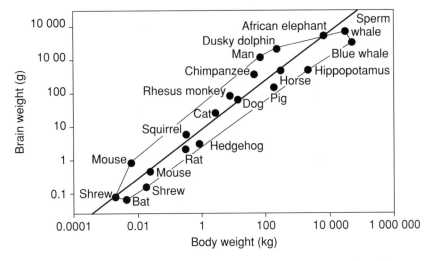

Figure 4.1   Relationship between brain size and body size for 20 selected mammals; the solid regression line represents predicted brain size for body size; mammals, such as humans and dolphins, that fall above the regression line are said to be more encephalized; the scales are logarithmic in order to encompass the large range in absolute brain and body sizes

Source: Roth and Dicke, 2005. © 2005 Elsevier Ltd

(Allman, 2000: 160). For those not mathematically inclined, this simply means that there is a direct and predictable relationship between brain size and body size. In his classic 1973 book, *Evolution of the Brain and Intelligence*, Harry Jerison plotted the brain and body weights of various vertebrate species on a log-log graph (he used log figures to compress the huge range of vertebrate body sizes and brain sizes). Mammals, as a group, fell around a regression line that was farther up the y axis (brain weight) than reptiles or fish; for any given body weight, a mammal has a brain that is eight to ten times larger than a reptile brain. This result is perhaps not surprising, but the sheer size of the difference indicates that mammalian brains have evolved to perform differently from reptile brains. What could require such a vast increase in brain power? The answer is related to thermoregulation and learning. Mammals maintain a relatively constant internal body temperature, and require neurological resources to do so. Mammals also rely very heavily on learned behavior, rather than pre-programmed instinctual responses, and this is the behavioral feature that is responsible for most of the dramatic increase in brain size. But, of course, mammals also vary in relation to one another (see figure 4.1 for a regression of mammalian brain weight to body weight). Primates fall above the brain weights predicted by their body sizes, with humans being especially large.

The brain weight/body weight regression is widely used in evolutionary discussions, but it does have its limits. For example, it is a meaningless number for comparing individuals of the same species to one another. Modern human brains vary in size from 1,100 cc to almost 2,000 cc, and there is no known correlation between brain size and intelligence, however one chooses to measure it. It is at the other extreme, taxonomically, that the relation is most informative, as in Jerison's comparison of major vertebrate groups.

The brain weight/body weight relation also allows us to predict what the brain size should be for any body weight and, more importantly, allows us to determine if a brain is larger or smaller than it "should" be for its body size. This difference between actual and predicted size is the encephalization quotient, or EQ. Any size increase beyond predicted values should reflect excess capacity not devoted to regulating basic metabolic functions (Jerison, 1973). This capacity must, therefore, be devoted to other brain functions of one kind or another, or so the argument goes. EQ has come to be the primary way in which brain size is compared, because of its presumed correlation with greater behavioral complexity. Exactly what EQ measures is a contentious issue in evolutionary science, but it does have comparative utility. EQ, like relative brain size, is most useful at the general taxonomic level – that is, when comparing major vertebrate groups. It is harder to use at finer taxonomic levels. Primates are a good example, and one directly relevant to human evolution. When we compare them to other mammals using the graph in figure 4.1, primates, on average, fall above the mammalian regression. Moreover, some whales and dolphins fall higher, on average, than primates. And, when it comes to correlating EQ with behavioral complexity, the relationship is much less clear than the one between mammals and reptiles. The EQ of humans and dolphins is very similar, for example. What does this mean? As it turns out, both do have very large brains for their body sizes, but very different parts of the brain have enlarged. We are encephalized for different reasons, and EQ alone does not take this into account. Nevertheless, there are some general trends in primate EQs which tell an interesting story, and which we will address later. There a number of ways to calculate EQ, determined primarily by the reference group used to define the regression line. In this book we will use EQ values calculated in relation to the average brain sizes of placental mammals. Finally, when it comes to plugging fossil brain sizes into the equation (literally and metaphorically), we not only have the problem of uncertain body sizes, we are also dealing with closely related species, a taxonomic level at which EQ may not be either reliable, or interpretable (Schoenemann, 2006).

Endocasts
At first consideration endocasts might not appear to have much potential for interpretation. They are, after all, impressions of the internal contours of the cranium, not actual fossilized brains, and while external brain features do come to be impressed on the cranial bone, the dura and meninges mute detail. Even the best endocasts preserve only gross features of brain anatomy, such as the lateral fissure, and the major lobes. Less pronounced features, such as the angular gyrus or the lunate sulcus, are often impossible to detect reliably. Paleoneurologists, the paleontologists who study endocasts, focus on two types of evidence. First, and most reliable, is the overall shape of the brain. The relative length, height, and breadth of the brain are important features of shape, as are more sophisticated geometric measures such as the length of various arcs and chords (Holloway et al., 2004). Paleoneurologists use overall brain shape for taxonomic purposes (assigning fossils to species and genera), and for interpreting neurological components of the adaptive niche. Much like brain size, endocasts have been most useful when making comparisons at the taxonomic levels of the Order (e.g., *Primates*) and higher. Features of brain shape do reflect an animal's way of life (Jerison, 1973). Moles, for example, have relatively large olfactory bulbs, and an expanded area of the motor cortex devoted to facial whiskers. Their visual cortex is much reduced. These features are preserved, to some extent at least, in endocasts. Of particular importance for primate evolution is the nature of cerebral asymmetry. As we noted in chapter 2, the left and right hemispheres are not mirror duplicates (indeed, symmetry is a pathology), and the patterns of asymmetry reflect cerebral specializations. At lower taxonomic levels, for example at the Family level, differences in overall shape are much more subtle. Humans have a primate brain, and our endocasts look like primate endocasts. There are differences between primates, but they are differences of degree. Humans have a slightly enlarged left occipital, and a slightly expanded right frontal lobe. This pattern can be recognized in endocasts (Holloway et al., 2004). Recently, Bruner (2003, 2004), using sophisticated

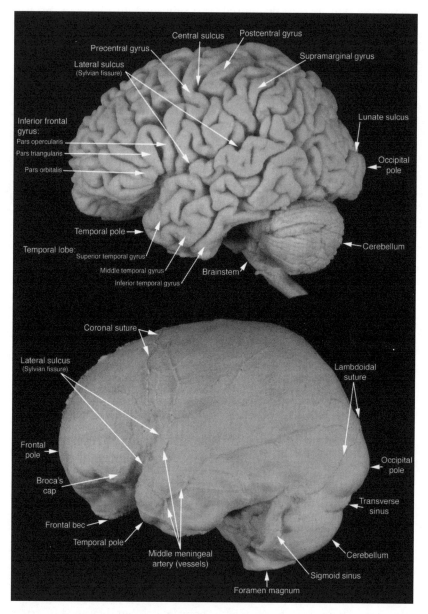

Figure 4.2   Modern human brain and its endocast; note that the endocast preserves only a minimum of detail

Source: Holloway et al., 2004. © 2004 John Wiley & Sons

neuroimaging techniques and equally sophisticated statistical analyses, has been able to demonstrate brain shape differences and even differences in arterial vascularization in brains between various hominins.

The second line of evidence consists of the locations of specific surface features of brain anatomy. Most often these are specific gyri or sulci. Identification of surface features on endocasts is fraught with difficulties, not the least of which is the variability presented by living brains in this regard (figure 4.2).

A feature of particular interest in hominin fossils has been the lunate sulcus, which marks the boundary between the parietal and occipital lobes. It is further back and lower on human brains than ape brains, reflecting the human's greatly expanded parietal lobes. If paleoneurologists could reliably identify the lunate sulcus on hominin endocasts it would be possible to trace the expansion of the parietal lobes over the course of human evolution. Unfortunately, it leaves such a subtle trace on endocasts, if it is there at all, that paleoneurologists rarely agree on its location. Gyri and sulci are so muted on endocasts that detecting them is almost more an art than a science. Columbia University anthropologist Ralph Holloway, arguably the leading US authority on hominin endocasts, once characterized the search for gyri and sulci as "the new phrenology."

In sum, although brain size and endocasts constitute the most direct evidence of vertebrate neurological evolution, neither is ideal. Moreover, they are weakest at precisely the level of analysis that concerns us in this book – the evolution of brains within a single subfamily of apes, the hominins. We will invoke brain size and endocasts in our discussion, but they will not be very helpful when it comes to cognitive evolution. For this, another line of evidence is actually more revealing – archeology.

Archeology

Behavior often leaves tangible traces that survive long after the actors are gone. These traces preserve something of the behavior itself, and can be used to reconstruct it. This is the basic principle behind crime-scene investigations, and also the basic principle behind archeology. Archeologists study traces and patterns in material evidence such as stone tools, pottery, burial goods, etc., that exist in the present in order to reconstruct actions and behavior that occurred in the past. Most archeologists are interested in the recent past and in developments in human history and civilization that have occurred within the last 10,000 years or so. But one group of archeologists, sometimes referred to as Paleolithic archeologists, is interested in an evolutionary scale of development. Among these are archeologists interested in the evolution of cognition, and often they are termed cognitive archeologists.

How can there be an archeology of cognition? Cognition is hard enough to study in the laboratory and in the field. How can we study the cognition of something or someone long dead, through the few bits and traces they have left behind? The answer is the same as it is for any rigorous discipline – by developing concepts and methods that allow identification and interpretation of patterns in the evidence. Actions are guided by cognition, and the traces of action preserve something of the underlying cognition. In certain circumstances cognitive psychologists already study traces of action to assess cognition. One example is the use of children's drawing to assess cognitive development. Another is the use of drawings to identify "lateral visual neglect" in people with possible brain damage. The cognitive archeologist takes a similar stance in relation to the evidence, asking what a particular trace or pattern reveals about the cognition of the actor.

The nature of the archeological record constrains the range of questions that cognitive archeologists can ask. Not all actions leave tangible traces, and only a limited range of traces survive for more than a brief period of time. A simple spoken conversation, for example, leaves no tangible trace, unless it is recorded somehow. As a consequence, archeologists have no direct remains of language until the advent of writing some 6,000 years ago. If we want to address the evolution of language, and some archeologists do, then we must rely on inference from indirect evidence – most often something that we believe to have required language, such as depictive art. Archeologists tend to rely heavily on those activities that preserve well, and thus give archeology a materialist bias. Paleolithic archeologists often seem obsessed with stone tools, for good reason. Virtually every stone tool made over the course of human evolution still exists, in theory preserving a complete sequence of human manufactures going back 2.6 million years. Of course, we have to find them, and place them in time, but these are practical matters of archeological technique. In practice, the sequence is far from continuous. Stone tools preserve the sequence of actions used to create them, and these sequences can reveal something of the minds that organized the action. The next most common traces in the Palaeolithic record are garbage, the remains of food, food processing, and disposal. This record is heavily biased toward meat consumption simply because animal remains (mostly bone) preserve much better than plants. From garbage and tools archeologists reconstruct subsistence – what our ancestors ate and how they got it – and this too can have implications for cognition.

Beyond technology and subsistence the archeological record becomes rather stingy. One of the themes we will emphasize in the section on primates is social cognition, which was also certainly a key player in human cognitive evolution. Archeology can detect some past social interactions, as when we identify the pattern of refuse produced when several individuals sit around a hearth, or when we find beads made from exotic shell that must have been traded in from a long distance. However, our ability to describe Palaeolithic social interactions is limited. We are even less adept at reconstructing the content of symbols. Archeologists, too, marvel at the spectacular cave paintings produced at Chauvet, France, 34,000 years ago. We suspect that they had profound meaning for the artists, and that modern symbolic behavior was involved. But we do not know what the symbols meant.

Cognitive archeology differs from other archeology in its use of cognitive science as a source of interpretive concepts. Traditional archeological concepts have been developed for a variety of goals – temporal ordering (e.g., Bronze Age), social complexity ("Classic" Mesoamerica), cultural affiliation (ancestral Puebloan), and others. Sometimes these concepts may carry cognitive implications (Upper Paleolithic is one we will discuss later), but because they were not defined with cognition in mind using them as such is potentially confusing. Cognitive science is rich in interpretive concepts (working memory is one!) developed to explain features of human cognition. It is the appropriate source for cognitive archeologists. Archeologists must take cognitive concepts and identify the archeologically visible consequences. What consequences, for example, would an enhanced working memory capacity have for the archeological record? How could we recognize it? This is the indispensable methodological step, and it must be done explicitly. It is not enough to claim that people in the Upper Paleolithic 30,000 years ago had modern minds because they painted cave walls. We must be explicit as to what cognitive abilities this activity required. And here we encounter a logical frustration. Archeologists can only identify the minimum competence necessary to produce the patterns we see. We are always at risk of underestimating ability. By the same token, it is unlikely that we will overestimate competence, assuming that we have defined our attributes correctly.

In this book we will emphasize the archeological record for a simple but important reason. Archeological traces are the only direct remains of prehistoric cognition we possess. As we will see below, features of modern cognition suggest certain evolutionary developments, and even certain evolutionary scenarios. But without actual evidence from the past these scenarios remain hypotheses. Yes, the archeological record is far from complete, and the traces are often enigmatic and hard to interpret, the more so the further back we look. But they remain the best evidence available for what our ancestors actually did, and how they thought.

Reverse engineering

The traditional methods of evolutionary science that we have just reviewed strike many behavioral scientists as too clumsy, or too off-target, or just too unreliable to provide acceptable accounts of cognitive evolution. The human mind is rich and complex, they would argue, and the bits of bone and stone offered up by paleoanthropologists are simply not up to the challenge of documenting cognitive evolution. Instead, the group of scholars we introduced earlier as "evolutionary psychologists" has opted to rely on a single method of enquiry known as "reverse engineering."

Reverse engineering, as the term describes, analyzes the form and structure of an object in order to discover its function. There are many famous historical examples. During the Korean War, a North Korean pilot flew his Mig-15 into South Korea, landed his jet at a United Nations base, and defected. US engineers analyzed the Mig in order to determine why it was superior in performance to the US F-86. The insights acquired were then used to modify future US fighters and tactics. This is reverse engineering; starting from the form of a designed object, analyzing it, and discovering its function. If we consider the human brain and cognition to be "objects" designed by natural selection, we can approach them in the same way. We start with a comprehensive description of the structure of cognition, identify what it is designed to do, and then use this insight to describe how and why it evolved.

Perhaps the most well-known example of this approach is Buss's (2003) discussion of the male preference for certain female body proportions. First, Buss established through controlled experiment that males (college students initially) were more attracted to silhouettes of individuals with waist to hip ratio of about 80 percent. He then documented that this preference was not culturally determined, but in fact was true for all human groups around the world, even though the standards of body pulchritude varied considerably (from thin to fat). He concluded that the human male perceptual system was designed to be sensitive to these body proportions. He could then ask why. His answer is not really surprising. The function of this perceptual sensitivity is to detect females who are healthy and fecund (reproductive potential). Over time, natural selection favored males who had a visual system sensitive to the body proportions of young adult females.

Over the last 20 years evolutionary psychologists have used reverse engineering to argue for the selective reasons behind a large array of human cognitive abilities, including spatial cognition (Irwin Silverman (Silverman and Eals, 1992)), language (Steven Pinker, 1997a, b), cheater detection (Leda Cosmides, 1989), and even religion (Pascal Boyer, 2001). They all share the conviction that the current structure of human cognition preserves traces of its evolutionary past. The methodological challenge is largely descriptive – establishing reliable details of the cognitive abilities in question. Most often this is accomplished through experimental protocols that isolate specific cognitive abilities. From there one can attribute function by linking the abilities to particular features of the human physical and social environment, or, more often, presumed features of an earlier physical and social environment, something termed the "environment of evolutionary adaptedness," or EEA. One of the major tenets of evolutionary psychology is that our minds are adapted to the EEA, a time of small hunting and gathering groups, not the modern world, and that this helps explain many psychological problems.

To one degree or another all evolutionary scientists use reverse engineering to generate hypotheses about function and the selective reasons for a particular anatomy or behavior. As we shall see later, for example, the most unusual derived feature of human anatomy is our upright posture and bipedal locomotion. Evolutionary scientists asked the basic reverse engineering question: What is bipedalism designed to do? For decades, the answer seemed obvious: an upright posture and bipedal locomotion freed the hands for tool use, which was an important derived feature of humans and our ancestors. This was a classic argument from reverse engineering. It was also wrong. Evolutionary scientists now know, from the fossil and archeological records, that bipedalism emerged several million years before evidence for extensive tool use. And the comparative evidence has revealed that other primates regularly use tools and are not bipedal.

An evolutionary factor that confounds reverse engineering is exaptation. Natural selection does not generate new structures, or behaviors, out of thin air. It modifies what already exists. We have already seen that some homologies are older than others. The anatomy of any organism is a complex mix of new, old, and older structures. Similarly, new functions are often performed by old structures. If we reverse engineer the human hand we might well conclude that our opposable thumbs were designed by natural selection to hold tools. In fact, it is an old structure that evolved with early primates some 50 million years ago, and is tied to arboreal locomotion, which modern humans seldom do. We only know this because of our knowledge of non-human anatomy and the fossil record.

Archeologists are especially suspicious of reverse engineering. The archeologist Nick Toth, who we will encounter several times in our exposition, likes to play a game with his house guests. He has a basket filled with unusual tools acquired from yard sales, begged off of friends, or just found. When an archeologist visits, he pulls out one of these tools and asks what its function is, that is, he asks his guest to do a bit of reverse engineering. The guest almost invariably fails. Why? After all, these people are specialists in material culture, and the tools were produced and used by people in their own culture. The answer is that the form of human tools is almost never determined solely by their function (Pye, 1964). Without knowing more about the context of the tool's manufacture and use, it is often impossible to reverse engineer. US Air Force engineers could reverse engineer the Mig-15 because they already knew almost everything about it. For reverse engineering of the human mind to work we need to know more about its evolutionary context than we can reliably recover from the design itself. Presumed features of the EEA are no substitute. It is important to learn as much about the actual context as possible.

Our intent here is not to denigrate evolutionary psychology, which has performed the invaluable service of forcing psychologists to confront evolution, thereby bringing psychology into accord with modern biology. Moreover, it has provided important insights into human evolution. But reverse engineering cannot stand alone. Whenever possible its conclusions need to be checked against the actual evidence of evolution: comparative, fossil, and archeological.

5

Primates

Human brains are primate brains, and human cognition is primate cognition. Much of our brain's anatomy and, indeed, much of the way we think is the way it is because we are primates. It follows that if we want to understand human thinking, and the evolution of human thinking, we must start with primate brains and cognition.

Primates are the Order within the Class *Mammalia* that encompasses monkeys, apes (including humans), and prosimians. From an evolutionary perspective this simply means that all living primates share a common ancestor, which in our case was a mammal that lived over 50 million years ago during the great expansion and diversification of mammals that followed the extinction of the dinosaurs. Most living primates are tropical, the two major exceptions being humans and macaques (e.g., Japanese snow monkeys). Most primates are also arboreal, spending some or all of their lives in the trees, a fact that is reflected in primate anatomy, including the anatomy of primates who no longer live in trees. This shared anatomy has a number of characteristics, the most important being grasping hands and feet for locomotion, and a well-developed visual system. Because primates have been around for over 50 million years they have had ample opportunity to evolve a wide variety of specific anatomies and adaptive niches. This variety reflects a continuum of ancestral (old) and derived (recent) adaptations, making primate comparative anatomy (and behavior) a fascinating topic in its own right. Our interest here is in the evolution of human cognition, so it is necessary only to review those developments, old and recent, that are directly relevant to our theme.

Brains

Primate brains are adapted to the demands of an arboreal way of life. The most salient developments occurred in the areas of the brain that process visual information. The center of a primate's retina is densely packed with photo-receptors, allowing detailed perception in the center of the visual field. Perceptual information passes from the retina through the lateral geniculate nucleus of the thalamus to the primary visual cortex of the occipital lobes. Here the "raw" data is processed initially and passed "forward" in the brain to the parietal and temporal lobes where more complex analysis occurs. Primates are particularly good at recognizing shapes and locating themselves in space. They also have stereoscopic vision. Primate eyes face forward with considerable overlap in the visual fields of each eye. By comparing the two slightly different images, the visual cortex is able to construct depth, an obvious advantage for an animal moving about in the tops of tropical trees. Of course, there is a serious downside to having front-facing eyes – primates cannot see to rear (which might be very useful for driving motor vehicles)! Primates also have hemifield (half-field) vision, which is a curious feature that is the source of "lateral visual field neglect" in humans. As we noted in chapter 2, each eye divides its own visual field, with the right side of the retina recording the left of the visual field, and the left the right. Information from the right side of each retina (left visual field) is then processed by the right hemisphere of the visual cortex, and vice versa for the left. This is unlike most mammals where the entire visual field of each eye is processed contralaterally. If, as occasionally occurs, an individual suffers brain damage in one hemisphere, he or she may lose the ability to process information on one side of the visual field – hence lateral neglect. No one is quite sure why the primate visual system works this way, though some speculate it is to avoid redundancy (Allman, 2000). Primate brains are also good at directing fine motor action; the part of the motor cortex controlling hand and finger movement (ventral premotor cortex) is expanded. In humans this bit of brain anatomy gets co-opted for the control of speech.

Anthropoid Brains

About 40 million years ago the large group of primates that includes monkeys, apes, and humans diverged from the earlier primates (who survive today as the prosimians). These anthropoids were larger than the prosimians, and developed a dietary focus on fruit and leaves, as opposed to the largely insectivorous niches of the prosimians. They also had larger brains, and in particular a larger neocortex. Understanding this expansion is one of the first steps in understanding the human brain itself.

Following the theme of visual acuity, anthropoids added two features to the primate ancestral repertoire – trichromatic color vision and a much-heightened ability to recognize faces and facial expressions. The former required a mutation (a gene duplication, probably) that added a third variety of cone to the retina, along with neural resources in the primary and secondary visual cortices. The result is the full range of color perception enjoyed by humans, and apes, and monkeys. It evolved in anthropoid ancestors as an aid to detecting food in complex forest canopies, most likely fruit. Heightened sensitivity to faces and expression resulted from an expansion of the infero-temporal visual cortex, the area of neocortex generally linked to shape recognition. It is part of what is sometimes termed the "ventral pathway" of visual processing, because information passes from the primary visual cortex of the occipital lobes forward to the temporal lobes, where more sophisticated visual processing takes place. The neurons involved in facial recognition are themselves linked to the amygdala, the structure that attaches emotional valence to perceptions (fear, for example) and this linkage is our clue to the importance of facial expression. The anthropoids use facial expression to communicate emotional states, which play an essential role in anthropoid social behavior. And it is social behavior that explains not just the anthropoid inferior temporal visual cortex, but also the increase in overall brain size and neocortex size.

On average, anthropoids have an EQ of about 2.1, meaning that their overall brain size is about twice as large as one would predict for a placental mammal of comparable size. However, there is a great deal of variability (as low as 1.05 for some Old World monkeys (Begun and Kordos, 2004; Roth and Dicke, 2005), and almost 6 for humans), and this variability both complicates the search for reasons and illuminates possible causes. Some of this variation in brain and neocortex size appears related to the total amount of visual information coming in from the eyes (Kirk, 2006), suggesting that visual specializations of various kinds may effect overall brain size. But some of the variability also appears to result directly from the evolutionary trade-off between brain size and gut length (Aiello and Wheeler, 1995). Leaf-eating (termed *folivory*) anthropoids have smaller brains and neocortices than fruit-eating (termed *frugivory*) anthropoids because leaves must be fermented in a very long gut in order to yield digestible carbohydrates. This requires a heavy metabolic investment in digestion, and because the balance cannot be recouped by decreasing reliance on hearts, kidneys, or livers (the other metabolically expensive tissues), brain size must be limited.

This explains why folivores have smaller brains, but why do frugivores need larger brains? Why not just opt for the metabolically cheaper variety? There are two ways of formulating an answer to this question. First, something about foraging for fruit *selected for* larger brains and neocortices. The best candidate appears to be "mental mapping," the ability to locate oneself and others, and navigate in complex forest habitats. In tropical forests, fruit is distributed in small, concentrated patches that ripen at different times throughout the year. Because fruit is high-quality nutrition, it is under great demand, and there is serious competition from birds and other mammals. If an anthropoid has a mental map of its territory, so the argument goes, it will be able to move efficiently between patches, remember where patches are and when they are likely to be available, and "plan" a foraging pattern that is more effective in the face of competition. This spatial mapping ability is a function of the parietal cortex, i.e., the dorsal pathway of visual processing. A second possibility is that the switch to the concentrated, easily digestible, high-quality nutrition of fruit *released selective pressure against* larger brains, freeing them to expand in response to other selective pressures. The leading candidate in this second scenario is social complexity.

There is no simple measure of social complexity; anthropoids live in a large variety of social systems, from the mostly solitary orangutan males to large multi-male, multi-female troops of baboons. One surrogate for complexity is group size, based on the reasonable assumption that more actors produce more interactions. However, when primatologists tried to correlate brain size (EQ to be precise) with social group size, they found no relationship; group size cannot be used to predict brain size, or vice versa (Allman, 2000; Barton, 2006; Barton and Dunbar, 1997; Dunbar, 1993). It is only when neocortex size is scaled to overall brain size, and the residual is correlated to group size, that a reliable pattern emerges. Group size does reliably predict relative neocortex size. The human neocortex falls just about where it should for a group size of about 150, which is the size of a large hunting-gathering band or, for modern humans, the community of regular personal contacts. Of course, evolutionary schemes are rarely so simple. There is more to evolution than adaptation, and developmental constraint casts this increase in brain size in a rather different light.

Brain size correlates very nicely with several life-history factors, including age at first reproduction and length of the juvenile period (Ross, 2004).

There are, again, several ways to explain this correlation. It could be that both brain size and maturation reflect an increase in body size; however, when body size is controlled the correlation remains. Alternatively, natural selection may have favored delay of reproductive age for reasons of niche complexity and the energetic costs of reproduction, and brain growth came along as a by-product. But most brain growth, in terms of numbers of neurons, occurs pre- and neo-natally, so a simple by-product explanation seems untenable. A third possibility is that selection for brain growth would require lengthening of juvenile periods and age of first reproduction, if only because of the greater amount of information to be learned. Or it could have been a combination of factors: when the number of neurons increases in the neocortex, the number of connections increases even faster, so that "white matter" increases faster than "gray matter"; moreover, to be effective these connections must myelinate, which takes a long time, extending even into late adolescence. What seems clear is that brain growth cannot have occurred simply through selection for more neurons in an adult individual. The process entailed changes in brain development, and physical development. It was not simple, and it was energetically expensive.

Ape Brains

Excepting humans, apes are today much less numerous and successful than the monkeys. Indeed, there are only four species of great apes (chimpanzees, bonobos, gorillas, and orangutans), along with several species of lesser apes (the gibbons and siamangs), all of which are declining in terms of numbers. They are, in a sense, a relic of an earlier age, the Miocene (23 million to 5 million years ago), during which these large, slow-reproducing anthropoids were most varied and successful. It is this slowness of reproduction (long gestation, increased inter-birth interval, and long juvenile period) that placed them at a disadvantage when competing with Old World monkeys, who reproduce much faster, and are almost as clever. Of course, as we have seen, long juvenile periods and late age of first reproduction correlate strongly with brain size. What is hard to unravel is whether apes have large brains because they have extended developmental periods, or whether their large brains required extended development for learning. Whatever the answer, we are in the somewhat unexpected position of suspecting that large brains may be partially implicated in the apes' recent evolutionary decline.

Large brains are expensive and have profound life-history consequences. If they no longer yield a competitive edge, their owners will, predictably, go extinct.

But what edge did ape brains initially possess? In general, apes are more encephalized than monkeys and have much larger absolute brain sizes, which some scholars see as equally important when comparing closely related forms (Begun, 2004; Schoenemann, 2006). Their relative neocortex volume and relative frontal neocortex volume fit a general anthropoid pattern (i.e., they fall on the anthropoid regression line). But there are some differences in more specific anatomical details. The brains of great apes have an expansion of the planum temporale (an area on the dorsal surface of the superior temporal lobe) and Brodman's area 44 (left ventral motor cortex). These have been linked to apes' more complex vocalizations (Brodman's area 44 becomes Broca's area in humans). There is also a marked difference in the cerebellum. The lateral cerebellum of apes is 2.5 times larger than that of monkeys. The cerebellum controls many basic postural functions, but is also involved in the cognitive planning of complex motor actions, sequential patterning, and procedural learning (MacLeod, 2004). Some have suggested that great ape encephalization is linked to suspensory locomotion in forest canopies (Povinelli and Cant, 1995), but others have proposed that it may be linked to "complex foraging," and access to embedded foods in particular (Byrne, 2003; Yamakoshi, 2004).

Chimpanzees are now well known as tool-users and tool-makers. They habitually use tools to access hard-to-acquire foods such as termites, hard-shelled nuts, and honey from well-defended nests. Their solutions vary from community to community, but all rely on complex motor manipulations of objects, often in hierarchically organized sequences, sometimes requiring a series of different tools (McGrew, 1992). Though most dramatically, and habitually, demonstrated by common chimpanzees (*Pan troglodytes*), orangutans have also been observed to use tools to break open nests. This use of tools to access hidden and embedded foods has been termed "extractive foraging" (Parker and Gibson, 1979) (figure 5.1).

But what about gorillas? Even though they rarely use tools, gorillas do use hierarchically organized, complex manipulations to gain access to the pith of nettles. Such manipulations require cognitive resources similar to those required for chimpanzee tool use (Byrne, 2004). It seems, then, that this pattern of complex feeding is shared by all of the great apes (Yamakoshi, 2004), and perhaps explains the very significant difference in the size of the lateral cerebellum, when compared to monkeys.

Figure 5.1 Chimpanzee using one of a series of tools to break into a nest of stingless bees; this is a good example of extractive foraging, an activity shared with early hominins and probably inherited from the common ancestor

Source: Sanz and Morgan, 2007. © 2006 Elsevier Ltd

The Machiavellian Hypothesis and Theory of Mind

The challenges presented by diet and foraging almost certainly selected for specific features of primate cognition; the examples we have mentioned are spatial mapping for fruit-eating anthropoids (including the apes), and extractive foraging for the great apes. There are undoubtedly others. However, these specific adaptive problems do not seem general enough to explain the increase in overall neocortex size true of all anthropoids, and the flexible problem-solving abilities we associate with apes. Specific problems tend to select for specific solutions. In the case of cognitive abilities, one might first expect selection for an encapsulated module, with dedicated neural circuitry, tied to the specific foraging problem. This would be the optimal solution energetically. Although it is possible that such circuitry could be diffuse, and not concentrated in any particular lobe, it seems unlikely

that it would select for overall neocortex expansion, with its heavy energetic cost. This mismatch between the apparent adaptive problem and the
neural solution led primatologists to search for features of anthropoid lives
and niches that might have selected for a general problem-solving ability.
The solution was social behavior. In 1976, Nicholas Humphrey suggested
that the complex social lives of anthropoids selected for their problem-
solving abilities (Humphrey, 1976), and in 1988 Richard Byrne and Andrew
Whiten pulled together various authors into a volume that summarized
evidence for the leading role of social behavior in primate cognition.
The volume was entitled *Machiavellian Intelligence* after the Renaissance
classic *The Prince*, in which Machiavelli set out the requirements, many
unscrupulous, for the successful head of state (Byrne and Whiten, 1988).
In a nutshell, the Machiavellian hypothesis argues that the most complex
part of a primate's daily life is the ever-changing nature of polyadic (more
than two individuals) social interactions. Primate social groups often consist of adult females, their offspring, and adult males. Success in reproduction,
and also access to high-quality foods, requires constant monitoring of one's
social standing. The most successful individuals monitor not only dyadic
relationships (how one relates to one other individual), but also polyadic
relationships (how A relates to B when C is present, how A's relationship
to B might affect D, and so on; if this sounds like your life, or a soap opera,
just remember that you are a good anthropoid primate). We have already
seen that there is a correlation between anthropoid neocortex size and social
group size that probably reflects the increasing complexity of polyadic
interactions in larger social groups. But what is it that is so mentally
challenging about polyadic interactions? Much research has focused on two
related abilities: tactical deception and theory of mind (ToM).

Tactical deception occurs when one individual misleads a second individual in order to obtain some immediate goal normally available to or under
control of the second. Tomasello and Call (1997) relate a classic example
observed by Kummer. A female baboon, apparently wanting to groom
with a subdominant male, slowly inched toward a boulder while in plain
view of the alpha male (who would not approve). When she reached a position from which the alpha male could only see her head, she successfully
groomed with the subdominant male. This is *tactical* deception because
the behavior was tailored to the immediate circumstances. Many organisms
deceive others (camouflage is a good example, as is feigned injury by mother
birds), but this kind of deception is not tactical because it is not a novel
response to a specific condition. Such tactical responses are impressive bits

of problem-solving, and it is easy to overinterpret them. One might, for example, conclude that the female in the example "knew" what the alpha male was thinking, and planned her action to reinforce his belief that she was simply foraging quietly. There is, however, a simpler explanation: over many similar situations she had learned that creeping behind rocks could yield mating opportunities otherwise impossible. Nevertheless, it is an impressive bit of learning. Almost all examples of tactical deception among anthropoids can be explained by learning (Byrne, 2003). Of course, humans regularly rely on an ability to predict what another person knows or believes when we set out to deceive, so the next logical question concerning anthropoids is whether or not they ever use a "theory of mind."

Theory of mind (ToM) is sometimes described as "mind reading." Over the last 15 years or so it has been a hot topic not just in primatology, but also in cognitive science, linguistics, and philosophy. And there is much disagreement. Most simply, ToM is knowing that other individuals have minds and beliefs and that these beliefs may differ from one's own beliefs. In developmental cognitive psychology, ToM is most often evaluated via the "false-belief test." A child is shown a scenario in which a doll watches as the experimenter places a piece of candy in one of two opaque boxes. The doll is then removed to a place from which it cannot see the table, after which the experimenter moves the candy to the second box (the subject child watches all of this). The doll is brought back, and the experimenter asks the child where the doll will look for the candy. If the child answers "the first box," she passes the false-belief test; she knows that the doll had not seen the candy moved, and therefore has a false belief. Human three-year-olds generally fail the test, but five-year-olds almost always pass. What about other anthropoids?

Giving a false-belief test to any non-human primate is fraught with methodological problems (Tomasello and Call, 1997), not the least of which is the impossibility of using language to ask a monkey or ape just what it believes. Comparative psychologists are quite clever, however, and have devised a number of experimental procedures that require the subject to construct what another individual knows. Tomasello and Call summarize a typical experiment:

> They had four chimpanzees, all with much human experience, witness an experimenter bait one of four cups behind an occluder (so that the chimpanzees could not tell which cup contained the food). Another human remained outside the room and consequently did not know which cup was

being baited. After this naïve human entered the room, subjects could choose either the naïve or the knowledgeable human to inform them of the whereabouts of the food. If they chose the knowledgeable experimenter, they invariably got the food; if they chose the naïve experimenter, they invariably did not. (Tomasello and Call, 1997: 325)

Three of the four achieved a 70 percent success rate on these tests, but only after 100–150 trials. Do results such as this suggest that chimpanzees can construct what another individual knows? The results are not easy to interpret. The success rate and number of trials certainly give one pause; human five-year-olds would almost certainly do much better. Tomasello and Call take a more skeptical view, and suggest that the chimpanzees may be learning to solve the test by other means (unintended cueing, for example) or the experimenter becomes a conditioned stimulus for food. In their own research they found that chimpanzees generally fail tests of false belief.

A concept of self is a prerequisite for a theory of mind, but presumably one a bit more basic than false belief. Do apes (or monkeys) have a concept of self? This is most simply assessed through a mirror recognition test. The subject is briefly anesthetized and a spot of paint placed above its eye. If, when presented with a mirror, it immediately touches the spot, it demonstrates that it knows that the mirror image is of itself, and hence passes the mirror recognition test. Monkeys and gorillas invariably fail. Chimpanzees sometimes fail, and sometimes pass. Interestingly, chimpanzees that are raised in human conditions are the ones most likely to pass, which suggests that experience with human objects plays a role. In other words, in the right circumstances chimpanzees are likely to pass the mirror recognition test. They almost certainly have some concept of self.

We have dwelt on theory of mind because it lies close to our general theme of the evolutionary development of higher cognitive abilities, executive functions and working memory in particular. ToM is related to executive functions. Children's performances on ToM tests and tests of executive functions have positive correlations between 0.30 and 0.60 (Bjorklund and Bering, 2003: 132). This correlation between ToM and general problem-solving ability suggests that ToM is not an encapsulated, domain-specific cognitive ability that evolved to solve a narrow adaptive problem, but arose from a need for flexible response to complex but generic problems. However, while this is arguably true for humans, it does not point to any likely evolutionary antecedents. What do anthropoids do that might have set the stage for ToM?

One possibility lies in the cognitive underpinnings of social recognition, tactical deception, and response inhibition. We have seen that anthropoids have expressive faces, and a neural network sensitive to differences in faces and facial expressions. Because this network is linked via the amygdala to centers of emotional processing, anthropoids communicate their mood via facial expression. This is still largely true for humans; try looking happy when you are very sad. Interestingly, anthropoid vocalizations are tied into the same emotive network. When chimpanzees vocalize they are expressing their current emotional state, and other chimpanzees can interpret these signals because they share these emotional states. One of the hardest things for an anthropoid to do is inhibit these responses because they are not voluntary. Apes would make terrible poker players because they would be unable to put on a "poker face." This may also explain their poor performance on many false-belief tests; they may find it impossible to select the object of false belief because their desire for the reward is very strong and cannot be inhibited, even if they "know" that it is the wrong choice for the test. Anthropoids do use tactical deception, but without ToM they are relatively poor liars. Liars must have the ability to inhibit their emotive response. Such "inhibition of a prepotent response" is one of the key components of executive functions (Barkley, 2001). The primate evidence suggests, then, that sometime after the evolutionary split from chimpanzees our ancestors acquired the ability to inhibit natural vocal and facial responses, that is, to hide their emotions. And the primate evidence also suggests that the selective agent may have been success in tactical deception.

Apes' minimal ability to suppress pre-potent responses should lead one to expect an equally poor performance on tests of working memory. There are, as always, methodological problems; many classic tests of working memory rely on recall of lexical items, a clear impossibility with apes. Moreover, most tests of working memory require considerable cooperation on the part of the subject, especially when they require maintaining attention in the presence of distraction. Of course, maintaining attention on one goal while distracted by another is the point at which response inhibition and working memory overlap. And given apes' poor performance on the former, the difficulty in motivating an ape subject to perform in the face of interference should not be a surprise. Apes do have working memory, however, and this capacity can be tested.

There have been only a few experiments designed to measure a chimpanzee's WM capacity. In the most interesting, Kawai and Matsuzawa (2000) tested the chimpanzee Ai's capacity to remember the location, on a screen, of a set of sequential integers (she had already learned to recognize the integers 0 through 9, and arrange them in ascending order, even when some were missing). She could reliably remember up to five locations. Note that the task has two components – ordering the integers and remembering the location. However, the memory portion of the task began only after Ai had selected the first integer in the series, at which point the remaining integers were masked. The memory tested only her spatial WM; she had ordered the series when the integers were visible. Based on her performance, Kawai and Matsuzawa suggested that chimpanzees' working memory capacity was five items, and contrasted it with the seven items often cited for humans. They also challenge this "magic number seven" for human spatial memory, and suggest chimpanzees are closer to us than many suppose. In many respects this experiment involves a classic "short-term" memory test, rather than a true working memory test such as reading span or three back. There was no distraction, or competing task, built into the experimental protocol. However, on one occasion Ai was inadvertently distracted after selecting the first integer by a screaming chimpanzee in a nearby room. After 20 seconds she returned to the four-item task and completed it successfully. While provocative, this cannot stand as a true measure of working memory capacity (nor do Kawai and Matsuzawa suggest that it is). What we can conclude from Kawai and Matsuzawa's work is that chimpanzees have, apparently, a shorter short-term memory capacity than humans – but, perhaps, not by much.

6

Early *Hominins*

What is a hominin, anyway? In current primate taxonomy, hominins belong to the subfamily *Homininae* (African great apes) and tribe *Hominini* (hominins for short). The *Hominini* include living humans, the direct ancestors of humans, and a number of closely related, but non-ancestral, species that lived alongside human ancestors for much of human evolution (indeed, until very recently in some parts of the world). Biological systematists place all of these into the same "tribe" because they share a number of distinguishing characteristics not possessed by other African apes. Anatomically, the most important of these "derived" features are linked to four adaptive complexes: locomotion, diet, reproduction, and behavior. Hominins are habitually bipedal. Our anatomy differs dramatically from that of other apes because we move on our hind legs alone. This very odd way of moving about presents problems of balance that have reshaped our feet, legs, hips, spines, and even our skulls. Hominins also have an unusual way of chewing, at least for an ape, termed "rotary chewing." When we chew our mandibles make a circular motion so that our lower molars grind past our upper molars. The enamel on our molars is thicker than that of an ape's, we have much smaller canines, and our palate (dental arcade) has an arch shape instead of the box shape of an ape. These are adaptations to heavy chewing, at least heavier chewing than we normally associate with fruit-eating apes. Hominins also have a derived reproductive strategy. The natural interval between births for a human female is actually shorter than that of a chimpanzee or gorilla (about two to three years vs. four to six years) (Knott, 2001). Exacerbating the problems that more young children present, human infants are "altricial," which means that they are less mature at birth, including their brains, than infants of other apes (Zeveloff and Boyce, 1982). In other words, the life-history pattern of hominins differs from that of apes, and this pattern has consequences for infant care and neural development. Hominins have very large brains for their body size. Because this encephalization is more or less what this book sets out to help explain, it is appropriate here to identify some of the derived behavioral characteristics that might have selected for larger brains. We will address them in more detail as the book unfolds:

- Language: Modern humans are the only apes that use a grammatical language. Language does rely on dedicated brain structures (Pinker, 1997a, b). However, these neural resources have evolved out of homologous regions in ape brains, so tracing their evolution is very difficult.
- Problem-solving and planning: Modern humans often use sophisticated planning in which errors are anticipated and contingencies developed ahead of time (Baddeley, 2007). We can also do thought experiments. These are largely a function of our enhanced working memory capacity.
- Expert procedural thinking: Modern humans are adept at learning and performing complex procedures, often at an astonishing level of speed and accuracy. Musicians, artists, chess masters, and athletes are experts at what they do, but what they do is often narrowly focused in specific domains (Ericsson and Kintsch, 1995).
- Symbolic culture: Modern humans invest just about everything with meaning, including technology (what does driving a Ferrari tell us about the driver?).

All of these are possible candidates for the agent, or agents, that selected for increased encephalization.

The Common Ancestor

Humans and chimpanzees share an ancestor that lived in Africa some 6 to 8 million years ago. We know, as Darwin did, that it lived in Africa because of our close similarity to the African apes, and we think it lived 6 to 8 million years ago because that is about how long evolution should take to produce the 1+ percent difference in DNA that separates us from chimpanzees. Paleontology has not yet provided science with a fossil of this ape, but this does not mean that science is completely ignorant about what is was like. Based on knowledge of living primates, apes in particular, and knowledge of humans, it is possible to identify characteristics of this elusive ape with a fair degree of reliability. It almost certainly possessed characteristics shared by all apes and humans: use of vocal communication, life with complex polyadic social interactions, expressive faces and reliance on facial recognition, use of tactical deception and hierarchically organized object manipulations. Because all African apes other than humans are forest dwellers who sleep in constructed nests, our common ancestor probably did too. Chimpanzees and humans share an additional set of derived features not known for gorillas, and the common ancestor almost certainly had them as well: extractive foraging (for insects, nuts, honey, etc.), tool use in foraging, exploitation of foods with a "patchy" distribution, and a concept of self, if not a complete theory of mind. We have emphasized characteristics that had cognitive/neural components because it is this package that the earliest hominins brought to their initial adaptive niches. And, as we will show, it is a package that did not change in its general features until relatively late in the hominin evolutionary story.

The Early Bipedal Apes: 7–2.5 Million Years Ago

The first hominins were bipedal apes. We pick up their trail soon after 7 million years ago in East Africa. The remains of the earliest examples are fragmentary, mostly jaws and teeth, with a few cranial fragments (though the enigmatic *Sahelanthropus* fossil from Chad is an almost complete cranium distorted during fossilization). They appear to have been smaller than modern chimpanzees and humans, and retained many ape-like features in their teeth (thin enamel on the molars, and canines that protruded above the tooth row). But they do appear to have been bipedal. These earliest known examples have been placed in three different genera: *Ardipithecus*, *Orrorin*, and *Sahelanthropus* (Brunet et al., 2003). We do not know much about them, except that they lived in a woodland environment, which is a habitat with many trees, but rarely a continuous forest canopy. After 4 million years ago the record improves significantly with the appearance of the genus *Australopithecus*.

Australopithecus afarensis is the name paleoanthropologists have given to a group of hominins who lived in East Africa between 3.9 and 3.0 million years ago (henceforth Ma). Paleoanthropologists have recovered hundreds of bones of this hominin, including the 40 percent complete skeleton of an adult female (well known as Lucy), and the remains of 17 individuals who all died at about the same time in the same place (sometimes referred to as the "first family," though this now appears very unlikely) (Johanson,

2004). Because of the comparatively large number of fossils, paleoanthropologists have a good idea of the basic anatomy and the range of variability. This, combined with detailed knowledge of the local habitat, allows reconstruction of the way of life of these early hominins.

Australopithecus afarensis was fully bipedal, but retained many ape-like features in its locomotor anatomy. Its arms were a bit longer in relation to its legs than is true for modern humans, its phalanges (finger bones) were slightly curved front to back, and its rib cage had a funnel shape rather than the barrel shape of modern humans. These suggest than afarensis still climbed into trees on a regular basis, perhaps to escape predators, and almost certainly to sleep. Below the waist it had anatomy typical of a biped. It is not entirely clear what may have initially selected for bipedal locomotion. It is certainly an odd way for a mammal to move about (indeed, hominins are the only examples), and it has definite disadvantages. There have been many hypotheses concerning the selective advantage of bipedalism. For decades, these hypotheses focused on the advantages of freeing the forelimbs for foraging, or for carrying tools, food, or infants. We now know that bipedalism long antedated the first appearance of stone tools, at least, and also the evidence for carrying food or infants. Recent arguments have focused largely on energetics. Bipedalism consumes less energy than knuckle-walking. A chimpanzee knuckle-walking at 5 kph consumes significantly more calories than a hominin of the same size walking bipedally (Rodman and McHenry, 1980; Sockol et al., 2007). For an ape that spent most of its days foraging on the ground, this difference would have yielded long-term selective advantages.

Bipedalism also has definite disadvantages, and these disadvantages are directly relevant to a discussion of cognitive evolution. It is slower than knuckle-walking, and increases an individual's visibility on the landscape, so it probably increased the dangers of predation. It also had negative consequences for reproductive anatomy. Under selection for bipedalism the hominin pelvis became lower (top to bottom), and wider side to side. This change in shape reduced the size of the birth canal, creating potential obstetric stress on hominin females (Lovejoy, 2005). This reduction in the size of the birth canal effectively selected against any significant increase in brain size. Unless encephalization produced a significant counteracting advantage it would never have occurred. And for most of hominin evolution, from 7 Ma to 2.5 Ma there was no encephalization. When it finally did occur, these obstetric problems forced a dramatic solution – the birth of immature offspring.

The teeth of *afarensis* indicate that hominin diets differed from those typical of the living apes. Large molars with thick enamel, and the rotary chewing complex yielded a dentition that was ideal for crushing and withstanding abrasion. Apes have thin enamel on the molars and, for the most part, consume relatively soft foods such as ripe fruit, with leaves and plant pith as fallback foods when fruit is unavailable (Laden and Wrangham, 2005). What kind of a diet selected for large molars with thick enamel? The two leading candidates are small, hard seeds (imagine chewing unpopped popcorn) or buried food. The relatively large, flat molars would have worked well for crushing seeds, and the thick enamel would have resisted fracturing (Teaford et al., 2002; Ungar et al., 2006). But this anatomy would also have been a benefit for a hominin consuming roots, tubers, rhizomes, and corms. These "underground storage organs" (USOs) are available in all seasons in the tropical woodlands, and if the hominins could get at them, they would have been a useful food source, especially in seasons when higher-quality foods were unavailable. The adaptive problems of this resource would have been tooth wear, and access to the USOs. The grit adhering to USOs would wear down molars rapidly, and selection for thicker enamel would be strong. Getting at USOs would have required finding them, and digging. Here the early hominins came pre-equipped. The mental mapping ability of the common ancestor, developed for foraging for ripe fruit with a patchy distribution, could easily have been applied to the locations of buried foods, and the ability to find and access hidden foods, often with tools, would have been precisely the abilities needed for USOs. One interesting bit of paleontological evidence supports the USO hypothesis: early hominin fossils are often found in the same geologic deposits with rodents (naked mole rats) whose primary food is also USOs, so the resource was clearly available.

Three fossil crania of *Australopithecus afarensis* are complete enough to measure or estimate cranial capacity. These are 400, 485, and 500 cc, with a mean of 478 (Holloway et al., 2004). Body weights for *afarensis* varied between about 30 kilos for a female to 45 kilos for an adult male (McHenry, 1992a, b). These figures yield an EQ of 2.2, compared to EQs of 1.54–1.89 for modern chimpanzees (Kappelman, 1996). These numbers suggest a modest increase in relative brain size, but they must be considered with caution; the sample is small, and given the statistical range of body-size estimates for *afarensis* there is no justification for concluding that *afarensis* was significantly more encephalized than the living apes. Studies of endocasts suggest that the shape of the brain differed slightly from that of the apes. On one particularly detailed endocast, Holloway has been able to recognize the lunate sulcus, which is in a more posterior position that it is in living apes. He attributes this migration to relative increase in the posterior parietal cortex, rather than a reduction of the occipital cortex (Holloway et al., 2004: 285). Holloway suggests that these shape differences document the beginnings of cerebral reorganization, which he argues preceded any significant increase in encephalization. This may well have been true, but again caution is in order; there is no compelling reason to assign specifically human behaviors based on this rather subtle difference in brain shape. All ape brains differ from one another in shape, and the functional reasons are rarely obvious.

Paleoanthropologists know close to nothing about the social behavior of *afarensis*. Our only useful evidence derives from sexual dimorphism. In general, sexual dimorphism in primates correlates with the degree of inter-male aggression; the greater the aggression, the greater the sexual dimorphism (Plavcon and van Schaik, 1997). Gibbons, who live in permanent pair-bonded couples, have almost no sexual dimorphism, and gorillas, who live in single dominant male harem groups, are extremely dimorphic. The postcranial evidence of *afarensis* indicates a range of body sizes, and a sexual dimorphism that exceeds those of both humans and chimpanzees. If true, then a social system based on pair-bonded adults seems unlikely. The degree of dimorphism argues for male dominance hierarchies, which almost always means a few males mating with many females. As this is more or less typical for anthropoids, it would not in itself present cognitive challenges that exceeded those encountered by modern apes.

In sum, the early hominins, as best exemplified by *Australopithecus afarensis*, were bipedal creatures who had adapted to a life in tropical woodlands. This way of life included a shift in diet away from that typical of apes, perhaps toward extractive foraging of buried foods. They brought to this new way of life the same basic brain and cognitive abilities still used by modern chimpanzees – a sophisticated knowledge of locations of food, and the ability to use hierarchically organized actions to extract them. But these abilities had been in place already with the common ancestor, and they had not yet selected for either a larger or a significantly restructured brain. These were truly bipedal apes.

The First Stone Knappers 2.6–1.5 Ma

Flaked stone tools were the first uniquely hominin technology. Hominins first produced them at least 2.6 Ma (Semaw, 2000), and for the next

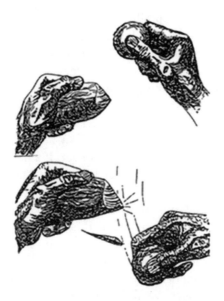

Figure 6.1   The basic stone knapping action or gesture

99.8 percent of the human story stone tools remained the central component of human technology. The basic principle behind flaked stone tools is simple; breaking rocks produces sharp edges. There are a number of ways to fracture stone. One can, for example, throw a rock at a hard surface, and if one throws hard enough the rock will fracture. Although this may have been an early phase of lithic (stone) technology, archeologists have never found evidence for it. The earliest known flaked stone artifacts were produced by a different procedure in which a "hammer" stone held in one hand struck a "core" held in the other hand. This gesture is known as knapping (figure 6.1).

Even though the basic idea is simple, it is not as easy as it might appear. Only relatively hard rocks break in a way that produces sharp, durable edges. The knapper must strike the core with considerable force, and he or she cannot strike it just anywhere. There are anatomical limits on the amount of force a knapper can deliver, and these effectively restrict knappers to breaking pieces off of the edges of cores where there are acute angles (see figure 6.1). Varieties of rock ("raw material') that have little or no crystalline structure were especially prized by knappers because they break in predictable ways not limited by the natural fracture planes in the stone. From the very beginnings of lithic technology stone knappers showed a clear preference for these kinds of stone (e.g., quartzite, flint, chert, even lava). Stone knapping produces three products that can be found by archeologists: (1) hammers, which were hard stones, often round in shape, and about 5–10 cm in diameter; (2) flakes, which were the pieces removed by knapping and which had the sharpest edges; and (3) cores, which were the stones being struck, and which might also have had sharp ridges left behind by flake removals (Schick and Toth, 1993).

What are stone tools good for? Stone flakes, especially flakes of high-quality raw material, are very sharp and can be used to cut just about anything a modern knife could be used to cut. If a flake has a sharp projection, it can be used to pierce or even bore holes. The heavier cores with sharp ridges are useful for crushing and smashing. Eventually, though not at first, hominins came to modify the edges of flakes in a variety of ways that made them effective as scraping and even sawing tools. Indeed, the vast majority of the history of technology is an account of increasingly elaborate ways to produce, modify, and use stone tools. By 2.6 Ma stone tools had become an important component of the hominin way of life, and like all features of an adaptive niche came to select for certain characteristics in hominin anatomy and cognition.

Stone knapping appears to have selected for specific derived features in the hominin hand. Anthropologist Mary Marzke (1996) has identified eight characteristics of the modern human hand, including features of the finger tips, thumbs, and bones of the palm, that differ significantly from those of other apes, and which enable the hand to "pinch" objects firmly and shift the position and orientation of objects. These abilities are just those required for manipulating hammers and cores during stone knapping. Three of the eight are present in the hand bones of *Australopithecus afarensis*, but the entire complement appears not to have evolved until after 2 Ma. From a cognitive point of view these anatomical changes have two important implications. First, regions of the motor cortex dedicated to fingers, thumbs, and palms must have evolved as well, including perhaps an overall relative increase in neural resources supporting hand postures and gestures. Second, these adaptations indicate that stone knapping was important enough to the adaptive niche of later hominins to have selected for specific anatomies. Might not the same pressures have selected for specific cognitive abilities unknown in modern apes?

Did stone knapping reshape, actually or metaphorically, the hominin brain in any significant way? Curiously, this is a research question that has only recently received any serious attention. We can begin by asking an even more basic question: just what parts of the brain are used when one knaps?

Dietrich Stout (Stout et al., 2000) attempted to answer this question using positron emission tomography (PET). He had Nick Toth, who is an expert stone knapper as well as an authority on early stone tools, perform the very basic task of knapping simple flakes off of a core. Stout then imaged Toth's brain use a PET scanner (Toth had been injected with the appropriate radioactive tracers prior to the task). The resulting image was informative, but not surprising. The areas of the brain most activated were primarily what "would be expected for a complex motor task requiring hand–eye coordination" (Stout et al., 2000: 1218). These included the primary motor and somatosensory cortices surrounding the central sulcus, visual processing areas of the occipital lobes, and the cerebellum. There was little activation of the prefrontal lobes, but there was significant activation of the superior parietal cortex, which is associated with spatial cognition. In other words, basic stone knapping is primarily a skilled motor task guided by spatial cognition. It is also important to note that Toth is an expert stone knapper, and because he is adept at the procedure, it did not tax the planning portion of his frontal cortex to any significant extent. This issue of expertise and skill is important to our argument, for it appears that expert performances of all kinds do not rely heavily on the executive functions of the frontal lobes. When a novice first struggles at a task, he or she must pay close attention to everything about it, but as expertise increases much of the procedure is passed to long-term memory (LTM), where it is accessed as needed, often with little or no demand on active attention.

Stout's study corroborates what many cognitive anthropologists have long appreciated. The cognition deployed during tool use has its own neurological basis, and it is a pattern that differs from that used in word problems or verbal tests. Much of "tool" cognition consists of procedural memories, which are a form of long-term memories acquired through practice and repetition (Keller and Keller, 1996). It is the same kind of "motor" memory that is used by athletes. Through repetition muscles learn sequences of action, and the higher the number of repetitions, the more reliable and accurate the actions become. Of course, muscles do not learn except in the limited sense that some muscle groups are strengthened and others not, which affects their patterns of use. It is the neurons that learn, but in the realm of procedural cognition the learning is of a very old kind in an evolutionary sense. Repetition and rhythm are key. By repeating a sequence of action again and again, the artisan or athlete reinforces the links in the chain of action and adds links to the chain. For reasons that are unclear, rhythmic repetition facilitates this learning, and rhythmic coordination is very, very old. It is in fact governed by mid-brain structures and the cerebellum. Stone knapping is a highly rhythmic task. Indeed, modern practitioners often comment on the pleasure it gives them simply to knap, and the very real tendency to continue flaking beyond the point at which an acceptable end product has been achieved.

Tool cognition is more than just motor memory. Like all artisans, the knapper must monitor the consequences of his or her action. But much of this assessment is non-verbal, in the sense that it does not consist of inner speech. Instead the knapper relies on visual, aural, and tactile patterns – how the surfaces and angles appear, what the blows sound like, and how they feel (Keller and Keller, 1996). If asked, a knapper may or may not be able to express in words what he or she is doing, and this has important consequences for learning. Most complex crafts are learned by apprenticeship, and knapping is no exception. Though some basic directions can take the form of sentences – "Do this." "Watch me." "Attend to this angle." – the novice acquires most of his or her procedural knowledge by observation and practice. Shared attention between the master and novice is also the rule for modern apprenticeship, but even this is not absolutely required. One can learn a great deal through anonymous observation and practice.

Are no frontal lobe functions required at all? In particular, did stone knapping ever tap into executive functions, or working memory, and if it did, is there evidence that this component evolved? This is the crux of the problem for those archeologists interested in studying cognitive evolution through stone tools. Basic rhythmic knapping required little in the way of frontal lobe function. However, more complex procedures probably did. In particular, knapping of some types of stone tools required reliance on more specific spatial relations, and eventually incorporation of shape recognition, and both almost certainly engaged, however fleetingly, the visuospatial component of working memory. In addition, response inhibition, which is an executive function, was required to interrupt the rhythmic sequences of action at the appropriate time, reorient the core, and begin anew. Both of these cognitive components clearly evolved over the course of human evolution.

But what of our initial question? Has knapping changed the brain? We have reviewed, briefly, the basic cognitive components of knapping, but is there any reason to think that the hominin brain has evolved to optimize these particular functions? As a starting point we must again turn to modern apes.

Kanzi and Panbanisha

Modern chimpanzees do not make or use flaked stone tools in the wild. They do use stone hammers to break open nuts, and do roll and even throw rocks during intimidation displays, but they do not fracture stones to produce sharp edges. Of course, they probably do not need to; their large incisors and canines are well suited for their primary diet of fresh fruit and fallback diet of leaves, pith, and insects. But if they needed to, could they? This question has a biomechanical component (can chimpanzee bodies do the task?), a cognitive component (can chimpanzee brains organize the action?), and a motivational component (would chimpanzees ever consider it worth the effort?). The first two components can be, and have been, addressed using experiments with captive animals. The most famous ape stone knapper is the bonobo Kanzi, who is also justly famous for his ability to understand spoken English, and to use a lexigram board to form sentences (Savage-Rumbaugh, Shanker, and Taylor, 1998; Schick et al., 1999; Toth et al., 1993).

In the early 1990s, Nick Toth (whose knapping brain was introduced earlier) and Sue Savage-Rumbaugh taught Kanzi to flake stone. Their intent was to teach him in as natural a way as possible. He was first allowed to watch Toth knap simple flakes and use the flakes to cut a cord that held shut a box with a visible reward. He was then given a hammer stone and a core of flint. Instead of hitting the core with the hammer stone, Kanzi threw the core forcefully onto the tile floor, where it shattered into several pieces. He then selected a sharp flake and cut the cord to the reward box. Only after carpeting the laboratory could Toth and Savage-Rumbaugh convince Kanzi to use the "normal" knapping gesture of striking a core, held in one hand, with a hammer held in the other. And he was ultimately successful. After some practice he could reliably knap a flake large enough to cut the cord. He could strike the core well enough, but seemed unable to place his blows in optimal places on the core. He did not appear to examine the core to find edges with acute angles that would knap successfully (figure 6.2).

He also seemed unable to deliver the blows with a great deal of power. But he did grasp the basic idea of breakage and sharp flakes. After the initial experiment (Toth et al., 1993), Toth and Savage-Rumbaugh allowed Kanzi to knap periodically for a number of years (indeed he still knaps) and, significantly, allowed him to develop and practice his own technique. He prefers to throw the hammer at a core because he can deliver much more power that way, which means in turn that he can produce larger flakes.

Figure 6.2   Kanzi caught knapping
Source: Toth et al., 1993. © 1993 Academic Press

His aim has also improved. His half-sister, Panbanisha, has taken up the trade. Interestingly, she is more willing to use the normal knapping gesture, and also examines the core more carefully before trying to remove a flake (Toth, personal communication, 2003).

These experiments with Kanzi suggest that humans have evolved capacities for knapping. We are naturally better at it than Kanzi; even novice human knappers quickly exceed Kanzi's abilities. Just what it is that has evolved is much less clear. As we have seen, hominin hands have evolved to be better at holding and shifting cores and hammers during knapping, and it is likely that hominin shoulders are better at delivering powerful aimed blows. Some of Kanzi's limitations are clearly biomechanical. But there may be a cognitive difference as well. This could be a poorer ability to detect particular edge angles on the visually complex core, or perhaps a poorer ability to interrupt the rhythmic action of knapping in order to shift the core. It is subtle, but Kanzi seems not to understand something about basic stone knapping. However, this lack is likely to be something closely tied to the procedural knowledge required for knapping itself, and not a more general planning ability. Kanzi "knows" what stone knapping is "for", and is quite capable of success at the overall task of manufacture and use, tied to a goal. Byrne and Russon (1998) have termed this kind of social learning "program level imitation." This kind of social learning is typical of wild apes in their extractive foraging routines.

The first stone tools

The oldest well-dated stone tools come from the archeological site of Gona in Ethiopia, and date to about 2.6 Ma (Semaw, 2000; Semaw et al., 2003). Even these earliest stone tools demonstrate a deftness at knapping that exceeded Kanzi's ability, so it is likely that hominins had started knapping earlier than this. The Gona artifacts consist mostly of cores and flakes, and it appears that the stone knappers had carried the cores to the site for the purpose of producing flakes, and that they probably tested the raw material at its source to asses its suitability (Semaw, 2000). At the slightly more recent site of Lokalalei, located in northern Kenya, archeologists Anne Delagnes and Helene Roche have been able to describe more complete sequences of action through the technique of refitting (Delagnes and Roche, 2005). See figure 6.3.

The Lokalalei sites, like Gona, are places where early knappers carried raw material and then produced flakes. There are two sites, dating to about 2.3 Ma, that were located on the floodplain of a local river at the time the sites were used. These were not campsites in the modern sense. There is no evidence of fire, but there is some poorly preserved animal bone, mostly teeth, that may reflect hominin activity. The sites were probably disturbed to some extent by natural processes prior to being buried by local stream deposits, but the lithic artifacts had not moved far. Delagnes and Roche were able to take the excavated flakes and refit them into the original core, very much like a three-dimensional jigsaw puzzle. This enabled them to reconstruct the exact sequence in which the flakes had been knapped and, equally important, identify the times at which the knapper reoriented the core. Such a reconstructed sequence – a *chaîne opératoire* in French – is invaluable to the cognitive archeologist because it documents a series of decision points that provide us with a small glimpse of the hominin mind at work. Several things were immediately obvious to Delagnes and Roche. First, unlike Kanzi, the Lokalalei knappers used a standard knapping gesture and were able to deliver well-aimed blows. There were only a few miss-hits (visible as small crush marks on the core). Second,

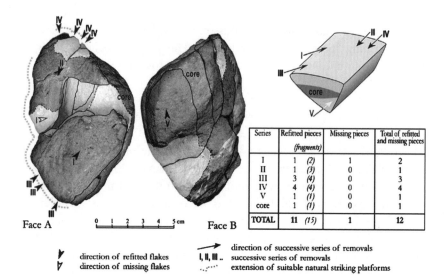

Face A   0 1 2 3 4 5 cm   Face B

Series	Refitted pieces (fragments)	Missing pieces	Total of refitted and missing pieces
I	1 (2)	1	2
II	1 (3)	0	1
III	3 (4)	0	3
IV	4 (4)	0	4
V	1 (1)	0	1
core	1 (1)	0	1
TOTAL	**11 (15)**	**1**	**12**

⟅ direction of refitted flakes
⟅ direction of missing flakes

⟶ direction of successive series of removals
I, II, III .. successive series of removals
...·'·· extension of suitable natural striking platforms

Figure 6.3 A refitted Mode 1 core from Lokalalei (*c.*2.3 million years old); note the sequence of flake removals from one orientation, followed by a rotation of the core, a second series of flake removals, and so on

Source: Delagnes and Roche, 2005. 2005 Elsevier Ltd

the knappers examined the cores and chose to knap edges with appropriate "platform" angles. Like the Gona knappers, these hominins had tested the raw material at its source, and indeed must have done some of the preliminary flaking there; the telltale flakes with cortex are mostly missing. The hominins removed as many as 16 flakes from a single orientation, but more commonly the sequence would be two to four removals before reorienting the core. This attests to the operation of two of the procedural features true of modern knapping. First was the rhythmic coordination of the knapping gesture itself, which produced in this case 2 to 16 flakes from the same orientation. Second was the ability to assess the success or failure of the gesture, and interrupt the rhythmic action of knapping to reorient the core. This is more similar to modern knapping than it is to Kanzi's personal solution (throw the hammer at the core and then search for useable pieces). The knappers were clearly monitoring the procedure itself. However, and this is the important bit, these abilities were probably part of the learned procedure itself. It is how these knappers always flaked cores. There is no reason to invoke advanced planning abilities, or even foresight (the term used by Delagnes and Roches) beyond the range of modern apes performing hierarchically organized manual tasks. But it may be necessary to invoke "action level imitation" in which a novice copies not just the goal and means (program level imitation) but also the specific motor procedures. It is far from clear how significant this development in social learning might have been. Yes, the knapping reconstructed at Lokalalei stretches the range of ape procedural cognition, but it was not qualitatively different. Indeed, Frederic Joulian (1996) compared the action sequences of chimpanzees cracking nuts with hammers to the action sequences required for knapping the earliest stone artifacts and found no qualitative differences between them – the *chaînes opératoires* of the chimpanzees are no less complex than those reconstructed for the Lokalalei hominds. Yet there is evidence that these knappers may have had larger brains, and the temporal coincidence between the appearance of knapping and the evolution of brain size is hard to ignore. Perhaps it was not knapping per se that selected for large brains; perhaps it was what the tools were used to do. For examples of Mode 1 tools, see figures 6.4–6.

Scavenging, meat eating, and expensive tissues

Some of the early sites with stone tools have also yielded fragmentary bones of other animals, including bones from a variety of small and medium, and occasionally large mammals. At Lokalalei there were bones from 12 different mammal species, along with fragments of tortoise shell and crocodile bones. The association of stone tools with bone is of course provocative,

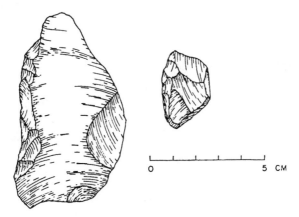

Figure 6.4   Mode 1 flake tool

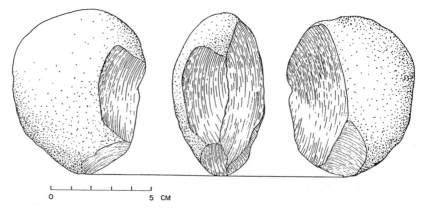

Figure 6.5   Mode 1 core tool (aka chopper)

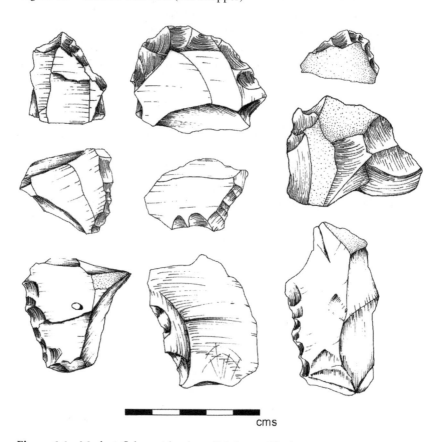

Figure 6.6   Mode 1 flakes with edges slightly modified

Source: de laTorre, Mora, Dominguez-Rodrigo, de Luque, and Alcala, 2003. © 2003 Elsevier Science Ltd

because it suggests that the tools might have been used on the animals or at least on their bones. However, association alone is not enough of a foundation to support the ascription of a radically new way of life to these tool-makers. All of the early sites were situated very near streams or lakes, and all of the animals whose remains have been found would have been regular visitors (especially the crocodiles!). The association might be simply fortuitous. But there is evidence that suggests it was not, at least not entirely. Some of the animal bones have evidence of butchery in the form of cut-marks. Superficially, scratches made by carnivore teeth and stone tools are similar, but under the microscope they look very different. There is one such cut-marked bone from Lokalalei, and one such bone from Gona, so it does appear that even the earliest stone tools were used in butchery, at least some of the time. Does this imply that the stone knappers were hunters? Unfortunately, these very early sites yield too few bones to resolve this issue, and it is necessary to jump forward several hundred thousand years before a clearer picture emerges.

The FLK site at Olduvai Gorge resembles the earlier sites at Gona and Lokalalei in many respects. It was situated very near a lake in an environment that included trees and many woodland species of mammal. It differs from the earlier sites in being larger and much better preserved. Archeologist Mary Leakey excavated hundreds of stone tools and thousands of fragments of animal bone from an area of about 315 m^2 (vs. Lakalalei 2C's 18 m^2) (Leakey, 1971). The remains include bones from a variety of small and medium mammals (antelope sized), but not all of the body parts of these animals are represented. There are very few bones from the axial skeleton – vertebrae, shoulder blades, pelvic bones – but lots of leg bones (Bunn and Kroll, 1986). It does not appear that the animals died there. Instead, someone had carried the legs or leg bones to FLK from elsewhere. Many of the bones have cut-marks, including cut-marks produced in removing meat from the bones (see, for example, figure 6.7).

But most of the bones had smashed and splintered in a way that suggests that marrow was a target. Many of the bones also have carnivore gnawing marks. In a few cases the cut-marks overlap the gnawing marks, and hence clearly came after, but in a few other cases the carnivore gnawing came second. So what can we conclude? It does not appear that the hominins were hunters. None of the stone tools would have made effective killing weapons, and the carnivore gnawing suggests that the hominins were not the first ones to use a carcass. Instead, they appear to have been scavengers, taking parts of animals killed by carnivores and carrying these body parts

Figure 6.7 Butchery marks on an antelope leg bone from FLK, a 1.75-million-year-old Mode 1 site at Olduvai Gorge

Source: Blumenschine, 1995. © 1995 Academic Press

to relatively safe places near water where they removed the remaining meat and smashed the bones for marrow (Blumenschine, 1987).

At first blush this scenario may seem radically different from an ape way of life, but in some important respects it simply expanded a strategy long used by apes – extractive foraging. Chimpanzee use of hammers to break into nuts has been extensively documented and is perhaps the best example of chimpanzees using hierarchically organized actions with tools to acquire an encased food. The hominins at FLK also appear to have been doing a lot of pounding. Among the stone tools are numerous cobbles and blocks of stone with battered surfaces. These are not typical hammer stones used in knapping but appear to have been used as hammers and anvils to smash bones, and perhaps nuts as well. Indeed, at some of the Olduvai sites such pounding equipment outnumbers the remains of stone knapping, attesting to the importance of pounding in early hominin activities (Mora and De la Torre, 2005; Parker and Gibson, 1979). The action sequence and goal orientation necessary to smash open a bone to get at the marrow is almost indistinguishable from that required for nut-cracking. Parker and Gibson (1979) have also suggested that cutting through skin to get at meat is a form of extractive foraging. In other words, these early hominins had simply shifted an established cognitive/action pattern to a new resource. They had not developed anything radically new that required a change in the cognition underpinning tool use. Neither stone knapping itself, nor using the tools to butcher animals, is likely to have selected for larger brains. But they may have released selection against larger brains.

The archeological remains document scavenging, but do not allow a very precise measure of how important it was to the diet. In a very general way, the debris of bone-cracking at these sites resembles the nut-cracking debris at chimpanzee sites, and nuts are a significant component of some chimpanzee diets. Most paleoanthropologists think that animal products were at least a significant minor component of the diet. Meat, and especially bone marrow, is high in fats and protein and is relatively easy to digest. Hominins who had access to a significant amount of this high-quality nutrition would not require the long guts of herbivores. Long guts are metabolically "expensive tissues," and calories devoted to digestion are unavailable to that other "expensive tissue," the brain (Aiello and Wheeler, 1995). So, even if tool-making and butchery per se did not select for larger brains, they did "release" selection pressure for retaining long guts, allowing individuals with shorter guts and larger brains to be reproductively successful.

Fossils of Early *Homo*

The fossil record of hominins living between 2.6 and 2.0 Ma is confused. Africa as a whole presents at least four different species; East Africa alone certainly had two, and perhaps as many as four (Aiello and Andrews, 2000). This attests to the overall success of the hominin lifestyle, as adaptive success often leads to divergence. One of these hominins was clearly a stone tool-maker who had begun to rely more on scavenged meat, but it is also possible that more than one of the hominin species had started down this adaptive path. After all, as we have seen, basic stone knapping and breaking into bones are well within the abilities of apes, and any or even all of the hominins could have used this tactic some of the time. However, paleoanthropologists suspect that one, perhaps two, had begun to devote more of their time and energy to this aspect of niche, and that this adaptive shift led to an increase in brain size, either through direct selection, or as a result of released selection on gut length. Unfortunately, no fossil from this period actually has a larger brain. Indeed, the best association between a fossil and stone tools is a hominin known as *Australopithecus garhi*, which had an ape-sized brain (Semaw, 2000). There are a few tantalizing fragments that attest to the presence of a larger brained form. Near Gona, paleoanthropologists have found a mandible that has dental features resembling larger-brained forms that lived after 2.0 Ma, and it is reasonable to suppose that this may have been the elusive tool-making scavenger (Kimbel et al., 1996).

Several fossils dating to between 2.0 and 1.8 Ma had larger brains and higher EQs than any ape or earlier hominin. Because of their brain size they have been attributed to the genus *Homo*. The cranial capacities of these individual fossils vary between 510 and 755 cc, a range that is well outside that of any living ape (Holloway et al., 2004). The mean size is about 630 cc. To compute an EQ it is necessary to have reliable estimates of body size, and here the situation gets tricky. Postcranial bones for these early *Homo* are scarce, and indeed it is difficult to link even one complete long bone with a known cranium (McHenry and Coffing, 2000). The greatest number of postcranial bones comes from Olduvai Hominin #62, which lacks a cranium. It has been assigned to early *Homo* on the basis of fragmentary bits of cranium, teeth, stratigraphic position, and because it almost certainly could not have been the remains of a *Paranthropus*, the heavier, more specialized hominin living at Olduvai at the time. OH 62 was a small hominin, about the same size as *Australopithecus afarensis*. If this was a typical body size for these large-brained forms, then the EQ was a relatively high 3.1 (Kappelman, 1996). But there are some fragmentary bones that suggest that some of the early *Homo* were larger than OH 62. Indeed, early *Homo* fossils present so much variability that many paleoanthropologists recognize two separate species, *Homo habilis* and *Homo rudolfensis*. Exacerbating the confusion are the recent fossil crania from Dmanisi in the Republic of Georgia. Not only does their brain size fall in the 550–750 range, but these hominins are associated with Mode 1 tools, and had left the African continent entirely (Rightmire et al., 2006)!

A few of the fossil crania of these early *Homo* are complete enough to allow endocranial casting. The resulting endocasts allow evaluation of overall brain shape and, more controversially, the identification of some of the major landmarks. As one might guess, interpretation is fraught with uncertainty. Philip Tobias, who has studied endocasts and brain evolution for half a century, argues that *Homo habilis's* endocasts present several human-like features. In particular, he identifies increased size of the frontal and parietal lobes, accomplished via increased breadth and height (Tobias, 1987). He also argues that the sulcal and gyral pattern was more human-like than ape-like, and that the brain regions controlling speech in humans were expanded relative to the same regions in apes and australopithecines. Other paleoneurologists are not as sanguine about their ability to read endocasts, and appear satisfied to suggest that early *Homo* brains show trends away from an ape-like shape and towards a human-like shape (though there is considerable disagreement about just how). Given the current state of our understanding of the factors controlling brain growth and shape, it is best to be cautious. The cognitive implications of these changes in brain shape are almost entirely unknown. Ironically, perhaps, we actually know more about cognition from the archeological evidence than from the brains.

Summary

We now know that a variety of hominins lived in Africa between 6 million and 2 million years ago. Although they differed from one another in size and diet, they were very similar in their basic adaptive pattern: they were all bipedal apes who lived in woodland habitats. Everything we know about them suggests that they also shared the same basic cognitive profile:

- They were slightly more encephalized than modern African apes; however, given uncertainties about body size it would be unwarranted to conclude that these early hominins differed from apes in raw computational power.
- They demonstrate a modest change in brain shape, with expansion of the parietal cortex relative to the occipital lobes, and perhaps a more human-like pattern of asymmetry with right frontal and left occipital petalias.
- Most of them probably incorporated extractive foraging into their adaptive niches. Some may have included underground storage organs such as tubers, while others extracted marrow from scavenged bones. Extractive foraging is characteristic of all African apes. Here the specific foods may have differed, but the overall pattern clearly antedated the appearance of hominins.
- Some made and used tools in foraging. This is again a pattern shared with apes, especially chimpanzees, and in using tools these hominins relied on coordinated sets of motor activity similar to those used by chimpanzees to open nuts, and those used by gorillas to access pith inside nettles. There is evidence to conclude, however, that some of these early hominins made more extensive use of tools, which in turn selected for anatomies in the hand, and perhaps appropriate neural structures in the motor cortex.

- What little we can reconstruct about social life and life history appears very ape-like. All were sexually dimorphic, suggesting social groups in which males competed for access to females. Individual developmental rates resembled the life-history pattern of African apes. Because adult brain size remained in the ape range, neonates could still have had brain sizes that were 40+ percent of adult size, which in turn indicates that newborns were not as immature as those of modern humans, and had a brain developmental pattern that was also ape-like.

A Grade Shift?

Evolutionary scientists sometimes use the term "grade" to refer to a group of related species who share the same basic phenotype and organizational plan (Collard, 2002). When we survey the evidence of these early hominins it is clear that they all shared the same basic phenotype and adaptive strategy. It is appropriate to lump them into the same adaptive grade, including the forms we label *Homo*. If we focus on just the cognitive component, we come to an even more conservative conclusion. These early hominins shared a cognitive phenotype that was indistinguishable in its major components from that of gorillas, chimpanzees, and bonobos. These bipedal apes occupied the same cognitive grade as their knuckle-walking cousins.

When a member of an evolutionary grade acquires a new adaptation, with a distinctive phenotype and organization plan, evolutionary scientists say that a "grade shift" has occurred. All evidence suggests that early hominins do not represent a cognitive grade shift away from apes. They differed from other African apes (just as the other African apes differed from one another), but they were still apes, in mind if not body. Of course, a grade shift does not occur miraculously without antecedents; instead, one species makes a minor adaptive change that opens up the possibility of a dramatic shift. We think we can detect this initial minor change in the fossils we attribute to early *Homo*. The change was an increased reliance on meat, probably attained through scavenging. This change in diet released the tight metabolic selection against encephalization. These early *Homo* were also adept at tool use and tool-making. And within a few hundred thousand years a dramatic grade shift did occur.

7

Homo erectus

Nariokotome

In 1984 Kamoya Kimeu, Kenya's most accomplished fossil prospector, noticed a bone eroding from beneath an acacia tree along a dry stream channel west of Lake Turkana. As field workers sifted nearby sediments and excavated beneath the tree, more and more bones emerged until, eventually, they recovered almost every bone from the skeleton of a single 11 year-old boy who had died 1.6 million years ago. This find, known as Nariokotome (named for the nearest town), is the most complete skeleton of an early hominin ever found, and his completeness has allowed paleo-anthropologists to reconstruct details of its way of life that are unavailable from the fragmentary remains that are more typical of the hominin fossil record. The anatomy of Nariokotome is surprising in many respects, and it corroborated a suspicion held by many paleoanthropologists that a dramatic change in way of life accompanied the appearance of this new variety of hominin.

From the shape of the pelvis, we know that Nariokotome was a male, and from the eruption pattern of his teeth, and the unfused condition of the growth plates of his long bones, we know that he was a pre-adolescent. The best estimate gives him an age of about $11^{1}/_{2}$ years. But even at this young age Nariokotome had developed pronounced areas of muscle attachment on his long bones, attesting to a very strenuous way of life. Perhaps the most surprising initial interpretation was his stature. He was 160 cm (5 ft. 3 ins.) tall when he died. If one extrapolates his adult height using standard human growth tables, he might have attained a height of 170 cm to 185 cm (from about 5 ft. 7 ins. to 6 ft. 1 in.). In other words, Nariokotome was modern in stature, even on the tall side of modern human stature variability. He was also very thin, with narrow hips, even for a boy, and had relatively long arms and legs for his height. In light of Bergmann's and Allen's laws for mammalian body proportions (cold-adapted mammals have compact bodies and shorter limbs to maximize heat retention and reduce heat loss), Nariokotome had a classic body type for heat loss. Indeed, the modern people built most like Nariokotome live in nearby Sudan, where they have adapted to a life in hot, open, tropical grassland. Like the Sudanese people, Nariokotome had an ideal body type for life in hot, open, habitats – very different from the smaller, woodland-dwelling, body types of *Australopithecus* and *Homo habilis*. A significant shift had occurred in where hominins were living (Walker and Leakey, 1993).

Nariokotome's endocranial volume was 880 cc. When the modest brain growth at adolescence is factored in, it produces an adult capacity of about 910 cc, clearly larger than the brains of *Homo habilis* (about 630 cc). Of course, Nariokotome was also considerably larger than the earlier hominins, so his relative brain size is only slightly larger than that of *Homo habilis* (an EQ of 3.3 vs. 3.1 for *habilis*). The endocast exhibits an asymmetric pattern of expanded right frontal and parietal lobes and expanded left occipital lobes. In addition, the lower left frontal lobe, generally assigned to Broca's area in modern humans, is larger than the corresponding region of the right (Begun and Walker, 1993; Holloway et al., 2004). In these features, Nariokotome presents an overall pattern that is basically modern. Holloway (1995) has argued that the important reorganizational changes in the human brain had all occurred by the time of Nariokotome, and that subsequent changes were a matter of increasing overall size. He also argues that Nariokotome probably did possess some language abilities. Begun and Walker (1993) are more cautious, suggesting only that the endocast's asymmetry reveals preferential right-handedness, and explain the expanded "Broca's" area as a reflection of the more complex motor sequences required for knapping stone tools.

One feature of Nariokotome's anatomy, his pelvis, has led to some controversial extrapolations that bear directly on our topic of cognitive evolution. Nariokotome had a very narrow pelvis, even for a boy, and also long femoral necks (the "arm" of the thigh bone that attaches to the pelvis) (Walker and Ruff, 1993). This produces a very efficient mechanism for striding and running. But it also produces a very small birth canal. Obviously Nariokotome was never going to give birth, but when we extra-polate his pelvic anatomy to that of an equivalent adult female, the birth canal would still have been very small. Add to this the increased brain size and the result would be obstetric trouble. The modern human response to this obstetric problem is to give birth to helpless, immature infants, with brains only 25 percent the size of an adult brain (brains of chimpanzee infants are 40–50 percent of adult weight). It seems likely that the population of which Nariokotome was a part did the same. The term that paleoanthropologists use for this alteration in developmental timing is secondary altriciality. Altriciality (the opposite of precocial or advanced behaviors for one's biological age) connotes helplessness at birth and the extended help of parents that is required until mature (Zeveloff and Boyce, 1982). Secondary altriciality refers to the fact that newborn humans have rapidly developing brains in the first year of life while all other primates' fetal rate of brain growth becomes much slower at birth. The attribution of secondary altriciality based on a juvenile male pelvis is controversial, as you might imagine, and paleoanthropologists are far from agreement on this point. But if the population from which Nariokotome derives was, in fact, altricial, it would have implications for brain development, cognition, and learning. Other anatomical features suggest that Nariokotome's life-history pattern was not entirely modern; the eruption sequence of his teeth and the maturity of his long bones suggest that he might not have gone through a dramatic "spurt" of growth at adolescence. In some respects at least he would have been more mature at 11 than a modern boy (Dean et al., 2001).

Homo erectus sensu lato

Nariokotome has been assigned to either of two species – Homo erectus or Homo ergaster. The reasons for two competing labels are rooted in two different interpretations of geographic and temporal variability. Homo erectus (sensu stricto) was defined on the basis of Asian fossils that differ in certain details of anatomy from most African fossils, which are therefore sometimes assigned to Homo ergaster. We prefer to use Homo erectus sensu lato as label because our interest is in general developments; the details of specific evolutionary histories are less relevant to us than overall trends. Some of the Homo erectus sensu lato were our ancestors. All were very similar in neural features (brain size and shape) and behavioral features (archeological remains, that we find so informative).

Homo erectus, as a species, presents many features, in addition to those true of Nariokotome, that distinguish them from earlier hominins. Most dramatic was their geographic distribution. The Dmanisi (Republic of

Georgia, adjacent to Russia) fossils indicate that an earlier *Homo* may have moved out of Africa, at least briefly (Gabunia et al., 2001). *Homo erectus sensu lato*, in contrast, lived in Africa, southern Europe, South Asia, East Asia, and South-east Asia. It had clearly developed a way of life that allowed it to adapt to very different kinds of habitat, from dry African savannas to tropical forests of South-east Asia. Moreover, it appears to have expanded very rapidly into these new areas. There are *Homo erectus* fossils from Java dating to 1.8 million years ago, earlier than Nariokotome in Africa. Indeed, though most paleoanthropologists consider Africa to be the original of *Homo erectus*, it is also possible that *Homo erectus* evolved out of an earlier *Homo* (like Dmanisi, perhaps) outside of Africa and then reinvaded the African continent (Dennell and Robroeks, 1996). And, after this rapid expansion, *Homo erectus* appears to have entered a period of relative stasis for perhaps as much as a million years. There was little change in anatomy, and only a very modest increase in brain size (Rightmire, 2004). Relative stasis can be viewed as a kind of evolutionary success; whatever *Homo erectus* was doing appears to have worked quite well.

Mode 2 Technology

As with the earlier hominins, the archeological record presents a parallel set of evidence from which it is possible to identify cognitive developments. And, as with the earlier evidence, the tools and fossils do not "match up" as nicely as paleoanthropologists might want. Nariokotome, for example, was associated with no stone tools at all. He almost certainly made and used them; he just did not die with any in his possession. Archeologists do have a number of sites from Nariokotome's time period (1.6 million years), and even Nariokotome's region in northern Kenya, but the stone tools at these sites resemble the earlier tools from the FLK site in the Olduvai Gorge, Tanzania. Indeed, there is nothing about the material culture of the earliest *Homo erectus* in East Africa that clearly sets them apart. But by 1.5 million years ago, this situation changed. A new and significantly different lithic technology emerged.

The hallmark of this new Mode 2 technology was the biface. This was a relatively large (> 10 cm) tool produced by trimming a core or large flake bifacially, that is, by knapping smaller flakes off of the edges onto both faces of the artifact. This produced a long, sinuous cutting edge, often encom-

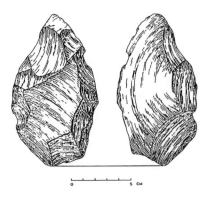

Figure 7.1a   Mode 2 bifaces: a 1.4-million-year-old handaxe from West Natron

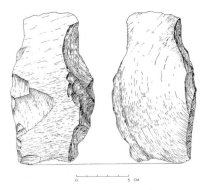

Figure 7.1b   Mode 2 bifaces: a cleaver of similar age to the handaxe in figure 7.1, from Olduvai Gorge; both were produced by trimming the margins of large flakes

passing the entire margin of the tool. In many cases this bifacial trimming produced an artifact with an overall symmetrical shape (figure 7.1a). In Africa, knappers regularly produced two different shapes: handaxes, which have a teardrop shape; and cleavers, which have an untrimmed bit instead of a narrow tip (figure 7.1b). In addition to bifaces, a Mode 2 technology included the same range of stone tools found in Mode 1 sites. Indeed, contemporary sites lacking bifaces, and there are several, are largely indistinguishable from the earlier Mode 1 sites (Schick and Toth, 1993).

Bifaces were the first tools that appear to have been clearly beyond the scope of ape abilities. As such, they occupy a significant place in the history of technology and cognition, and warrant a close look. Many of the earliest bifaces were made on large flakes, some weighing several pounds. Archeologist Peter Jones (1981) rediscovered the technique for producing these flakes; the knapper places a large core on a boulder anvil, and then strikes the core with a large hammer stone using a powerful, over-the-head, two-handed blow. This is a modification of the basic knapping gesture, and probably developed over millennia of experience with stone and hard hammer knapping. The resulting large flakes would have been very useful in their own right because of their long sharp edges. But the stone knappers often modified the edges with bifacial trimming. In most respects this trimming used the same technique that had been in place for a million years, and indeed the resulting trimming flakes themselves make useful tools. There were, however, a few refinements. The knappers were more deliberate in placing the trimming blows, often in a sequence that produced a continuous, sinuous edge. The earlier Mode 1 knappers focused on flake production; these Mode 2 knappers were also interested in the effects trimming had on the edges of the cores and, often, the overall shape of the artifact. In the case of cleavers, the knappers trimmed the sides and butt of the artifact, and left the "bit," or business end, with an unmodified sharp, flake edge. In the case of handaxes, they trimmed to produce sides that converged to a pointed tip. Sometimes, but not always, they attended to the bilateral symmetry of the plan shape. We know this because on some handaxes and cleavers the trimming on one side was placed to mirror a configuration on the opposite edge.

Archeologists often overlook a fact about bifaces that is really quite important. They were the first tools that probably existed in the minds of their makers *as tools*. In non-human and Mode 1 tool use the target was task completion – cracking open a nut or butchering a carcass – and the tools were components of those procedures. They did not exist as things apart from those contexts. But bifaces did. Hominins made bifaces, carried them around, and used them again and again as tools and as sources of flakes. The role of tools had changed. Instead of being elements in a procedure, tools themselves had acquired the status of permanent objects in hominin daily life, even when not in use. But what were they used for? Archeologists try to answer this question by identifying what the tools are associated with, by examining their edges for residues and wear patterns, and by experimentation. The results of these analyses are not really surprising given the ubiquity of bifaces in the archeological record; they were multi-purpose tools. Nick Toth has demonstrated in dramatic fashion that they are effective butchery tools; he and assistants actually used bifaces to butcher an elephant that had died of natural causes in a Zambian game park (Schick and Toth, 1993). But we also know that bifaces were used to cut and shave wood; Dominguez-Rodrigo and associates (2001) recovered the residue of acacia wood on the edges of bifaces from Peninj, one of the earliest Mode 2 sites in East Africa. Some have even suggested that bifaces were projectiles (O'Brien, 1981; Calvin, 1993), though most archeologists are skeptical of this interpretation. Bifaces have occasionally been called the "Swiss army knives" of the Paleolithic, but this is misleading. Swiss army knives consist of several quite distinct tools. Bifaces were a single very adaptable tool, and one that hominins carried around in anticipation of *potential* future use. This change in basic approach to tools was a very significant event in technological evolution because it brought tools into contact with other aspects of hominin lives, and this development would have interesting ramifications down the road.

Bifaces remain a perennial puzzle for archeologists. On the one hand their "toolness," and imposed shape, were very different from what apes do and suggest that *Homo erectus* had a very different relationship with tools. On the other hand, the complete absence of innovation, and the dogged conservatism of the form (for well over 1 million years!), indicate that the relationship was also very different from the one modern humans have with tools. In this sense, at least, *Homo erectus* was neither ape nor human.

Other Mode 2 archeology

Despite being more recent, early Mode 2 archeological sites do not often present as detailed a picture of hominin activity as the earlier Mode 1 sites. This is largely the consequence of their different sedimentary context. Early Mode 2 sites are most often situated in sand or gravel deposited by streams, rather than the finer silts deposited by lakes. Because streams are higher-energy depositional agents, they move artifacts and garbage much farther than lakes, destroying the natural associations, and destroying or damaging the more fragile items. So, somewhat paradoxically, we know less about the activities that occurred at early Mode 2 sites; there is, for example, no site comparable to FLK at Olduvai Gorge. There are a few early Mode 2 sites with bone, and the much-abbreviated picture of activities at these sites resembles that of the earlier Mode 1 sites. There is no reason, based on this limited evidence, to conclude that the hominins hunted, rather than used some form of scavenging. It is possible that there was more hunting, but we just do not see it. Some archeologists speculate that the wood residue on the Peninj handaxes may be the result of sharpening acacia branches for spears (Dominguez-Rodrigo et al., 2001). This is possible, but it is equally possible that the hominins sharpened digging sticks used to acquire underground storage organs (USOs).

The different sedimentary context of Mode 2 sites does corroborate a conclusion derived from fossils such as Nariokotome. *Homo erectus*, the presumed knapper of Mode 2 tools, had invaded hot, open savannas. We find bifaces in stream deposits because *Homo erectus* used streambeds regularly as foci of activity. Availability of water, essential to hominin survival in open country, was an obvious draw, and stream channels supported the only available shade. They were also the only relatively secluded places on the open savanna and, even though *Homo erectus* was considerably larger than earlier hominins, predation must still have been a serious danger. Mode 2 sites also occur at higher elevations, and in a greater variety of geographic settings than earlier Mode 1, corroborating the greater adaptability suggested by the distribution of *Homo erectus* fossils (Cachel and Harris, 1995, 1998).

Handedness

Another feature of this period is that the stone tools start to show a more pronounced right-hand preference of their makers (e.g., Corballis, 2003). Life in trees would have almost demanded ambidextrous hand and leg movements. With the transition to life on the ground, hand-preference symmetry would no longer be a requirement of successful living. For example, it has been argued that bipedalism would have allowed the hands and arms to gesture. Corballis argued that the incorporation of gestures along with vocalizations might have served as a foundation of language. He also postulates that the left hemisphere's predilection for vocalization probably occurred much earlier in time. As a consequence of the incorporation of manual gestures with vocalizations, language could then evolve beyond simple manual gestures, although, interestingly, modern humans often still gesture while speaking and show a right-hand preference for gesturing. Toth (1985) found a right-hand preference ratio (57:43) in stone tools from 1.9 to 1.4 million years ago that is not close to the modern ratio of 9:1 of right-handers to non-right-handers. This discrepancy and other factors led Corballis to suspect that true syntactic modern speech was not to evolve until a million or more years later.

Fire

Homo erectus may have used fire. The evidence for this is very controversial. Archeologists have yet to discover the remains of a compact hearth (campfire) with telltale charcoal filling a nice pit, or surrounded by a stone ring, that dates back 1.8 million years. Indeed, the oldest feature of this sort is only about 350,000 years old. But use of fire does not require structured hearths. The South African site of Swartkrans has the remains of burnt animal bone dating back to about 1.4 million years, and the site of Chesowanja in Kenya has patches of heat-altered soil that are hard to explain through natural bush fires (Brain and Sillen, 1988). These bits of evidence are tenuous, but when we consider the location of most early *Homo erectus* and Mode 2 sites – the beds of ephemeral water courses – then the dearth of charcoal is not as surprising. We think it likely that *Homo erectus* used fire. They need not have been able to make fire, just capture it from natural burns (e.g., lightning-caused). The use of fire has several benefits. One is warmth, though this may not have been important until *Homo erectus* left the tropics. Another is discouraging predators. *Homo erectus* had moved away from the woodlands, and was too large, and lacked the upper-body anatomy, to have done much climbing. They almost certainly slept on the ground, and fire would have been a very useful deterrent to carnivores. If used in cooking, fire can break down the chemical defenses of many plant foods (including USOs) and aid the digestion of meat (Wrangham et al., 1999). And keep in mind that *Homo erectus* needed to feed its enormous brain. Fire also had a potential social consequence. In positioning themselves close to fires, *Homo erectus* had new social opportunities. Members of a group could see one another, and communicate visually and vocalize quietly – all necessary in the presence of predation risk. Perhaps, more importantly, *Homo erectus*, as a hominin, would have maintained the need for social bonding, and modern apes and monkeys use physical grooming to accomplish this task. Around communal fires, *Homo erectus* might also have fulfilled social grooming requirements. Psychologist Matt Rossano (2006) has speculated that fires may also have aided communal attention, served as a form of meditation, and aided the development of consciousness. Would *Homo erectus* have told stories or sung, activities that are characteristic of so many modern hunters and gatherers? That speculation is tempting but has no evidential basis – for the present.

The *Homo erectus* Adaptive Niche

A general consensus has emerged among paleoanthropologists that the emergence of *Homo erectus* represented a major adaptive shift in hominin evolution, and a giant step away from an ape-like way of life (Anton, 2003). Primates like *Homo erectus* had never been seen before. They were not just a variation on an old theme; they were something altogether new. Evolutionary scholars often use the terms "grade shift" to characterize such a significant change, and we maintain that the grade shift represented by *Homo erectus* included developments in cognition, and also opened up many new possibilities for cognitive development. Part of the argument for a grade shift is based on facts we know about *Homo erectus*, and part is based on reasonable inferences. Based on Nariokotome, other fossils, and the archeological record, we know that *Homo erectus*:

(i)   was larger than earlier hominins;
(ii)   had reduced sexual dimorphism (females had a much increased body size);
(iii)   had a larger brain, absolutely, than earlier *Homo*, and a slightly larger EQ;
(iv)   had smaller teeth, and a smaller face;
(v)   had a body build adapted for efficient cooling;
(vi)   lived in a wider variety of habitats, including hot, open, savannas;
(vii)   had dispersed rapidly to many tropical and subtropical regions of the Old World;
(viii) made and used tools of much greater complexity.

From these facts about *Homo erectus*, it is possible to formulate a number of reasonable inferences concerning *Homo erectus*' way of life:

1. *Homo erectus* diets almost certainly contained more high-quality foods than those of earlier hominins; the increase in brain size alone would more or less require this. Most paleoanthropologists assume that animal fat and protein were key elements. Unfortunately, the archeological record is not as helpful as it was for early *Homo*, though there are sites, such as Konso-Gardula (Ethiopia) and Peninj (Tanzania), that hint at a greater emphasis on animal carcasses than was true for earlier hominins (Dominguez-Rodrigo, 2006). If *Homo erectus* had increased its reliance on animal products,

especially if it had added hunting to aggressive scavenging, then it would have been in competition with large carnivores. This would have required utilization of much larger territories, and probably use of deceptive techniques; even though they were bigger, it is unlikely that *Homo erectus* could have killed lions, or even leopards (let alone the saber-tooth cats that were on the African landscape at the time).

2.   The home range of *Homo erectus* groups was up to 10 times larger than the home ranges of australopithecines and other apes. Increase in body size alone would dictate an increase in home range, and when one takes into account greater reliance on animal products, the necessary territory to support a group increased dramatically (Anton and Swisher, 2004; Anton et al., 2002). Exact size of the home range is very difficult to determine, and would vary according to local conditions, but, if *Homo erectus* ranges were 10 times larger than those of chimpanzees, they could easily have exceeded 100 square miles. Such an expansion would have come with energetic costs, dramatically implied by Nariokotome's anatomy – increased bipedal efficiency, strenuous activity, and the necessity for efficient cooling. Indeed, Bramble and Lieberman (2004) have suggested that many of *Homo erectus'* derived features (e.g., long legs and tall, narrow body form) may have been tied to endurance running, which would have enhanced its ability to exploit larger territories. There would also have been social costs. Maintaining social cohesion within a group would have been difficult, especially if *Homo erectus* foraged in small subgroups the way modern chimpanzees do. Unfortunately, we know little about group size. All apes are exogamous, indeed all are male philopatric – females leave their natal group and join another at adolescence. Simply finding a neighboring group outside a territory of 100 square miles would have presented problems – even encounters at boundaries would have been rare. Rather than maintaining hostile relations toward neighboring groups, as chimpanzees clearly do, *Homo erectus* may have had to establish and maintain mating networks.

3.   The energy budgets of both males and females – the number of calories taken in and expended – had almost certainly changed. For almost all primates, males are larger than females. This sexual dimorphism is linked to greater caloric demands on females (pregnancy and lactation), and greater size demands on males (intra-group aggression). There is a good correlation between degree of intra-group male aggression and sexual dimorphism. Sexual dimorphism was considerably reduced in *Homo erectus*, but not

because males had become smaller; indeed males were much bigger than earlier hominin males. Females had grown even more, and this is the telling point. Given the large home ranges, and strenuous activity in hot climates, the size increase in females would have dramatically increased their caloric intake requirements. Aiello and Key (2002) have estimated that this increase was on the order of 50 percent above that of an australopithecine female. There had to have been some way to compensate for this increase, either through an increase in caloric intake, or a decrease in energy expenditure. An increase in meat consumption might solve the problem, but only if it did not also require an increase in expenditure. Aggressive scavenging or hunting could be the solution if relatively large quantities could be acquired with minimal effort, and herein lies the problem. Aggressive scavenging and hunting both require considerable energy expenditure – finding, killing, or driving off carnivores. For females who are pregnant, carrying infants, or nursing, there are large risks in this kind of foraging. About the only way a *Homo erectus* female could support her body size and reproduce effectively would have been through assistance. One hypothesis, known as the grandmother hypothesis (O'Connell, Hawkes, and Burton Jones, 1999), suggests that the problems of female energy budgets were solved via provisioning by mothers' mothers. If a woman gathered and carried food to her pregnant or nursing daughter there would be immediate benefits to both in terms of reproductive success. In effect, two adults would be foraging in support of one offspring. Of course, this would work only if the grandmother were not herself pregnant or nursing. This scenario has the added advantage of accounting for an unusual feature of human life histories – postmenopausal women. It should be noted that this hypothesis is based more on knowledge of what actually occurs in modern hunting and gathering societies, where grandmothers are primary providers for grandchildren, than on what we know about *Homo erectus*. The grandmother hypothesis also has an interesting corollary. It would only work if the groups were female philopatric, that is, if females remained with their mothers at adolescence, and adolescent males left the group to find and join new groups. This is the way most Old World monkeys handle exogamy. The male side of the equation is problematic, however. Female philopatry usually selects for increased male size, and increased sexual dimorphism, because males must fight their way into the dominance hierarchy of their new group.

Many paleoanthropologists believe that the reduction in sexual dimorphism implies that males provisioned females. If males acquired meat via aggressive scavenging and/or hunting, the argument goes, there would be enough to carry back to females to share. If a male and a female had developed a pair-bonded relationship, even if only temporary, this would reduce selection for male size. The results would be the same, more or less, as those of the grandmother hypothesis, except that there is no necessity to invoke a dramatic change from male philopatry to female philopatry. The weakness of this scenario, somewhat ironically, is that meat and animal products are not particularly reliable sources. Indeed, among modern tropical and subtropical hunters and gatherers meat constitutes a smaller part of the total caloric intake than plants, often by a wide margin (O'Connell, Hawkes, and Burton Jones, 1999), and these hunters have bows or other relatively sophisticated killing systems not possessed by Homo erectus. So, we are left with a conundrum. Somehow Homo erectus females must have increased their caloric intake. Some form of cooperative system in which pregnant and nursing females were provisioned by others appears likely. However, the two leading hypotheses, grandmothering and male provision-ing, both have weaknesses in light of what we know about modern apes (male philopatric) and modern tropical hunters and gatherers (heavily plant dependent). For our purposes, it is unnecessary to solve this puzzle. It is sufficient to know that Homo erectus must have used some kind of cooperative, social provisioning.

4. There must also have been a change in life-history pattern. As we saw earlier, some paleoanthropologists have argued that Homo erectus had secondary altriciality. Such a change in developmental timing would mean that Homo erectus had helpless infants, just as modern human infants are helpless. Such a change would have placed even greater demands on females, who would have had to carry helpless infants who could not hang on. And given that evolution had selected a body type suited for heat dissipation, it seems likely that these Homo erectus had lost the dense body hair typ-ical of apes, so there may have been little to hang onto! Altriciality would also place demands on lactation because postnatal brain growth would have depended on high-caloric nursing. About the only way that this could have worked would have been through social assistance. Altriciality fits the evidence for increased female size nicely. Unfortunately, it is far from clear that Homo erectus was altricial. The pelvic and brain-size evidence suggests that it was, but the only young juvenile in the Homo erectus fossil record, Mojokerto from Indonesia, seems not to have been altricial, though this interpretation has been challenged (Leigh, 2005). Nariokotome's tooth eruption pattern suggests that he may not have undergone a "spurt" of growth

when he entered puberty (had he lived to do so) but would have had a more gradual growth curve. The implications of this are not clear, though it would seem to indicate a more gradual ontogenetic development of adult abilities, and commensurate shorter childhood during which it relied heavily on parental provisioning.

5.   *Homo erectus* would have encountered cognitive challenges. The most obvious would be organizing action in large territories, both to find food and to maintain mating contacts and networks. If the energetic requirements of females were met through greater group cooperation of some kind, as seems likely, then the demands on social relations would have increased significantly. And the change in life history, whatever it was, may have changed the learning environment in significant ways. *Homo erectus* did have larger brains than any earlier hominin, and we suspect that the reasons for this increase lay in the challenges just enumerated.

The Weed Hypothesis

This suite of adaptive developments has led several paleoanthropologists to suggest that the evolution of *Homo erectus* represented a grade shift away from previous, more ape-like, ways of life (Anton, 2003; Aiello and Key, 2002; Wood and Collard, 1999; Collard, 2002; Rightmire, 2001). Cachel and Harris (1995) have proposed a provocative hypothesis for the niche of *Homo erectus*, a hypothesis that dovetails nicely with the evidence for a grade shift. They suggest that *Homo erectus* was a "weed" species, especially adept at invading disrupted environments, such as those common in the Pleistocene, and new locales. This characterization has recently received added support from Wells and Stock (2007), who also see rapid colonization as an essential component of the *Homo erectus* niche. An essential element to this was the ability to learn new territories very rapidly. "It is tempting to infer that, if relative brain size increase in genus *Homo* is associated with an enhanced ability to map important resources and predict their availability across a home range, this might explain the greater dispersal ability of this genus in comparison to the australopithecines" (Cachel and Harris, 1995: 59). However, they also observe that there is no correlation between dispersal ability and brain size in other animals, and focus on the increase in body size and culture as the important factors. We think that they abandoned the neurological factor too quickly.

Homo erectus Cognition

It is our contention that the evolution of *Homo erectus* was accompanied by significant changes in cognition. We are certainly not the first to try to characterize something about the cognitive abilities of *Homo erectus* (Donald, 1991; Mithen, 1996). Our approach differs from earlier attempts in the specificity of its description. We try to identify a few fairly narrowly circumscribed abilities, along with some of the neurological systems that enable them. We do not pretend to provide a comprehensive account. Most of *Homo erectus* cognition remains inaccessible. But we do strive to provide a description of those cognitive abilities that are available to us through the paleoanthropological record.

Homo erectus had a more sophisticated spatial cognition than apes or earlier hominins (Wynn, 2002). Our evidence for this is direct, through artifacts, and indirect, through the reconstruction of range size and geographic distribution. Bifaces were the first objects with imposed shapes. The knappers paid attention to more than just the nature of the edge; they were concerned with the overall shape of the artifact. There has been some disagreement among archeologists concerning just how "intentional" this was, and some have suggested that even the bilateral symmetry was an unintended consequence of using large flake blanks as cores (Noble and Davidson, 1996). Much of this hesitation appears driven by an unwillingness to grant *Homo erectus* "mental templates." The concept of a mental template is an old one in archeology and is based on the common-sense presumption that in order to make any kind of regular shape one must have a precise, pre-existing mental image of the object. To our knowledge, mental template appears nowhere in the psychological literature of either perception or procedural knowledge; it is a common-sense notion with relatively little interpretive power. No precise mental image of a finished biface is necessary for their manufacture. All that would have been required is that the knapper attended to the shape as he or she flaked the artifact. A regular shape could emerge from the procedure. The cognitive implications of this are reasonably clear. Basic stone knapping is primarily a motor task guided by spatial thinking (Stout et al., 2000). As Stout's study revealed, this is primarily a motor cortex task guided by parietal lobe spatial networks (the dorsal pathway of visual processing). Shape recognition, and symmetry in particular, constitute a separate set of cognitive connections situated primarily in the temporal lobes (the ventral pathway of visual processing). So, to make a biface, the knapper had to coordinate these two pathways. What is not at all clear is just how and where, in a neurological sense, this coordination took place. The solution modern humans would undoubtedly use at first would be coordination in the active attention of working memory; later, after the task had become routinized, the coordination would become largely pre-attentive (a procedural memory). There are reasons for thinking the *Homo erectus* solution may have been entirely pre-attentive. The task, and the shape of the artifacts, remained essentially unchanged for over 1 million years. Innovation and creativity was not a component, and these are functions of modern working memory. We maintain that the coordination of visual and spatial information was part of the procedural memories of these hominins. They were accessed when needed and held in visuospatial attention only. Note that this account does not require explicit knowledge, or declarative memories. *Homo erectus* juveniles could have learned by observation and practice, incorporating the entire sequence of actions into procedural memory. Some neural connection had to have evolved to enable shape information to be coordinated with knapping action. But why? What selective advantage could this possibly have provided?

There is strong evidence that *Homo erectus* territories were up to 10 times larger than those of apes. Earlier we saw that fruit-eating primates have larger brains than leaf-eating primates, probably because of the cognitive challenge of remembering and monitoring locations of fruit patches scattered in the forest. A *Homo erectus* faced with a much larger territory, and a more unpredictable food source in the form of herbivore carcasses, would have an even greater challenge in conceiving of spatial relations. Although this was almost certainly true, it does not help us much. First, while it may select for more powerful spatial thinking, it would not require shape recognition. Second, although there is some correlation, cognitive abilities used in conceiving large-scale, landscape-sized spaces appear to be different from those used to think in terms of small-scale spaces such as objects (Silverman and Eals, 1992). So, although selection for large-scale spatial thinking probably did occur, it does not solve the problem at hand. For this we need to consider what shape recognition evolved to do.

Shape recognition is important for the social life of primates. Facial recognition is a critical component of neonates bonding with mothers, and, for juveniles and adults, facial identification of individuals is an important component of social life (Allman, 2000). Neural resources in the temporal lobes are dedicated to this task, and have evolved over the 50 million plus years of primate success. Symmetry plays an additional role. It is a component of mate assessment (Gangestad, 1997). Individuals who deviate significantly from bilateral symmetry (faces, bodies, etc.) are likely to be less healthy and make poorer candidates for mating. Primate shape-recognition systems have evolved to be particularly sensitive to bilateral symmetry. Given that primate shape recognition appears to be tied closely to mating systems, which in primates are highly social, parsimony requires us to ask whether or not shape *imposition* on bifaces might not also have been socially driven. What if *Homo erectus* made shapely bifaces not for mechanical reasons, but for social reasons? How might this have worked? Kohn and Mithen (1999) have suggested that it might have been via straightforward sexual selection. Handaxes signaled technical competence, and shapely, elegant handaxes signaled high value as a mate (are you initially more attracted to someone driving a 10-year-old Saturn or a Ferrari?). This would have been a relatively simple shift in a cognitive sense because symmetry was already in the repertoire (and brains) of *Homo erectus'* mate-recognition systems. At first blush this may seem far-fetched. But it fits the evidence very nicely; indeed, it solves several nagging problems about bifaces:

1. Bifaces are "standardized," in the sense that thousands of knappers made the same basic shape over an immense geographic range, in different habitats with different resources, and over an immensely long period of time. Even though they are not anatomical traits, they "act" like anatomical traits.
2. Even though good at butchery, archeologists actually find relatively few at butchery sites, which instead are dominated by simple flakes and cores.
3. Many, indeed most, show few signs of heavy use.
4. Archeologists often find sites with hundreds of bifaces, but little else in the way of remains.
5. Bifaces did get nicer and prettier over time, improvements that did nothing at all to their usefulness as tools. In an experimental study, Machin et al. (2006) were unable to demonstrate any relation between degree of symmetry and effectiveness in butchery.

Much later in human prehistory, artifacts do take on symbolic roles in marking status and social group membership. We do not think *Homo erectus'* bifaces did this – they vary like anatomy, not like clothing styles. But the possibility, indeed we think probability, that tools had entered social life is one of the most provocative developments that can be linked to *Homo erectus*. And it appears to have selected for the ability to coordinate shape and spatial information.

Homo erectus tools also reveal some more mundane things about cognition. The two-handed, over-the-head, knapping gesture required to produce large flakes suggests developments in skill, which probably played out in the expansion of appropriate areas of the motor cortex. It probably also selected for anatomies of the arm and shoulder. The manufacturing sequence, the *chaîne opératoire*, was also more complex than that of earlier Mode 1. Knapping a large flake, then trimming that flake into a shape, constitute two distinct steps. At a minimum, the procedures, held in long-term procedural memory, were longer than those of Mode 1. Longer technical sequences would benefit from more long-term memory capacity. Beyond this the *chaîne operatoire* appears to have been fairly simple; there is no evidence for significant changes in procedure as the artifacts were knapped. The knappers proceeded with the same basic flaking procedure until an acceptable result was achieved.

What about planning and working memory, which, after all, are the themes of this book? Recall that Baddeley's basic model of working memory includes two main subsystems, an articulatory processor that keeps words in active attention and visuospatial processor that does the same for image and spatial information. A central executive holds the output in the episodic buffer for further processing. Is it possible to reach any conclusions about *Homo erectus'* working memory? Given the role of linguistic processing in Baddeley's model, we need first to address the issue of *Homo erectus'* language.

Language remains perhaps the most significant unknown concerning *Homo erectus*. There is little hard evidence on which to base a solid argument, one way or the other, about this most human of abilities. No one doubts that *Homo erectus* communicated with one another vocally – all primates do – but beyond this there is no agreement. Recall that for a communication system to qualify as a language it must use symbols and have a grammar. Both are very hard to detect in fossils. Nariokotome's brain was larger than that of an ape, its pattern of asymmetry was essentially modern, and Broca's area was larger than that of other primates and earlier hominins. Surely this triumvirate points to language. Unfortunately, it need not. The greater length and complexity of sequential motor action in tool-making and other activities could account for the expansion of the left inferior premotor cortex. There is just no telltale piece of gross brain anatomy upon which we can hang the hat of language. But, many paleoanthropologists have argued, the stone tools, especially the arbitrary shapes of handaxes, would have required either grammar-like rules or linguistic instruction (e.g., Holloway, 1969; Isaac, 1976). Again, this is wishful thinking. The only thing that technical thinking and language share is sequential production. Technical sequences are produced by procedural cognition, which is learned through observation and practice. Complex procedures require lengthy training and practice to consolidate the links in the sequence into long-term procedural memories. They are not generated by grammar-like rules; this is a misleading metaphor. This is why apprenticeship (guided imitation) remains, to this day, the primary mode of technical learning. And, in apprenticeship, linguistic communication is secondary (Keller and Keller, 1996; Gatewood, 1985). Indeed, many procedures can be learned by observation and practice alone. So, as much as archeologists may fervently wish it, bifaces did not require language. But they are perhaps not entirely mute.

Bifaces may not have been symbols, or required grammar, but they did have a potential communicative role, even beyond any role in sexual selection. They would have been natural indexes of their own use (Byers (1994) prefers the term *warrants*). Because they were permanent tools, carried from place to place, they were no longer restricted to specific contexts of use. They could, then, stand for past use and potential future use, and this reference to past and future is something no chimpanzee has ever been observed to do. A simple act of gesturing with a biface, using the motor pattern typical of use, would have communicative power. We do not know if *Homo erectus* ever did this, but the potential was there, day after day, for hundreds of thousands of years. Add to this a new social group configuration of cooperative provisioning, and aggregating near fires, and the communicative potential of gesturing with tools would have increased dramatically.

There is no reason to conclude that *Homo erectus* had a modern articulatory processor as a subsystem of working memory. But could it have had a less powerful processor, one with less capacity, but which still handled meaningful vocal or gestural units, a kind of proto language, in Bickerton's (1990) sense? As we noted in chapter 3, Aboitiz et al. (2006) noted that the phonological storage system represents a short-term memory ensemble that can be phylogenetically tracked to earlier homologues in hominin evolution and to current primate brain systems. Further, they postulated that an expansion of the short-term memory system may have allowed the processing of sounds, transmission of more elaborate meanings, and eventually participation in syntactic processes. There is also some evidence for a modern pattern of left-hemisphere enlargement. The only honest answer to this question is that we just do not know. It seems unlikely that the modern articulatory processor evolved whole cloth one day via a massive mutation; some proto-system seems likely. But the paleoanthropological evidence shows neither what it was, nor when it occurred. We are on slightly firmer ground with the visuospatial processor (visuospatial sketchpad – VSSP) and the central executive.

One of the more puzzling results of experimental research on working memory is that it is more difficult to isolate VSSP performance from central executive performance than it is to isolate the articulatory processor. VSSP and central executive performance always correlate strongly. We suspect that this may reflect the greater evolutionary antiquity of VSSP. We suspect, for example, that neural resources that were to become the modern VSSP were the ones that coordinated the spatial and shape information necessary for biface manufacture. In isolation, the VSSP would operate in a pre-attentive, implicit fashion. The sexual selection scenario of Kohn and Mithen (1999) could still play out (big handaxes are sexy), but it would play out very slowly in an evolutionary sense. Intentional innovation would require the full attention of a central executive. For innovation, the central executive must hold in mind not only the goal, but also the available cognitive and practical resources, and alternative resources for comparison. *Homo erectus'* central executive probably just could not handle all of that information. When it had a task to perform, it could hold a goal in attention (so can apes, so this is not new), and access a procedure, held in long-term memory. Part of the procedure in biface manufacture included the VSSP coordinating shape and spatial information, and this was new, but this coordination need not have required *extended* central executive functions.

Lack of innovation does not mean lack of flexibility. Long-term memory can hold a large range of alternative procedures and implicit knowledge, all learned by observation and repetition. Indeed, the domain of expert performance in the modern world is largely a domain of pattern recognition tied to well-practiced responses (Ericsson and Delaney, 1999, Ericsson and Kintsch, 1995). Working memory in the narrow sense plays only a limited role. *Homo erectus* must have had a very flexible adaptive niche. After all, they used it to expand very rapidly into regions with new resources and new problems. But this kind of adaptability does not require innovation or contingency planning. Macaques, for example, have adapted to an equally large range of habitats (including cities!) without an enhanced working memory. *Homo erectus'* rapid dispersal relied on a large corpus of procedures held in long-term memory and accessed through a comparatively small central capacity. In this scenario, an increase in brain size would accommodate more and longer procedures. In other words, the encephalization of *Homo erectus* may have been largely a matter of increasing long-term capacity, especially the capacity for procedural memory and expertise. This cognitive strategy was very successful, and indeed was the primary theme of cognitive evolution for the next million years.

8

The First Major Leap in Cognition: The Tree-to-Ground Sleep Transition

Imagine you are suddenly placed in a "Survivor"-like episode in Africa, where woodland meets a vast savannah, and you suspect you will be there for a long time. This is the very scenario that faced the reputed descendant of *Australopithecus afarensis, Homo erectus.* What would you like to have with you? When I (FLC) posed this question to my brother, he said "beer?" As we noted in the last chapter, *Homo erectus* had invaded hot, open savannas, and water was essential, especially stream channels because they also provided shade. Furthermore, even though *Homo erectus* was considerably larger than earlier hominins, predation must still have been a serious danger so stream channels may have also served as a form of protection.

In the previous chapter, we argued that the advent of *Homo erectus* represented a dramatic change in the way of life of our ancestors, a grade shift in evolutionary terms. We noted the significant change in anatomy and in where this hominin lived, and the probable expansion in the size of its habitual territories. We emphasized the new features of Mode 2 technology, especially the reliance on the first true tool type, in the sense of a category that existed in the minds of its makers. These bifaces had a variety of possible uses: for heavy butchering, for sharpening digging sticks, as a source of sharp flakes, and perhaps for social display and/or sexual selection. We also mentioned the use of fire for protection, warmth, and food preparation. The communal use of fire may have promoted communication, also a vital requirement of life on the ground. But now, back to our survivor question: what else would you require? The idea that early humans were prey as well as predators has been strongly emphasized by Hart and Sussman (2005). As we have descended from very small primates living in trees, and we remained relatively small compared to many other animals (who might be weighed in tons), life on the ground must have presented extraordinary predation risks. The adage "there's safety in numbers" comes to mind. So we might expect that group size expanded after the transition to a terrestrial life; however, there is little or no anthropological evidence for this expansion. But the evidence for reduced sexual dimorphism, and the possibility of more helpless, altricial infants, strongly suggests that something must have changed in the social behavior of *Homo erectus* compared to that of earlier hominins. Again, this fits with the grade shift in adaptive niche. Robin Dunbar (1993) has argued that if social group size increased beyond that of normal primate groups, the typical primate method of maintaining group bonds, physical grooming, would no longer have been effective (too many individuals to groom). This would have been an evolutionary impetus for social use of language, especially gossip, as a means of social discourse. Perhaps, such phrases as "nice day," "nice hair," "nice handaxe!" served the same original purpose as did physical grooming in early primates. Although the evidence is equivocal, what we know of the brain (Broca's area) and vocal tract of *Homo erectus* suggest it may, in fact, have relied more on vocal communication than other apes.

Earlier we also noted that the home range of *Homo erectus* was up to 10 times larger than the home ranges of australopithecines and other apes, perhaps as great as 100 square miles. *Homo erectus* was faced with a much larger territory and a more unpredictable food source in the form of herbivore carcasses; thus there was greater challenge than ever in conceiving of spatial relations, mapping new territories, and memorization of important locations of resources and dangers. It seems likely to us that *Homo erectus* was highly mobile, but this mobility may have presented a new set of dangers, especially in open country whose trees were few, far between, and small. We think this new life on the ground had another subtle yet profound consequence: *Homo erectus* slept on the ground.

The First Leap: The Tree-to-Ground Sleep Transition

Other than slightly larger brain cases and relatively simple Mode 1 tools, there is presently no other evidence for clear behavioral differences between the *Australopithecines* and earliest *Homo* such as *Homo habilis*. Because *Homo habilis* retained the same general body type as *Australopithecus*, with a relatively light body and long arms compared to the length of their legs, but with bigger brains, it suggests that hominins such as *Homo habilis* could only have evolved so far while generally maintaining a life in trees. It apparently took the new demands of life on the ground to cause a real grade shift in our evolution. However, as we have vividly noted, life on the ground was inordinately more dangerous. We think *sleeping* on the ground was an important component of the grade shift. The tree-to-ground sleep transition certainly allows individuals to grow in height and weight, but ground sleep also ameliorates one of the more dangerous effects of sleeping in trees – falling out of them! However, in order to appreciate some of the other deleterious effects of tree sleep, let us review the physiological aspects of a night's sleep.

Characteristics of Sleep

Researchers typically characterize sleep by five distinct EEG stages. Stages 1 and 2 are considered light stages of sleep, as people are easily awakened from them. Stage 1 is typically brief and usually occurs at the onset of sleep. Stage 2 accounts for about 50 percent of sleep and is distributed fairly evenly throughout a typical eight-hour sleep period. The brain waves during these stages are of lower amplitude than other stages but higher in frequency (i.e., > 15 Hz). Stage 2 is also characterized by sleep spindles, which are periodic brief bursts of 12 to 16 Hz, occurring at a rate of about two per minute. Humans can report thoughts, ideas, and dreams after awakening from these stages. Stages 3 and 4 are considered deeper sleep stages and are also referred to as slow-wave sleep (slow in the sense of wave frequency). Slow-wave sleep has a frequency of 0.5 Hz to 3 Hz (called delta waves) and high amplitude (compared to other sleep stages). In humans, it is the stage in which it is least likely that coherent stories or vivid dreams are reported, and it diminishes sharply after the age of about 60. There appears to be an activation of the parasympathetic nervous system during slow-wave sleep and less activation of the cardiovascular system, with decreases of respiration, heart rate, and blood pressure. Activity of the gastrointestinal system accelerates, and there are increased movements of the gastrointestinal tract (Beatty, 1995). Most slow-wave sleep occurs during the first third of a human's eight-hour sleep period. Besides a nearly complete absence of vivid dreams in slow-wave sleep, it is also the most difficult stage from which to awaken sleepers.

The fifth stage of sleep is not labeled as such. It is called rapid eye-movement sleep or REM sleep, and it appears to be a newer evolutionary development compared to the other stages. Winson (1990) argues that it arose approximately 140 million years ago in a context of early mammalian evolution, whereas slow-wave sleep may date back as much as 200 million or more years. The brain waves in REM sleep are similar to Stage 1 sleep with low amplitude and higher frequencies. However, there are periodic bursts of eye movements, and when human sleepers are awakened during REM, they often report vivid dreams and often see themselves actively participating in their dreams. These reports are usually qualitatively distinct from the thoughts and snippets of ideas in Stages 1 and 2 (e.g., Hobson, 1988). REM sleep predominates in the later third of a human's eight-hour sleep period (see Dement and Vaughn, 1999 or Ellman and Antrobus, 1991, for more elaborate descriptions of sleep and dream research). Human REM constitutes 25 percent of the total sleep time.

Interestingly, the onset of sleep in most primates (including modern humans) is often accompanied by a hypnic or hypnagogic jerk, which is a sudden muscle reflexive movement that frequently awakens the sleeper. Although the ultimate cause of the hypnic jerk is unknown, a common hypothesis is that it is an archaic reflex to the brain's misinterpreting the muscle relaxation accompanying the onset of sleep as a signal that the sleeping primate is falling out of a tree. The reflex may also have had selective value by having the sleeper readjust or review his or her sleeping position in a nest or on a branch in order to assure that a fall did not occur (e.g., Coolidge, 2006).

The onset of sleep, even the lightest of stages, Stage 1, and the other sleep stages are accompanied by muscle relaxation. However, an even deeper muscle relaxation occurs at the onset of REM sleep. In the language of sleep researchers, it is called muscle atonia or muscle paralysis. Jouvet (1980) explored the role of inhibitory neurons upon voluntary muscle systems in preventing these systems from acting out dreams. Morrison (1983) demonstrated that selective destruction of these inhibitory neurons allowed cats to act out predatory actions, presumably the content of their REM dreams. A similar disorder has been noted in humans, the REM sleep behavior disorder (Sforza, Krieger, and Petiau 1997). Also, some sleeping people can become aware of this muscle paralysis during REM sleep, and their accompanying dream themes often reflect the interpretation of muscle atonia, such as being paralyzed by aliens or being crushed by ghosts (e.g., Wing, Lee, and Chen, 1994). In their study of over 600 Chinese undergraduates, over 93 percent had heard of the ghost oppression dream and 37 percent claimed to have experienced it.

It has also been suggested that one of the most common themes of all adult dreams, falling, may in part occur because of the sleeper's interpretation of the complete muscle atonia that accompanies the onset of REM sleep (e.g., Van De Castle, 1994). The other suspicion, of course, is that the falling theme is connected to our arboreal (tree-living) hominin origins, as falling out of a tree was an event that an early hominin should not have taken lightly nor have easily forgotten (e.g., Sagan, 1977).

An evolutionary speculation for muscle atonia and the differentiation of slow-wave and REM sleep comes from the work of Kavanau (2002). He proposed that as ambient temperatures during twilight portions of primitive sleep rose above an animal's core temperature, the thermoregulatory need for muscle contractions became superfluous. With the absence of muscle tone, he proposed that selection may have favored fast waves during nocturnal twilight sleep. These fast waves may have reinforced motor circuits of evolving warm-blooded organisms without the concomitant, sleep-disturbing muscle contractions. Through these and other mechanisms, twilight sleep may have become REM sleep, and the daylight sleep may have become slow-wave sleep and non-REM sleep.

It also appears that the motor paralysis during REM sleep is accompanied by specific deactivation of some of the central executive's functions. As we noted in chapter 2, a distinction is often made between the executive functions of the dorsolateral prefrontal cortex and the ventromedial prefrontal cortex, with the former considered cognitive executive functions (complex problem-solving, decision-making, etc.) and the latter considered affective executive functions (decision-making when people and their feelings are considered). Neuroimaging studies have shown that there is deactivation of the dorsolateral prefrontal cortex but activation of the ventromedial prefrontal cortex, the amygdala, and the anterior cingulate gyrus. The amygdala, as previously noted in chapter 2, is involved in fear and startle reactions, and the anterior cingulate gyrus mediates attention and some interpersonal decisions. The latter gyrus is also phylogenetically older than the prefrontal cortex so it is interesting to ponder why it is active during REM while the phylogenetically newer PF cortices are truly "asleep" during REM. Perhaps these differential brain activations allow the dreamer to remain in a quiescent physical state, unable to select and attend freely to particular internal stimuli (a dream's content) and external stimuli, and yet accept often bizarre dream scenarios as reality. For example, interacting with long-dead people we have known or people we have not seen for years is not rationally challenged while we dream, nor are we easily able to become aware that we are dreaming when we encounter these unlikely dream scenarios (e.g., Franklyn and Zyphur, 2005).

As for the function of sleep, Lima, Rattenborg, Lesku, and Amlaner (2005) have noted that most evidence has supported an important restorative basis, although an overview of this literature also supports mnemonitive and innovative functions as well (Coolidge, 2006; Walker, 2005). Furthermore, it appears unlikely that sleep would have a single function, as multiple and interactive reasons for sleep are more probable, given the latter's long phylogenetic history, and behavioral and physiological complexities.

Importantly, Lima et al. pointed out the anti-predator function of sleep, i.e., sleep serves a protective role when an organism cannot be useful performing other activities. For example, with relatively poor night vision compared to some other animals, it might be better for early hominins to be out of harm's way and sleeping rather than stumbling about in the dark. This "immobilization" hypothesis is entirely consistent, as being inert in a predatory environment can still be risky. Lima et al. propose that the dramatic differences in sleep stages, e.g., light Stage 2 evenly distributed throughout the night, deep Stage 4 (slow-wave sleep) predominating early in a sleep period, and REM sleep predominating later in a sleep period, reflect an evolutionary trade-off between more vigilant states of sleep (Stage 2) and less vigilant states (Stage 4 and REM).

Primate and Hominin Nesting

Virtually all animals sleep, but the nature of sleep is best documented and understood for vertebrates, especially birds and mammals. Both spend a significant portion of their time asleep, and selection of sleeping sites is therefore a significant feature of adaptive niches. Various considerations come into play in selection or construction of sleeping sites, including thermoregulation, nearness to and/or protection of food resources, social interactions, parasite threat and risk of predation. All of these come into play for primates, but there is considerable variability within the order in solutions to the sleeping-site problem. Many prosimians nest, but most anthropoids do not (Kappeler, 1998). Instead, monkeys and lesser apes select sleeping sites, but do not modify them. For monkeys such sites are often high in trees or on cliff faces, sites which present a real risk of falling, but which, for the same reason, reduce the risk of predation. One apparent effect that this has had for many monkeys is a predominance of early stage, light sleep (Anderson, 1998).

Construction of sleeping nests appears to be a derived feature for the great apes. Orangutans, chimpanzees, and bonobos typically construct nests in trees, while gorillas typically build nests on the ground. Fruth and Hohman (1996) report an average above-ground height of 10–20 meters for the arboreal nests, while Groves and Sabater Pi (1985) report a range of 3 to over 25 meters for chimpanzees. Chimpanzees construct individual nests in new locations every night (infants sleep with mothers) and rarely re-use earlier efforts. When constructing nests chimpanzees most often start at a fork in the branches and bend down and weave nearby branches into a stable platform. Chimpanzees build the nests before nightfall and stay in them the entire night. The members of a traveling party build nests near to one another, and often vocalize in the evening after settling down, and in the morning before rising. In contrast, gorillas nest on the ground, a fact probably linked to gorillas' size. Gorillas also construct a nest each night, usually by bending over leafy vegetation. Chimpanzees do occasionally nest on the ground (6.1 percent of the time in one study (Koops et al., 2007)), and gorillas, usually females, do occasionally nest in trees, attesting the variability present even within communities. All great apes sleep in a horizontal position, probably because muscle relaxation is a general characteristic of the onset of sleep, and nests undoubtedly aid in both sleep comfort and the prevention of sleep mishaps (i.e., falling out of a tree).

The same considerations appear to go into great ape nest construction as go into the selection of sleeping sites by other primates. Great apes often nest near food sources (Fruth and Hohman, 1996), and occasionally in fruit-bearing trees (Basabose and Yamagiwa, 2002). Predation risk is also real for most studied groups of chimpanzees, with leopards being the major threat (Fruth and Hohman, 1996; Koops et al., 2007). However, it has proven very difficult to assess the role of predation risk (Anderson, 1998), and there are no known cases of predation on chimpanzees from nests (McGrew, personal communication, May 2004). Social considerations are clearly important in selection of nesting sites; the number and propinquity of nest sites closely reflects the make up of foraging groups. Significant social interaction takes place after settling down for the night, often via vocalization (Anderson, 1998), enough so that Fruth and Hohman (1996) consider this as a potential evolutionary source for information exchange among hominins. It is less clear that thermoregulation considerations come into play for great apes (they do for monkeys). The one tested chimpanzee case found that selection of ground nests was not influenced by windy or rainy conditions (at this site there was no predation risk) (Koops et al., 2007).

In part based on modern evidence of nest building in great apes, Sabater Pi, Veà, and Serrallonga (1997) proposed that early hominins probably also nested in trees. Additional support for arboreal nesting among early (before 2.5 million years ago) hominins rests on the evidence of hominin postcranial anatomy. As we saw in chapter 6, the hominin fossil record from Africa has yielded numerous examples of postcranial bones. For many of these examples, it is possible to assign taxonomic status, and for some (e.g., AL 288 (Lucy) and WT 15000 (Nariokotome)) it is possible to attribute bones to single individuals. Several limb features are reliable indicators of the hominin locomotor profile. In particular, climbing selects for more robust front-limb features, longer arms relative to legs, a higher brachial index (length of forearm relative to upper arm), a more cranially (head-ward) orientated glenoid (shoulder) cavity, and curved fingers (Stanley, 1992). These features are clearly represented in the anatomy of our nearest relatives, the common chimpanzees and bonobos, who forage, sleep, and nest in trees, but who travel on the ground between food sources.

All of the early hominins retain features of a climbing anatomy (McHenry and Coffing, 2000). *Australopithecus afarensis*, though clearly bipedal, retained robust fore limbs and long arms relative to femur length. As we have seen, a variety of hominins evolved in Africa between 3.8 million years and 2.5 million years ago, including a robust group (generally assigned to genus *Paranthropus*) and a more gracile group (assigned to genus *Australopithecus*). All were clearly bipedal, but all also retained features of a climbing anatomy (McHenry and Coffing, 2000; Stanley, 1992; Wood and Collard, 1999). Current hypotheses for the evolutionary advantage of bipedalism now focus on features of woodland niches, rather than the open grasslands favored by earlier hypotheses, and a variety of proposed explanations remain tenable (Richmond, Begun, and Strait, 2001), though the weight of evidence now favors the energy-expenditure hypothesis. What one can conclude with confidence is that these early hominins must have spent more time, and traveled longer distances, on the ground. But prior to the advent of *Homo erectus* they all lived in habitats with trees, and do not appear to have exploited treeless savannas. Their teeth document an adaptation to heavy chewing, perhaps of small hard seeds, or buried, gritty foods, and they may have spent much of their foraging time on the ground. Their climbing anatomy would then have been linked to predator avoidance and nesting (Stanley, 1992). In other respects these early hominins were ape-like. Their growth rates resemble those of chimpanzees (Wood and Collard, 1999), and there is no evidence (prior to 2.5 million years ago) for extensive tool use. Thus, because of their climbing anatomy and other evidence, it appears likely that these early hominins nested in trees and, by extension, retained an ape-like pattern of sleep.

Early *Homo* and *Homo erectus*

The earliest fossils assigned to the genus *Homo* are harder to assess, largely because the record of postcranial anatomy is poor; there are few examples *in toto*, fewer still that can be reliably assigned to an individual, and few complete examples of individual bones, requiring that measures of relative limb proportions be made from estimated lengths (Haeusler and McHenry, 2004; McHenry and Coffing, 2000). Nevertheless, studies of early *Homo* indicate that its postcranial anatomy was much like that of an *Australopithecus*. It, too, retained features of a climbing anatomy, though it may have been more human-like than the australopithecines (Haeusler and McHenry, 2004). Complicating the picture is the likelihood that there were two species of early *Homo* in Africa between 2.5 million years and 1.8 million years ago. One, *Homo rudolfensis*, may have had a more modern postcranial anatomy, if an isolated and fragmentary humerus is a reliable indication (McHenry and Coffing, 2000). Both forms continued to live in the wooded environments favored by earlier hominins, though they may have occupied a wider range of specific habitats (Reed, 1997). Early *Homo* had larger brains than the australopithecines, and at least one of them made and used stone tools. There is, however, no reason to conclude that *Homo habilis* and *rudolfensis* had given up sleeping in trees.

But *Homo erectus (sensu lato)* almost certainly had. This conjecture is supported by the postcranial anatomy of Nariokotome, which we discussed in chapter 7. As we noted, he was tall and thin, with an ideal body type for heat dissipation, and had led a rigorous life (Walker and Leakey, 1993). Otherwise, his limbs were little different from those of a modern human – he had the anatomy of modern bipedalism, and no remnants of climbing anatomy in his forelimbs (McHenry and Coffing, 2000; Wood and Collard, 1999). Moreover, his maturation pattern (tooth eruption sequence, etc.) was more like that of modern humans than it was like that of apes and may have included secondary altriciality. Other *Homo erectus* postcranial remains indicate another important step toward modernity. *Homo erectus* females were closer to males in size than was true for earlier hominins (Aiello and Key, 2002; McHenry and Coffing, 2000). The anatomical features of *Homo erectus* alone indicate that a profound shift in adaptation had occurred. It is the anatomy of a hominin adapted to hot, open environments, and to traveling longer distances on the ground. It was larger than earlier hominins, and had lost all remnants of climbing anatomy. The advent of *Homo erectus* was clearly one of the most significant transitions in human evolution. We suggest that it almost certainly included a transition to ground sleep.

To our knowledge, Fruth and Hohmann (1996) were the first to propose that primate nest building may have been a "great leap forward" in the evolution of cognition. Specifically, they proposed not only that the proximate functions of nests may have aided the transfer of information but also that nests themselves may have helped establish memories through increases of slow-wave and REM sleep. We are proposing that the full ground-sleep transition may have further aided increases in slow-wave and REM sleep and preserved the general integrity of the sleep period (e.g., less fragmented sleep by being subjected less to the vagaries of tree sleep such as strong breezes, bad weather, etc.). Furthermore, we hypothesize tripartite benefits from sleep on the ground: (1) threat simulation, social rehearsal, and priming; (2) creativity and innovation; and (3) procedural memory consolidation and enhancement, including procedural memories for visual-motor skills and visual-spatial locations.

Threat Simulation, Social Rehearsal, and Priming

Dream reports of modern children provide possible insights into the life and consciousness of early hominins. Van de Castle (1983) and Domhoff (1996), in large surveys of children's dream reports, found that animal characters made up the largest proportion of children's dreams (approximately 20 percent to 45 percent). They noted that the animals in dreams tended to be those that were not often encountered in children's actual lives, e.g., monsters, bears, wolves, snakes, gorillas, tigers, lions, and biting insects, although children do often dream of commonly encountered animals such as cats and dogs. The authors also noted that college students and older individuals, whose percentage of animal dreams was much lower, tended to dream of animals more likely to be encountered in real life, e.g., horses, dogs, and cats. Children's dreams also had higher rates of aggression than adult dreams, and higher rates of aggression involving animals. Revonsuo (2000) interprets these findings in terms of a threat-simulation theory, which states that the present dream-production system simulates threatening events in the ancestral environment.

The recurrent dreams of adults, nightmares in particular, may also present a glimpse of ancestral dream life. Robbins and Houshi (1983), in a study of college students, reported that the most common recurring dream theme was anxiety in the context of being pursued or threatened. The most common themes in nightmares, of course, contain high levels of anxiety but also appear similar to recurrent dream themes such as being threatened, chased, or attacked. Revonsuo (2000) argued that the waking lives of most of these dreamers were unlikely to have high levels of real daily threats, especially attacks by wild animals. He hypothesized that the dreamers were reliving archaic dream themes, particularly ones that would simulate the real dangers of the ancestral environment, including falling, violent encounters with natural disasters, and being threatened by strange people and wild animals. He reasoned that through natural selection, dreaming came to be a biological function that rehearsed threat perception and threat avoidance. The selective advantage would come from a dream theme repetition that would enhance and prepare waking threat-avoidance skills, which experimental psychologists call priming. A recent study (Malcolm-Smith and Solms, 2004), in part designed to test Revonsuo's hypothesis, may provide some support for it. University students were polled for threatening dreams and about 9 percent of the sample reported a realistic physical threat in a dream and about 3 percent reported a realistic escape response in the face of the threat. Stronger support for the threat-simulation hypothesis comes from Revonsuo and Valli (2000) and Valli et al. (2005).

We also argue that even Freud (1900/1956) provides evidence for Revonsuo's threat-simulation hypothesis, albeit a weaker case. Freud noted at least two dreams that may have had ancient ancestral roots: (1) the examination dream; and (2) the embarrassment of being naked dream. In both instances, we would posit that the dreams serve to prime the dreamer to be prepared in his or her subsequent waking life. In the examination dream, the dreamer is unprepared for an examination about to be taken. Freud noted that the dream may appear years after any actual examinations had been taken and that they may represent neurotic (anxiety) fears of being punished for being unprepared by our parents or schoolmasters. Freud interpreted the dreams of being naked or partially clothed as repressed sexual wishes. We posit that both dreams probably had their origins in the ancestral hominin environment. Hunters who were improperly dressed for hunt might die in a sudden and harsh weather change. Hunters without proper stone tools or weapons might also regret their lack of preparedness. The replay of these themes may have served to prime the dreamers so they were less likely to actually commit these errors upon awakening. It is probably impossible to determine whether some of our present dream themes are rooted in our past, but no more impossible than being able to determine they are solely a function of recent events in our lives. In all likelihood, our dreams are a combination of both.

Would regular confrontation with a threatening environment increase dream themes of danger and threat? There is evidence from the dream reports of contemporary hunter-gatherers that daily confrontations do increase dream themes of aggression and anxiety. Domhoff (1996) reported the results of dream studies conducted in the 1930s on Yir Yoront, a group of native Australian hunter-gatherers. The dreams of the adult males had significantly higher percentages of dreams with animals, aggression involving animals, and physical aggression than did those of male American dreamers. Gregor (1977) analyzed the dreams of Mehinaku Indians of Central Brazil. He found significantly more aggression and animal-aggression themes than for those of American dreamers. Gregor estimated that about 60 percent of the dreams of the Mehinaku males had threatening themes, while only 20 percent of their dreams involved non-threatening or non-aggressive activities. In a classic study of one adult woman of the contemporary !Kung hunters and gatherers of the Kalahari desert in southern Africa, Shostak (1981) recorded over 10 dreams with recurring and threatening themes of sexual infidelity, jealousy, omens and divinations, and falling (while climbing a tree and falling into a well). These findings are again consistent with Revonsuo's threat-simulation hypothesis, and it appears highly probable that threatening ancestral environments helped sustain threatening dream themes in early hominins.

Franklin and Zyphur (2005) have recently broadened Revonsuo's hypothesis. They contended that differential brain mechanisms during REM sleep, consisting of activation and deactivation of the prefrontal cortex, anterior cingulate cortex, and amygdalae, allow dreamers not only to remain asleep but also to remain unaware that they are dreaming despite the often bizarre and illogical nature of dreams. They proposed that dreaming may not only serve to simulate threats but may also serve as a more general rehearsal mechanism, whose virtual variations in dreams of scenarios encountered in daily life, subsequently and positively influence waking encounters. They noted that the common inability to remember dreams does not necessarily invalidate their hypothesis, as dreams may shape behavior subconsciously, and through the priming effect (as we noted earlier) our waking decisions may be biased or primed by the mere prior exposure to dream stimuli. Finally, Franklin and Zyphur noted that this virtual rehearsal mechanism might have had its most profound effect in social situations, conferring greater survival value on those who could interact with others with minimal interpersonal conflict and confrontation, allowing them greater access to resources in their group (e.g., food or mates). Physiological evidence for their hypothesis comes from the increased activity during sleep of the ventromedial prefrontal cortex, amygdala, and anterior cingulate cortex which, as we previously noted, mediate affective executive functions thought to play a strong role in social and interpersonal decision-making and evaluations.

Creativity and Innovation

Clear evidence for the intimate relationship between creativity and dreaming is nearly as old as written records. A Sumerian king in 2,200 BC preserved at least two of his dreams on clay tablets. They reveal that the king had a puzzling dream and reported that he searched with a goddess for its meaning. This record serves as one of the first examples, in what was to be a rich history, that dreams may be divinely inspired and that answers to waking problems may be sought in dreams (for a more complete historical review of Near East dreaming see Oppenheim, 1956). Mesopotamians and ancient Egyptians had long traditions of dream incubation, where patrons would go to an incubation temple to sleep and dream and subsequently have their dreams interpreted by a practiced dream interpreter. Solutions to problems and even treatments for diseases were sought in dreams, and it was also believed that dreams could be used to prevent or change future misfortune. The Chester Beatty Egyptian papyrus, which dates to about 1,500 BC, contains a glossary-like index of over 200 dreams, divided into two groups of good and bad dream omens. From about 1,000 BC to 750 BC, it was apparently popular in Egypt to have scribes prepare small oracular amulets, which were to be worn about the neck. Two thirds of 21 known oracular papyri were commissioned by female patrons. Their contents frequently contain dream messages and decrees that appeal to gods and goddesses to protect the owner from diseases, and one of the most common forms was "make every dream which [he or she] has seen good and make every dream which someone else has seen for [him or her] good." The tradition that dreams contain important messages and answers, and the notion that they may be divinely inspired continues throughout later written history. The Jewish Talmud, roughly contemporary with the Christian Bible, about 300 BC to AD 200 contains over 200 references to dreams, and both old and new testaments of the Bible contain dream references along these same themes (for a more complete description of the history of dreaming, see Coolidge, 2006; Van De Castle, 1994).

Modern evidence for creativity and dreams is largely anecdotal but replete throughout the arts and sciences. Artists who claimed their work was based on a dream include Dürer, Goya, Blake, Rousseau, Dali, and Magritte among many others. Musicians who claimed a work was based on a dream include Mozart, Wagner, Keith Richards (lead guitarist for the Rolling Stones claimed the musical riff to "[I Can't Get No] Satisfaction" came in a dream), and Billy Joel, again, among many others. The eighteenth-century violinist Tartini reported his inspiration for his most famous violin work, "Trillo del Diavolo" ("The Devil's Trill"), came to him during a dream in which the devil played a particular violin riff. Upon awakening, he reported that he excitedly tried to duplicate the devil's trill.

A number of writers have claimed the inspiration for a work came in a dream. Robert Louis Stevenson wrote that while pondering a duality that exists in all humans, he dreamt the story for Dr Jeckyll and Mr Hyde in a dream. Samuel Taylor Coleridge claimed that his poem "Kubla Khan" came to him in a dream and that upon awakening he wrote down about 40 lines before he was interrupted by someone, and thus left the poem incomplete (in fairness, it is not known to what extent opium addictions may also have played a role in some anecdotal dream reports; see Hartmann, 1998, for more complete descriptions of creativity, dreaming and critiques).

Two chemists have anecdotally reported their most famous discoveries resulted from dreams. In the nineteenth century, the Russian chemist Dmitri Mendeleyev said he conceived of the periodic table in a dream (Van de Castle, 1994). Also in the nineteenth century, German-born and later French chemist Friedrich Kekulé had been pondering the structure of the benzene molecule. He knew that it had six carbon atoms but neither a branching chain nor a straight alignment would account for its chemical properties. In a dream, he saw snake-like "confirmations" writhing together. He reported that one of the snakes had seized its own tail and "whirled mockingly" before his eyes. He said he awoke in a "flash of lightning" and began working out his famous solution to the problem, the benzene ring. It has been suggested, however, that Kelulé may have made this claim to avoid accusations that he had borrowed the idea from the work of others. Again in the 1800s, American Elias Howe reported that he had worked for five years trying to create an automatic sewing machine. He said that he could not figure out how to get the machine to grab the thread once it had pierced the material. In his dream, he said he was a missionary captured by natives. They stood around him dancing with spears that had holes in their tips. Upon awakening, he said that he recognized that this was the solution to his problem, a needle with a hole in the tip (Hartmann, 1998).

There is also a plethora of anecdotal reports of creative ideas and solutions for problems arising from dreams. For example, Krippner and Hughes (1970) found, in a survey of contemporary mathematicians, over 50 percent reported that they had at least once solved a mathematical problem in a dream. The Indian mathematician Ramanujan (1887–1920) said that the goddess Kali gave him solutions to theorems in his dreams, although there was some suspicion he said so for politico-religious reasons. There is also the phenomenon of lucid dreaming, where dreamers can become aware that they are dreaming within a dream, and thus control the direction or outcome of the dream. This technique has reportedly been used successfully as a psychotherapeutic technique, or so its proponents have claimed (e.g., Cartwright and Lamberg, 1992; LaBerge, 1985). However, lucid dreams are very infrequent, and lucid dream control requires strong motivation for success (e.g., Coolidge, 2006).

Hartmann (1998) speculates that dreaming allows the dreamer to make connections between disparate and often contradictory ideas. These connections, he proposes, are often more broad and inclusive than during wakefulness. By the nature of cognition, some intent and coherence is imposed and guided by the emotions (and limbic structures) of the dreamer. Thus, Hartmann believes dreams contextualize emotions and, by using visual and spatial pathways, create an explanatory metaphor for the dreamer's emotional state. He offers, as evidence for his theory, dreams following traumatic events like the Holocaust and other horrific tragedies.

Whereas there exists a plethora of anecdotal evidence and personal speculation for the general claim that dreaming, problem-solving, and creativity are linked, there have been few experimental attempts. Dement (1972) gave 500 undergraduates a problem to solve 15 minutes before sleeping. In the morning, they reported their dreams and any solution to the problem. Of 1,148 attempts, it was reported that the solution came in a dream on only seven occasions (less than 1 percent). Blagrove (1992) presented a critique of problem-solving in the dream literature and concluded that there is little empirical evidence that new and useful solutions to waking problems are created in dream sleep. He did propose that psychological solutions may be correlated with dreaming, but it did not imply a causative relationship. He counter-argued that solutions may more often occur while awake, and subsequent dreaming merely reflects the solution. In summary, there is no wealth of compelling experimental evidence for the link between creativity and dreams; however, the preponderance of anecdotal and other sources of evidence makes it a difficult hypothesis to dismiss completely, and a recent empirical study has revived the idea.

In that study of sleep and creative problem-solving, Wagner, Gais, Haider, Verleger, and Born (2004) gave adults a cognitive task that required learning stimulus-response sequences (which they deemed an implicit procedural memory task) where improvement, as measured by reaction time, was evident over trials. Participants could improve abruptly if they gained insight into a hidden abstract rule. After initial training, participants either slept for eight hours or stayed awake (at night or during the day) for a similar period. Twice as many participants who slept became aware of the hidden rule than those who stayed awake, regardless of time of day. Based on a slowing of reaction times in the sleep group, the authors postulated that the participants' greater insight was not a strengthening of the procedural memory itself but involved a novel restructuring of the original representations. They speculated that the restructuring was mediated by the hippocampus, related medial temporal lobe structures, and prefrontal cortex. These structures have been previously shown to play an important role in generating awareness in memory. Wagner et al. suspected that cell assemblies representing newly learned tasks were reactivated by the hippocampal structures during sleep and incorporated by the neocortex into pre-existing long-term memories. They hypothesized that this process of incorporation into long-term storage formed the basis for the remodeling and qualitatively different restructuring of representations in memory. Thus, in their opinion, sleep may serve as a catalyst for insight.

Procedural Memory Consolidation and Enhancement

Consciousness is a continuum from awake to asleep. Wakefulness obviously varies from very aware to semi-aware (some freshmen in lectures), but sleep also varies in levels of awareness. Vivid and elaborate dream reports are nearly entirely absent in slow-wave sleep, but REM sleep often includes "paradoxical awareness," which is the state of being selectively aware of some aspects of our external sleeping environment (for example, muscle atonia, or strange sounds or our names), yet sleeping through most other sounds and stimuli. Furthermore, we can become aware that we are dreaming but, more often than not, we accept our dream and our awareness of it as reality. Because learning and memory formation are aspects of consciousness (although there is some evidence for some types of learning without awareness), there is reason to suspect that memories are stabilized and consolidated during sleep, both slow-wave and REM. Indeed, it would not be reasonable to suspect that these activities would stop altogether during sleep, although it also seems plausible that these activities might be reduced during sleep (particularly active learning).

The first strong empirical research for REM's role in memory consolidation comes from the work of Winson (1990). He demonstrated in animals that a theta rhythm (6 Hz) arises from the hippocampus associated with specific and important functions such as exploratory behavior of rats, predation in cats, and rigidity in rabbits. In research on sleeping rats, Winson found that theta rhythms in hippocampal neurons fired in patterns similar to their awake firing while learning mazes. Because exploratory behavior in rats appears critical to their survival, Winson reasoned one purpose of REM sleep might be the strengthening and consolidation of these visual-spatial (procedural) memories. Thus, in arboreal nesting hominoids, including early hominins, the increases in REM sleep that were associated with nesting may have strengthened waking memories critical to survival, such as memories for sites of food, safety, resources, and predators and other dangers. In arboreal hominoids, as with other mammals, the hippocampus would also have played a dominant role in the consolidation of procedural memory skills such as nest building, and also any tool-making and tool use (as it does with modern apes).

General support for Winson's hypothesis comes from a gene study by Ribeiro, Goyal, Mello, and Pavlides (1999). They studied the expression of a plasticity-associated gene zif268 during the slow-wave and REM sleep of rats that had been exposed to an enriched sensorimotor experience in a preceding waking period. In this context, plasticity refers an ability of neurons, under the control of genes, to make lasting structural and functional changes in responses to a stimulus or an experience. They found that non-exposed control rats showed a reduced zif268 gene expression during slow-wave and REM sleep, whereas the exposed rats showed upregulation in zif-268 during REM sleep in the hippocampus and cerebral cortex. They interpreted this finding as evidence that REM sleep opens a window of increased neural plasticity, presumably enhancing and/or consolidating the memory of the enriched experience.

The evidence for the enhancement (or even acquisition) of declarative memories (i.e., the memories for facts and verbal material) during the sleep of humans is less persuasive. For example, there is only minimal evidence for the ability to learn verbal material during sleep, and in any case, it appears to be a highly inefficient method of learning (e.g., Levy, Coolidge, and Staab, 1972). Most studies that have found any positive effect of slow-wave or REM sleep upon declarative memories have used a sleep-stage deprivation paradigm, and thus, the confound of sleep deprivation exists in nearly all of these studies. Reviews of these and other studies of declarative memory enhancement during sleep in humans tend, on the whole, to be skeptical that there is any acceptable evidence (e.g., Coolidge, 1974; Siegel, 2001; Vertes and Eastman, 2000; Walker, 2005). However, episodic memory (also known as autobiographical memory), that is, memory that is recalled like a written story of a time, place, and emotional state, which is often considered to be a type of declarative memory, may be affected by dreaming (e.g., Franklin and Zyphur, 2005; Wagner, Gais, and Born, 2001; Walker and Stickgold, 2004). Indeed, one critical variable in the paucity of evidence for REM and/or slow-wave sleep affecting declarative memories may be the emotional valence of the stimuli. Wagner, Gais, and Born found that memories with a strong emotional valence were retained better than emotionally neutral memories across periods of REM sleep but not for slow-wave sleep.

However, empirical evidence for the enhancement of various kinds of procedural memories in human sleep continues to mount. Walker (2005) argues that the initial acquisition phase of learning and memory does not appear to rely fundamentally on sleep. This initial stabilization stage (which itself follows acquisition) is characterized by the formation of durable memory representations, resistance to interference, and, like acquisition, develops as time passes. But there is a second stage, consolidation-based enhancement that may show additional learning benefits without further rehearsal. Walker proposes that consolidation-based enhancement may fundamentally rely on several specific sleep stages (but, presently, only for procedural memories). The specific stages involved may themselves depend on the type of procedural memory, and slow-wave sleep, REM, and Stage 2 have all been implicated (Walker, 2005).

Karni, Tanne, Rubenstein, Askenasy, and Sagi (1994) first demonstrated consolidation-based enhancement in humans on a procedural visual-spatial discrimination task. Learning was enhanced after a night of sleep but not after a period of wakefulness. They also established that selective disruption of REM sleep, but not non-REM, resulted in a loss of these memory gains. Stickgold, James, and Hobson (2000) used the same task as Karni et al. and found that the consolidation enhancement was dependent only on the first night of sleep following acquisition, and learning was correlated with both the amount of slow-wave sleep and the amount of REM sleep. Again using the same task, Gais, Plihal, Wagner, and Born (2000) deprived participants of sleep early in the night (presumably of predominately slow-wave sleep) and later in the night (presumably REM and Stage 2). They concluded that consolidation-based enhancement might be instigated by slow-wave sleep, whereas REM and Stage 2 may solidify and add to the enhancement effect, but that slow-wave sleep was a necessary component. If the latter conclusions are true, then the presently proposed further increases in both slow-wave and REM sleep and the general integrity of a sleep period, as a result of the ground-sleep transition, would have been advantageous for the consolidation-based enhancement of the procedural memories.

In the first of two studies of procedural motor skills, Walker, Brakefield, Morgan, Hobson, and Stickgold (2002) again found consolidation-based enhancement for normal-length periods of sleep immediately following acquisition. They found no enhancement effect during an awake period following acquisition. When sleep-stage amounts were correlated with enhanced learning, they found that Stage 2 amounts were most strongly and positively correlated with learning. In a second study, Walker, Brake-field, Seidman, Hobson, and Stickgold (2003) found that a majority of the consolidation-based enhancement occurred after the first night of sleep following acquisition, but that additional delayed learning did occur on subsequent nights. Fischer, Hallschmid, Elsner, and Born (2002) replicated these findings and supported the conclusion that a full night's sleep after acquisition is critical to the delayed enhancement effect. However, they found that learning was positively correlated to REM sleep, but not for Stage 2.

In another procedural visual-motor task, Smith and MacNeill (1994) found that selective deprivation of late-night sleep, particularly Stage 2, impaired retention. Maquet, Schwartz, Passingham, and Frith (2003) used a similar task and again demonstrated the sleep-dependent enhancement of memory, and the effect was present after three nights of sleep following acquisition.

Aubrey, Smith, Tweed, and Nader (1999) proposed that the degree of task complexity may be one determining factor in whether slow-wave, REM, or Stage 2 sleep are critical to the enhancement of memory. They suggested REM might be more critical to procedural tasks of greater complexity, such as visual discrimination, whereas Stage 2 might be more critical to more simple procedural tasks like motor skills. Walker (2005) surmised that if memory enhancement were one of the critical functions of sleep then evolutionarily it would make sense that the different sleep stages were exploited for their differential advantages for various tasks.

Peigneux et al. (2004) used an episodic/spatial procedural memory task in which the participants were trained to find a personally meaningful target (e.g., a Buddha medallion) in a computer-generated virtual town. The authors used positron-emission tomography to estimate regional cerebral blood flow in the subjects' hippocampal neurons and found that the amplitude of hippocampal reactivation in slow-wave sleep correlated significantly with their performance the next day on route retrieval measures. Peigneux et al. concluded that enhanced hippocampal activation after a spatial memory task during post-training, slow-wave sleep reflected the sleep processing of spatial memory traces, which led to enhanced performance upon awakening.

A summary of the research on the relationship between sleep and memory leads to the following conclusions: (1) there is little evidence that neutral semantic declarative memories are consolidated or improved by sleep or any of its stages, although episodic, affectively charged declarative memories may be consolidated and/or enhanced by dreaming and/or sleep; (2) there is increasing evidence that some types of visual-motor procedural memories may be consolidated and/or enhanced by stages of sleep or the sequences of stages of sleep; however, it is not yet clear which stages or stage sequences are critical to which tasks; and (3) the most recent research suggests that visual-spatial procedural tasks may be enhanced by slow-wave sleep and hippocampal reactivation post-training.

Thus far we have proposed that the ground-sleep transition may have aided the general integrity of an extended and less fragmented sleep period, increased the amounts of REM sleep and perhaps Stage 4 sleep, and it may have aided the integrity of the sequence of Stage 4 and REM. As a function of these sleep changes, and by means of the phenomenological contents of sleep (dreaming): (1) early *Homo* may have been primed to escape and avoid threatening events in the their waking environments, and early *Homo* may have rehearsed social scenarios, thus becoming more efficient in their waking endeavors in obtaining food or mates and/or interacting with others with less confrontation; (2) REM and/or dreaming may have promoted creativity and innovation (the notion that REM and dreaming are synonymous is contentious, and our arguments do not hinge on their equivalence; for greater detail on the debate, see Antrobus, Kondo, and Reinsel, 1995; Cicogna, Natale, Occhionero, and Bosinelli, 1998; Hobson, Pace-Schott, and Stickgold, 2000; Solms, 2000); and (3) these sleep changes may have aided procedural memories, including memories for motor skills, visual-spatial locations and discriminations, and episodic (personal) memories, without any further acquisition or practice.

Walker and Stickgold (2004) have recently proposed a homeostatic hypothesis for the relationship between sleep and learning that helps further our arguments. In a review of numerous human and animal studies, they proposed that not only is there strong evidence that sleep consolidates and/or enhances learning but also that learning may enhance sleep. They noted that daytime learning of both declarative (emotionally valent) and procedural memories can trigger subsequent increases in particular sleep stages, suggesting a homeostatically driven demand on sleep-dependent memory consolidation (e.g., Peigneux et al., 2004). Thus, in the transition to ground sleep, i.e., better sleep, visual-motor procedural memories and episodic declarative memories may have been enhanced. The latter ability may have included greater success in subsequent waking behaviors in harm avoidance, better mate selection, acquisition of resources, enhanced exploration abilities, greater diversity of experience, and even creativity. These enhanced learning experiences, according to Walker and Stickgold's homeostatic hypothesis, reciprocally enhanced sleep.

In sum, we believe that the paleoanthropological evidence supports one strong conclusion and one weaker conclusion concerning the evolution of sleep. The strong conclusion is that selective pressure *against* lengthened Stage 4 and REM sleep was released with the transition to ground sleep by early *Homo erectus*. An extended period of muscle atonia during sleep would no longer have been a handicap. Of course, gorillas also nest on the ground, and probably do not demonstrate lengthened REM sleep (as no monkey or great ape species studied to date has shown a greater REM sleep percentage than *Homo sapiens*). It is therefore also necessary to account for some selection pressure *for* lengthened Stage 4 and REM sleep, and this is the more difficult of the two pieces of the puzzle to identify. Our admittedly weaker argument concludes that features of the *Homo erectus* adaptive niche selected for lengthened Stage 4 and REM sleep, and perhaps other stages as well. Our reasons are both general and specific. In general, *Homo erectus* represented a new evolutionary grade, with profound changes in anatomy, sexual dimorphism, life history, behavior, and cognition. Such a profound shift may well have included selection for lengthened sleep stages. More specifically, *Homo erectus*' behavioral repertoire included more complex technical procedures, movement within larger territories, and perhaps the ability to learn new landscapes very rapidly, all of which might have benefited from the memory consolidation and enhancement that may have accompanied an extended sleep period. Furthermore, if Lima et al. (2005) are correct in their assumption that dynamic changes in sleep states reflect trade-offs in reducing sleep debt with costs of predation, then the role of Stage 2 sleep as a more vigilant state of rest becomes more prominent. As we noted earlier, Stage 2 is considered a lighter stage of sleep, constitutes 50 percent of all sleep, and is fairly evenly distributed throughout a full sleep period.

Concluding Thoughts

After the transition to complete ground sleep, hominins may have spent up to 33 percent of their total existence in sleep, about 9 percent of their total lives in REM sleep, and about 13 percent in slow-wave and REM sleep. If problem-solving, learning, and memory consolidation persist throughout waking and sleep (which appears likely), and dreaming provides for novel connections between ideas (for which there is overwhelming anecdotal evidence and some empirical evidence), it is possible that some sleep-linked innovative developments appeared as early as the period between 2 million and 1.5 million years ago. For example, Wynn (2002) noted that there is little evidence for transitional forms between Oldowan and Acheulean stone tools. Mode 2 tools (bifaces) appear rather suddenly as if in a punctuated event. In fact, there are some indications that they may have occurred as the result of a creative burst. Could it be that the idea for the imposition of symmetry came as the result of a dream in a sleeping hominin? Could it be that the neural mechanisms and structures were already in place by the time of the creation of Mode 2 tools and all that was required was the right dream? Could an expert *Homo erectus* stone-tool knapper have been perplexed by the lack of large, sharp cutting tools? Did his or her answer come in a dream? It is more difficult to imagine that Mode 2 technology was not aided by sleep and dreams and was restricted to wakeful states alone.

We have proposed that changes in sleep stages, patterns, and the general integrity of a single sleep period may have played an important role in hominin evolution. First, changes in the quantity and/or quality of dream sleep, which may have included simulated threatening waking experiences and virtual interpersonal interactions, may have better prepared individuals for the actual events. Second, abundant anecdotal evidence – and recent empirical evidence – suggests that sleep and dreams may provide unique and creative solutions that might otherwise not be provided, or aid the solutions to problems that arise while waking and are better reflected during sleep by dreams. Third, the neurochemical nature of the sleep stages and their sequences may have aided the consolidation and/or enhancement of procedural memories, and there is currently strong empirical evidence for the enhancement by sleep of visual-motor and visual-spatial procedural memories. The sudden appearance of Mode 2 tools and the clear ability of *Homo erectus* to explore and invade new territories undoubtedly were instigated by some biological, genetic, or environmental factors. Why could it not be that some might have occurred as a direct consequence of the enhancement of sleep and dreams during the tree-to-ground sleep transition?

9

Homo heidelbergensis and the Beginnings of Modern Thinking

In 1994, German archeologist Hartmut Thieme published a discovery that astonished the paleoanthropological world. While doing archeological reconnaissance in an area destined to be added to the Schöningen open-cast coal mine in Germany, his team of field workers discovered the remains of four spears (Thieme, 1997). Whoever had made these spears had used stone tools to sharpen both ends of 2-meter long spruce shafts that had been scraped smooth. These spears were associated with the carcasses of horses. More startling, they were almost 400,000 years old – the oldest reliably identified hunting weapons ever discovered (figure 9.1).

Since then, excavation has revealed three more spears, and a shorter bipointed "throwing" stick (Thieme, 2005). Archeologist Miriam Haidle of Tübingen University has carefully documented the steps necessary in the production and use of these spears, and the complexity of this procedure rivals that of modern non-industrial technologies (Haidle, in press). Tool use had become far more modern than that evident for *Homo erectus*. The hominin responsible for these masterpieces of Paleolithic craft was *Homo heidelbergensis*.

Figure 9.1   One of the Schöningen spears (*c.*350,000), shown next to part of a horse pelvis; production of this spear required a series of routines and sub-routines that were more complex than those required for contemporary hand-axes

Source: Thieme, 1997. © 1997 Nature Publishing Group

The Evolutionary Fate of *Homo erectus*

The *Homo erectus* strategy had proved remarkably successful, so much so that it enabled them to adapt quickly to environments hitherto unoccupied by hominins. The distinctive *Homo erectus* anatomy characterized the earliest known occupants of south, south-east, and north-east Asia, and also southern Europe. These areas boasted different climates, different vegetation, and different animal communities, and yet *Homo erectus* was successful in all of them. But this stability in the face of variability extended beyond geographic differences; it carried across some of the most dramatic and rapid changes in climate that the earth had experienced in tens of millions of years – the geologic epoch known as the Pleistocene.

Pleistocene Climate Change

The earth's climate changes constantly. The causes of these changes are many and complex, as anyone familiar with the science behind the global warming crisis knows all too well. Only very recently have anthropogenic effects on climate come to be significant, but natural causes have always been in play. These include earth-centered processes such as the position of the continents, height of the continents (mountains) and distribution of the continents (and major ocean connections), and amount of volcanic activity. All of these affect the amount and distribution of solar radiation reaching the earth's surface, which is the engine that drives the earth's climate (Zachos et al., 2001). Some of these geologic factors cycle at periods between 10^6 to 10^7 years, and some occur on immense cycles of hundreds of millions of years. Some of their long-term effects were important in the early phases of hominin evolution, especially the long-term cooling and drying trend that reduced the extent of the African forests. However, a set of shorter-cycle causes were the primary governing factors for Pleistocene climate change. These are the Milankovitch cycles, named for the Serbian astrophysicist who first identified and championed them 80 years ago.

Earth's orbit and orientation to the sun change in a regular and cyclical way (Zachos et al., 2001). The shape of the orbit fluctuates from rounder to more elliptical and back again (with a periodicity of about 96,000 years), the tilt of the axis fluctuates by several degrees ("obiquity"; periodicity about 40,000 years), and the position in the elliptical orbit where a particular season falls (say, northern summer) shifts (periodicity of about 21,000 years) (Anderson et al., 2007). These cycles reinforce and counteract one another in a complex way, the result being an overall cycle of about 100,000 years between peak periods of solar radiation. This periodicity is just the right size to pose potential evolutionary obstacles, but only if it produces significant changes in habitat.

During the Pleistocene epoch (1.8 million years to 11,500 years ago), the Milankovitch cycles were especially effective in producing climate change. The reasons for this are complex, but appear linked to geographic factors, including continentality and distribution of mountain ranges. Overall, earth's climate had been slowly cooling for almost 50 million years, and at the beginning of Pleistocene it crossed a kind of threshold after which the Milankovitch cycles, always there, produced much more profound effects. The most dramatic were the Ice Ages. Again and again, continental glaciers thousands of meters thick formed and retreated in the northern hemisphere. At the height of one of these ice ages, glaciers extended south into central Germany and covered most of the British Isles (and in North America as far south as central Illinois). The water trapped in these massive features did not return to the oceans, and sea levels dropped as much as 150 meters, dramatically changing the margins of continents, redirecting ocean circulation and exacerbating climate change (Anderson et al., 2007). In the tropics no glaciers formed, but the amount and yearly distribution of rainfall fluctuated, expanding and contracting forests, grasslands, and deserts. It is within this dynamic, rapidly changing context, that *Homo erectus* came to be successful. Just how remains a bit of a puzzle, but we contend, and are not alone in this, that the key lay in *Homo erectus*' minds.

Stasis or Change?

Stasis is the macro-evolutionary term applied to periods of little evolutionary change within a lineage. It has often been applied to *Homo erectus*, even though the 1.5 million-year duration of the lineage is actually too short to qualify, if we use the standards applied in general paleontology. There is a common misconception that stasis is a period of no change. In fact, organisms in stasis continue to undergo non-directional changes in genes and morphology, so that the long-term paleontological pattern (usually several million years) is one of fluctuation around an average phenotype (Gould, 2002). The adaptive implication is that organisms in stasis have stable niches that do not change. Not surprisingly, the classic examples of stasis are mollusks living stably in marine habitats. Given the roller-coaster nature of terrestrial climates during the Pleistocene, one would expect to see patterns of rapid evolutionary change as organisms adapted to chang-ing conditions, and this is what we do see for many mammalian taxa. But not for *Homo erectus*, at least not dramatically.

The argument for stasis in *Homo erectus* hinges on cranial size and shape, and also on the archeological record. East Asia has yielded many late *Homo erectus* fossils, some of whom lived until well after half-a-million years ago (Westway et al., 2007). Their anatomical features closely resemble the first *Homo erectus* who colonized the region over one million years earlier. The east Asian archeological record was also largely unchanged over this time span. Stone tools consisted of relatively simple cores and flakes. Even bifaces are missing or rare for most of East and south-east Asia. Pope (1989) has suggested that handaxes fell out of use when *Homo erectus* encountered bamboo, which is a versatile raw material for all kinds of prehistoric tasks, but which does not preserve in the archeological record. The fate of brain size is an unresolved puzzle. Depending on the dates one favors for each fossil, and which calculations of cranial capacity, the pattern can appear static, or with a slight upward slope (Rightmire, 2004). In East Asia, at least, it is possible to argue for a long period of relative stasis for *Homo erectus*, implying a successful, stable adaptation even in the face of dramatic environmental change.

The picture of morphological change in Africa and Europe was more dynamic (Rightmire, 2004). By 600,000 years ago, and perhaps even ear-lier, the million-year stasis of *Homo erectus*, to the degree that it was ever really true, had begun to change. This is evident in the fossil record, and in the archeology. The fossil record is actually rather confusing. In Africa fossils were found that bore heavy *Homo erectus*-like faces, but which had large cranial capacities (the Bodo skull found in Ethiopia and the Kabwe skull from Zambia are examples). In Europe, the fossils from Gran Dolina at Atapuerca in Spain had modern faces, but were otherwise *Homo erectus*-like in appearance. This confusing pattern of variation has always been difficult for paleoanthropologists to sort into realistic species and phylogenetic relationships (Arsuaga et al., 1999; Carbonell et al., 2005). Disagreement abounds concerning who is ancestral to whom, and who is an ancestor of ours, if any.

From our parochial perspective of cognitive evolution, two bits of anatom-ical evidence are of special interest: brain size and shape. Here we follow

Rightmire, who is the authority on Middle Pleistocene hominins, and brain size in particular. In the early 1980s, Rightmire suggested that brain size had remained statistically unchanged from the first *Homo erectus* until well after 500,000 years ago (i.e., he could not reject the null hypothesis of no significant increase in brain size; Rightmire, 1981). However, 20 years later, with a larger sample of fossils and better chronological control, he has revised this conclusion. Instead, he places pre-modern *Homo* into two groups. The first encompasses early *Homo erectus* in Africa and Europe, and all of *Homo erectus* in East Asia. In this group, brain size evolved, but very slowly, at a rate of perhaps 165 cc per million years (Rightmire, 2004). But a second group presents a larger cranial capacity and EQ than would be predicted from a *Homo erectus* statistical regression procedure. Indeed, all are in the modern range and some, such as Kabwe at 1,280 cc, had brain sizes close to the modern average. Rightmire places them into the taxon *Homo heidelbergensis*. What led to this spurt in brain growth? Perhaps not coincidentally, the European members of this taxon were the first to live in northern Europe (Roebroeks et al., 1992), where the climatic fluctuations of the Pleistocene were most dramatic. More significantly, at this time climatic swings became larger, with more severe environmental consequences (Anderson et al., 2007). But just how did *Homo heidelbergensis* cope? Their response was to perfect and fine-tune the old strategy of expertise. The fossils do not tell this story, but the archeology does.

Middle Pleistocene Archeology

From one perspective, that of the typological study of stone tools, nothing much changed in Europe and Africa between 1.4 million years ago and 300,000 years ago. Hominins made the same types of tools they always had – handaxes and cleavers, and a range of flake tools where the emphasis continued to be on the characteristics of the edge. In some sites flakes dominated in percentages, and in others bifaces dominated (Kleindienst, 1961), but there were never any "new" tool types – just varying percentages of the same ones. Because of this apparent conservatism, paleoanthropologists often described this technology as essentially changeless, a kind of technological stasis. But the typological approach missed very real developments in lithic technology that made this period, if not innovative and dynamic, at least not quite as mind-numbingly dull.

Two developments clearly spanned the period of supposed stasis: technique and refinement. Technique encompasses the procedures used to produce the tools, rather than the final products themselves. One such development was the introduction of soft hammers made of wood, bone or antler (or even softer stone, though this is harder to detect). When a knapper uses a soft hammer, the resulting flake is thinner, with a less pronounced bulb of percussion (the thickening at the percussion end of a flake). Thin flakes tend to be sharper than thick flakes, and this has clear advantages, but use of a soft hammer also enables greater control over the edge of the core. A second technique was the development of platform preparations, in which the knapper removed a number of small flakes from a core edge, or crushed the core edge, or even ground the core edge, in order to increase control of the results of a subsequent knapping blow. There were other technical developments, including prepared core techniques, which we will describe in much greater detail later. The precise timing of these developments is unclear, but they all occurred between 1 million and 400,000 years ago, during the time of supposed stases.

The second major development was in refinement. Most simply put, the bifaces became prettier over time. Two-dimensional symmetry became three-dimensional symmetry (plan, profile and cross-section), the symmetry itself became more precise, the edges became more linear in profile, and the thinning of the bifaces produced some truly beautiful artifacts (figure 9.2).

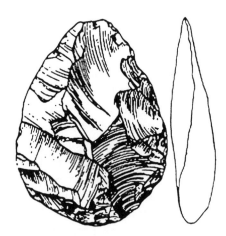

Figure 9.2   A late handaxe with a twisted profile. It is roughly equivalent in age to the Schöningen spears

Source: Roe, 1970

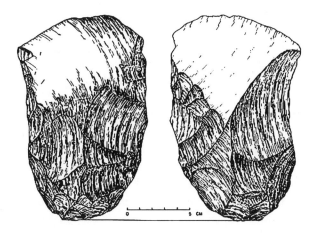

Figure 9.3 A "bent" cleaver from Isimila in Tanzania; it is about 300,000 years old

By 400,000 years ago, knappers could produce very thin bifaces, with three-dimensional symmetry, and even violations of symmetry such as twisted profiles, or "bent" plan shapes (figure 9.3).

This development in refinement appears to have been gradual. The 1-million-year-old bifaces from Gombore in Ethiopia were more regular than the 1.4-million-year-old bifaces from Olduvai in Tanzania, but not as refined as the 400,000-year-old bifaces from Boxgrove in England, or the 300,000-year-old bifaces from Isimila, Tanzania, and Kalambo Falls on the border of Zambia and Tanzania.

In other words, the stone tools do not really provide a picture of stasis. True, the range of stone tools did not change much, if at all. But the manner of tool production did. This apparent conundrum suggests that the range of tasks had not changed, but that the hominins may have become better and better at doing them. The technological component of the niche had become more effective, but its role in hominin way of life may not have changed significantly. This fine-tuning of the niche selected for appropriate cognitive abilities.

The bifaces of Homo heidelbergensis

Archeology's understanding of lithic technology rests heavily on two methods of investigation – experimental replication and refitting. In experimental replication a modern stone knapper attempts to reconstruct the actions necessary to produce a particular kind of flake or core. Such experimentation requires the knapper to develop the motor skills necessary for stone knapping, and to be adept enough to experiment with a variety of materials and procedures. This is the method by which archeologists identified most of the techniques and procedures we now associate with the Paleolithic. Experimental replication does have some drawbacks, the most significant of which is equifinality: the same products can often result from different procedures. In these cases, how can archeologists determine which of them the Palaeolithic knappers actually used? In a cognitive analysis the only solution is to invoke Occam's razor, and conclude that the least complex procedure was responsible. "Refitting" avoids the problem of equifinality by identifying some of the actual sequences of knapping that occurred in prehistory. In well-preserved Palaeolithic sites archeologists often recover thousands of stone flakes that were produced on-site by the prehistoric knappers. Archeologists can often refit these flakes – a kind of three-dimensional jigsaw puzzle. Refitting can be incredibly tedious, especially if the raw material is consistent and uniform (e.g., all the same color), but it yields actual sequences of action from the past. Most commonly, archeologists are able to refit flakes into small groupings of fewer than 10, but occasionally it has been possible to reconstitute the majority of flakes into a complete core. In these cases archeologists can recover long sequences of knapping action, and identify points in the procedure when the knapper made significant decisions. Using refitting and experimental replication, archeologists have been able to describe complete technological sequences, a source of information that is especially useful in a cognitive analysis.

Refitting studies have added some interesting insights into the bifaces manufactured by *Homo heidelbergensis*. In a study of English handaxe sites, Hallos (2005) has been able to demonstrate that the hominins carried finished handaxes to some sites; no knapping *debitage* is present at these sites, which means that the handaxes had been made elsewhere. At other sites, such as Boxgrove, the entire reduction sequence took place at a single location (more on this below). But the most common pattern that Hallos found was a pattern of sequential reduction. In these cases the knapper carried a partially formed handaxe to a site, reduced it some more, and then carried it away (i.e., archeologists find only part of the reduction sequence in the refits). This is a puzzling pattern if we use modern tools as a source of understanding. Why make a tool a little at a time? The answer is that there must have been more to bifaces than just the final tool. Australian

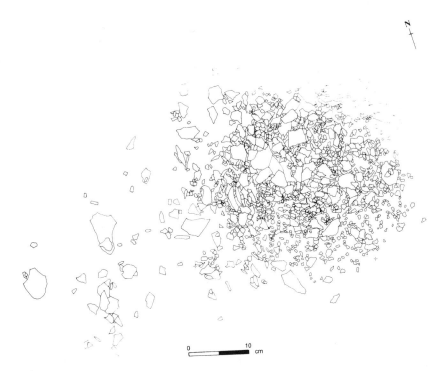

Figure 9.4 A *debitage* pile from Boxgrove, about 400,000 years old; a single knapper sat in one spot and finished a handaxe; at the same time he or she monitored the procedure for large, useable flakes

Source: Roberts and Parfitt, 1999. © 1999 The Boxgrove Project

archeologist Iain Davidson and neuropsychologist William Noble (1996) and others have long argued that handaxes were just cores – sources of flakes – and that the final shape was an accident of the procedure. Refit evidence now suggests that they are at least half right. Bifaces were a source of flakes. But they were also finished tools with a different role to play. This dual role of bifaces is nicely corroborated by a single refit sequence from the site of Boxgrove.

One day about 400,000 years ago a *Homo heidelbergensis* sat on a sandy dune near the coast of what is today the English Channel and knapped a handaxe. In the process he or she produced about 1,750 flakes over 5 cm in maximum dimension, and thousands of smaller fragments and chips (figure 9.4).

Because there are no cortical flakes (from the surface of a flint nodule) among these flakes, we know that the knapper must have carried in a rough-out (roughing out was often done at raw material sources – probably to test quality and reduce weight). The knapper at Boxgrove sat, apparently with legs apart, and reduced the rough-out to a finished handaxe – the telltale thinning and finishing flakes are all there – and then carried the handaxe away. But while making this handaxe, the knapper did something else. He or she kept a lookout for large useable flakes. Off to the side of the *debitage* heap was a small pile of larger flakes. When the knapper produced a nice, large, thin flake, he or she set it aside. The largest of these are also missing, carried away by the knapper. So why not agree with Davidson and Noble and conclude that the handaxe was just a core? The presence of many small finishing flakes, knapped to finish the edge, regularize the shape, and thin the core, would not be needed if flakes were the only goal. The knapper at Boxgrove did produce a finished artifact, while at the same time producing many other useful flakes (Roberts and Parfitt, 1999).

façonnage *and* debitage

A significant shift in stone knapping occurred about the same time as the appearance of *Homo heidelbergensis*. This was the shift from *façonnage*, the French term for shaping, to *debitage*, the French term for flaking. Handaxe production was primarily *façonnage* – the knapper removed material to achieve a particular result and, as we just saw, *Homo heidelbergensis* used *façonnage* to produce some truly beautiful artifacts. *Façonnage* had been in the hominin technical repertoire for over a million years, since the appearance of the first bifaces, and was the hallmark of Mode 2 technology. True, many bifaces started as large flakes, but the subsequent modification treated these large flakes as cores, so the term *façonnage* is still appropriate. And it is also true that bifaces were often the source of flakes, but this role occurred as an additional goal in the *façonnage* strategy.

Debitage is the production of flakes, and in a narrow sense was not new at the time of *Homo heidelbergensis*. Hominins had produced flakes since the advent of lithic technology 2 million years earlier. So the term *debitage* is slightly misleading. The intent is to emphasize the advent, and subsequent development, of techniques for managing core volumes to maximize their productivity and, sometimes, to control the size and shape of flakes. Secondarily, the *debitage* strategy also encompasses the increasing attention given to the edges of flakes, and the increasing variety of tools made on flakes. It is the core-management techniques that are most interesting from a cognitive perspective. During the million-year reign of *façonnage*, *Homo erectus* produced flakes by searching on cores for optimal places to use as striking platforms. Judicious selection would allow *Homo erectus* to remove many flakes from a core, but the nature of these flakes changed as reduction continued (e.g., they often became smaller), and eventually the core reached a point where no useable platforms could be found. This was an expedient, one-flake-at-a-time, approach. In core-management strategies, a knapper devoted attention to making sure that the core continued to be a productive source of flakes. This could be as simple as breaking the core to produce a new platform surface, and as complex as controlling the size and shape of subsequent flake removals by preparing the shape of an entire core surface. The latter are termed "prepared core" techniques, and it is these that characterize the *debitage* approaches used by *Homo heidelbergensis*. Most prepared core techniques used one or both of two kinds of preparation. The first prepares the overall shape of the core itself, often by removing small flakes, so that there is a convex surface that is optimal for "flake propagation"; the dome-like configuration guides the path of the force traveling through the core after striking. The second technique prepares the striking platform – removing small, often tiny, flakes from the platform so that the shape and the angle formed with the core surface (the convexity) are also optimal.

Prepared core techniques appeared in Africa, Europe, and south Asia by 300,000 years ago. There is some dispute among paleoanthropologists about whether there was a single origin followed by rapid spread (Foley and Lahr, 1997), or whether there were multiple origins. The differences in detail between the earliest African and European examples would appear to favor the latter explanation, but a resolution to this problem is tangential to our argument. *Homo heidelbergensis* in both areas (and India) used prepared cores, and that is the important point.

The flakes produced by prepared core techniques were useful as tools but were often further modified into a variety of edge types. Over time the variety of these flake tools increased, and the number of handaxes declined.

Non-lithic technology

Given the nature of preservation, the archeological record for *Homo heidelbergensis* has yielded few artifacts made of material other than stone.

There are exceptions, including an apparent club from Kalambo Falls (Clark, 2001), and a plank-like tool used as a lever at Gesher Benot Ya'aqov in Israel (Goren-Inbar et al., 2002). The most spectacular examples are the wooden spears found by Thieme at Schöningen in Germany (Thieme, 1997). There are eight of them, and they are complete (Thieme, 2005). Each is about 2 meters long, carved out of spruce, with both ends sharpened. The carvers selected the hardest wood of the spruce, the heart wood near the base, and used stone tools to shave and scrape the shafts into shape. As we noted earlier, they apparently used these spears to kill horses – the spears were found among the remains of horse carcasses.

In Europe, at least, *Homo heidelbergensis* controlled fire and built shelters. Archeologists have found hearths at the German site of Bilzingsleben, and the French sites of Terra Amata and Lazaret (Gamble, 1999; Mania, 2005). The latter two sites also present evidence of possible huts in the form of post molds – discolored patches of sediment produced by decayed wood, and at Lazaret an internal pattern of remains that also suggests an enclosure. These remains are controversial – the patterns are not as coherent as some have suggested (Villa, 1983). They certainly do not represent the kinds of well-organized, substantial huts that characterize the European record of the late Paleolithic, but they do suggest that *Homo heidelbergensis'* technology extended beyond stone tools to include materials and knowledge to mitigate the effects of cold in these higher latitude areas.

The spears and associated horse remains at Schöningen indicate that higher-latititude *Homo heidelbergensis* were hunters, a conclusion corroborated by faunal remains at several other sites, including Boxgrove. Scavenging may still have been an important component of foraging. It is often difficult to distinguish the two from faunal remains alone. And, as always, the plant component of foraging is almost invisible in archeological remains that are this old. As a consequence, archeologists must be cautious when describing diet and foraging activities. Nevertheless, it now appears that *Homo heidelbergensis* did hunt large mammals, a behavioral addition that may have been necessary for survival in higher latitudes during the Pleistocene.

Landscape use

When documenting activities that occurred hundreds of thousands of years ago, archeologists are almost never able to identify more than a single location used by a specific social group of hominins; most sites are separated in time by thousands of years. A notable exception is the English locality of Boxgrove, one of whose knapping scatters we presented earlier. The geologic deposit that overlies the scatter accumulated over a very short period of 20–100 years – perhaps only a single generation – and archeologists have been able to trace this bed for hundreds of meters, identifying a number of archeological locales (Pope and Roberts, 2005). These sites were presumably produced by the same group of *Homo heidelbergensis*, presenting a pattern of structured landscape use. To the north the landscape was bounded by a cliff, at the base of which was a scree of flint nodules that had eroded from the cliff face. The hominins tested these nodules by striking off a few flakes. If the nodule was poor in quality they abandoned it; if of good quality they carried it away or roughed out a handaxe, which they carried away. At another locale a few hundred meters away, there are the remains of a horse that the hominins had butchered. There are 10 discrete lithic scatters where hominins had knapped handaxes (we know this from refits), to be used, presumably, along with the larger of the flakes to butcher the horse. But the handaxes themselves had all been carried away. Each scatter appears to be the product of a single hominin, not a small group, so even if 10 *Homo heidelbergensis* were there, each seemed to be doing his or her "own thing." A third locale consists of the edges of a freshwater pond that had formed in a low spot in the sand. All around the edges of this "water hole" archeologists found lithic remains, sometimes in dense patches, and the remains of various butchered animals. In this case, it was not a single carcass, just scattered bones. And here archeologists did find handaxes, many of them in fact, along with smaller tools made on flakes.

From this pattern of contemporary remains archeologists have been able to reconstruct something of the group's movements on the landscape. The hominins carried cores and handaxes from place to place, in varying degrees of reduction. It seems clear that the handaxes were both tools in and of themselves, but also sources of flakes. When butchering the horse they knapped handaxes, and then carried them away. Pope and Roberts (2005) have reasoned that the hominins removed the handaxes because the horse carcass was a temporary activity to which the hominins might never return. The water hole, on the other hand, was a permanent landscape feature to which the hominins regularly returned. As such a handaxe discarded there would be available for use at another time. Indeed, Pope and Roberts suggest that the presence of handaxes on the surface might have acted to mark the locale as a special place on the landscape. The overall pattern of temporary and re-used locales indicates that *Homo heidelbergensis* had a structured approach to landscape use, and repeated habitual patterns of action again and again. They certainly did not wander aimlessly around their world, but kept to a regular and predictable pattern.

Non-utilitarian technology

Modern human culture is immersed in symbols of all kinds. Indeed, the human mind arguably achieves many of its most impressive feats by manipulating symbols. The origin of this ability is a core issue in human evolution, but also one of the most frustrating and contentious. Archeologists have a perennial problem identifying symbolic artifacts, and often base their arguments on what have been termed "non-utilitarian" artifacts. These are modified objects for which archeologists can identify no obvious role in the technological or foraging activities of the hominin in question. A telling example is the Berekhat Ram figurine, recovered from a site in Israel estimated to be about 400,000 years ago. It is a small lump of lava (< 3 cm) that has a number of scratched grooves; from some angles it resembles a woman (Marshack, 1997) (see figure 9.5). Microscopic analysis (d'Errico and Nowell, 2000) confirms that the grooves were produced by a stone tool.

Some scholars accept this object as the earliest example of depictive art; others reject it. We come down on the skeptical side, not because we are committed to a position of non-symbolic culture for *Homo heidelbergensis* (indeed, some symbolic ability would fit nicely into our arguments), but because this bit of evidence is so poor. Yes, the object has hominin-imposed grooves, but it takes considerable imagination to see a female figure. The object is also very small, about the size of the end of a thumb, and this strikes us as odd for an artifact with symbolic meaning; the symbolism would only work if it could be seen, and no one more than a couple of meters away would ever recognize this one. Finally, it is one-of-a-kind. There are no others like it at Berekhat Ram, or in the Middle East, or indeed anywhere. It could not have been a symbolic system, or archeologists would have other examples.

Evidence for use of mineral pigments is more compelling. These are minerals that concentrate in various sedimentary contexts and that produce colorful powder, either naturally or by scraping and grinding. The

Figure 9.5   The enigmatic Berekhat Ram object; a few of the scratches on the surface were produced by a stone tool; some consider this an iconic image of a woman; the object has a maximum dimension of about 2.5 cm

Source: Francesco d'Errico and Nowell, 2000. Reprinted by permission of April Nowell and Francesco d'Errico

most common in archeological contexts are the ochres, a general term that encompasses a range of specific iron oxides such as hematite and specularite. They produce a range of colors from red through yellow and brown, and even purple. Magnesium dioxide is another pigment, which is a good source of black. The earliest well-documented evidence for mineral pigment use comes from the central African site of Twin Rivers, which dates to between 266,000 and 400,000 (Barham, 2002). The site yielded over 300 pieces of hematite, limonite, and specularite. These minerals were not present in the deposits naturally and had to have been carried in. Some of the specularite pieces have striations produced by grinding; the specularite is the hardest of the minerals and does not produce powder by simple rubbing.

Why did *Homo heidelbergensis* use mineral pigments? Various practical explanations have been proposed, from medicinal uses, to use as a binding agent in adhesives, to use in hide processing (Wadley et al., 2004). However, the range of colors evident at Twin Rivers (red, yellow, brown, black, and purple), and the effort expended on specularite when easier pigments were at hand, suggest that the hominins were interested in the colors themselves. From this starting point, the presence of mineral pigments in African sites is virtually continuous up the historic period, an archeological fact that has some very interesting implications.

Cognition at 400,000 Years Ago

The archeological record for *Homo heidelbergensis* does not present as clear a picture as that of early *Homo erectus*, and this may seem paradoxical. After all, 400,000 years ago was much closer to us in time. The lack of clarity stems from the much greater number of sites and the greater geographic extent of hominin occupation. The result is more evidence and more variability (and, a cynic might add, a greater variety of national research traditions that do not all ask the same questions!). Some of this variability was idiosyncratic, some reflected different habitats and resources, and some may have resulted from different behavioral repertoires of different hominins. Nevertheless, we believe it is possible to make some generalizations about the cognitive abilities of *Homo heidelbergensis* as an evolutionary grade.

Spatial cognition

Homo heidelbergensis relied on a number of spatial abilities not used by earlier *Homo erectus*. One is allocentric perception, which was required to produce the three-dimensional symmetries true of the finer bifaces. Allocentric perception is the ability to imagine points of view not centered on one's own view. To make a three-dimensional symmetry the knapper needed to control the shape of the artifact from many different angles and perspectives, some of which were not directly available (e.g., cross-sections of the artifact that could not be directly sighted). A second ability is that of spatial quantity. The finer handaxes have a congruent symmetry in which one side is a virtual duplicate of the mirrored side. This suggests attention to spatial quantity. Here a fairly specific spatial concept, that of size, has been coordinated with the shape-recognition ability. From a cognitive neuro-psychological perspective, this implies a more sophisticated coordination of the dorsal and ventral pathways of visual processing. Indeed, it appears necessary to invoke visual imagery, in the sense used by Kosslyn (1994). The knappers of the fine three-dimensionally symmetrical handaxes almost certainly had a visual image of an end product that guided their action.

In using allocentric perception and spatial quantity to guide their actions, *Homo heidelbergensis* were using a Euclidean understanding of spatial relation; in other words, they used modern spatial thinking. A Euclidean space is one in which spatial quantity is held constant and objects and actors move with an invariant spatial frame. It is not necessary that *Homo heidelbergensis* had concepts of coordinates and measurement intervals – these are cultural constructs invented by us (well, the Greeks) to formalize our intuitive understanding of the structure of space – but it was neces-sary for *Homo heidelbergensis* to have the intuitive understanding itself. Certainly, many animals have evolved to perceive and navigate in a three-dimensional visual world, but *Homo heidelbergensis* may have been the first to have understood space in this way, and used this intuition to guide and control their actions.

But why? What was it about the way of life of *Homo heidelbergensis* that selected for a Euclidean understanding of space? One of the more com-pelling hypotheses has been proposed by Irwin Silverman and colleagues (Choi and Silverman, 2003; Eals and Silverman, 1994; Silverman et al., 2000; Silverman and Eals, 1992) as part of a more inclusive attempt to explain the well-documented sex difference in spatial cognition. They hypothesize that the inherent division of labor in hunting-and-gathering societies selected for specific spatial abilities. As in other arguments from the evolutionary psychological perspective, the hypothesis rests on the theoretical stance that the human mind is massively modular, and that natural selection designed each module to solve a particular evolutionary problem. Silverman and colleagues have identified a narrow ability they designate "space constancy" as underpinning the sex difference in spatial cognition, and argue that the male need for effective wayfinding while hunting selected for the difference. They support their hypothesis with experimental evidence for a male advantage in wayfinding, and the statistical correlation between wayfind-ing and other tests of space constancy, mental rotation in particular. Even though this hypothesis focuses on the modern sex difference in spatial cognition, it is also implicitly a selective hypothesis for a specific spatial ability, the same ability that underpins all Euclidean thinking, and as such can be checked against the paleoanthropological record.

As we have seen, the archeological record of stone tools supports Silverman's emphasis on space constancy. Space constancy encompasses "all of the processes involved in maintaining the stability of the surrounding environment while in locomotion" (Silverman et al., 2000: 205), including maintenance of the constant size and shape of objects. It is clear that the *Homo heidelbergensis* who made the fine three-dimensional handaxes had this ability. The archeological record even supplies some weak support for the contention that hunting was part of the selective milieu – the Schöningen spears and horses are good evidence for hunting. So there was a coincidence in the paleoanthropological record between evidence for hunting and evidence for space constancy. However, though the coincidence is provocative, there is a weak link in Silverman's chain of inference. The scenario hinges on hunters being able to travel directly back to a starting point on the landscape after traveling through several intermediate points. If the hunter had space constancy, he (and remember it was a "he" for the hypothesis) could conceive of a route from any point in space to any other. So it was not hunting per se that was the selective agent; it was wayfinding. Is there any reason to conclude that *Homo heidelbergensis* used such advanced wayfinding? The answer is no, there is not. First, when we look at what modern hunters in hunter-gatherer societies do, it turns out that they almost never travel directly back to a starting point using a novel route; instead, they invariably use established routes and trails. And these are modern humans. The archeological evidence for *Homo heidelbergensis* suggests only opportunistic, encounter hunting, the kind one could accomplish following familiar routines. Much later in the Paleolithic there is evidence for intercept hunting, where hunters moved to landscape features in anticipation of the arrival of animals, and this could have relied on advanced wayfinding (though established routes and trails are still more likely).

The cognitive processes we have just described are the province of the visuospatial sketchpad in Baddeley's model of working memory. The ability to maintain and manipulate images and spatial relations is the *sine qua non* of this subsystem, and *Homo heidelbergensis'* performance in such image manipulation would appear to be comparable to performance on, say, a modern mental rotation task where the subject rotates an image of a three-dimensional solid in order to match a target answer. Must we then conclude that working memory at the time of *Homo heidelbergensis* was also modern? We think not. The visuospatial sketchpad is just one of the components of working memory. The reader should recall that experimental results can fairly easily isolate the visuospatial sketchpad tasks from verbal tasks. It is more difficult to isolate the visuospatial sketchpad from the central executive – this is one of the more curious problems in working memory research – but the visuospatial sketchpad does appear to be a discrete cognitive system. There are no a priori reasons to conclude that the visuospatial sketchpad could not have had its own evolutionary trajectory; indeed, the archeological evidence would appear to require this. Even though *Homo heidelbergensis'* spatial cognition appears to have been modern in scope, little else does. There is no evidence for the kinds of executive functions that are enabled by fully modern, enhanced working memory – no evidence for long-range contingency planning, and no evidence for innovation or use of thought experiments. In the absence of compelling evidence otherwise, it is necessary to take the artifactual evidence at face value and conclude that spatial cognition and the visuospatial sketchpad had evolved before other components of the modern mind. But it was not the only precocious cognitive ability.

Technical cognition

Spatial cognition may have evolved early because it was a component of technical cognition, closely linked to the manufacture of tools. Archeologists have often emphasized the advent of the *debitage* strategy, and some have suggested that it marked a significant development in cognitive evolution. Few, however, have attempted to specify just what this cognitive development might have been. White and Aston (2003) come closest in their discussion of the origin of prepared core technique in Europe. They note that the specific lithic technique used in core preparation (invasive flaking and edge preparation, for example) initially arose as techniques for biface thinning and finishing. At some point knappers began to apply these *façonnage* techniques to core management. "This represents an innovative conceptual leap whereby principles previously limited to *façonnage* are exapted to systems of *debitage*" (White and Ashton, 2003: 606). Use of the term "innovative" is provocative, and White and Ashton probably intended it to be so. Paleoanthropologists have often reserved innovation for the cognitive repertoire of modern humans. Moreover, we (Coolidge and Wynn, 2005) have argued that innovation is an executive function enabled by enhanced working memory. So must we grant modern cognition to *Homo heidelbergensis*?

The application of *façonnage* techniques to *debitage* does suggest an inventive scenario. At some point while knapping a core, a *Homo heidelbergensis* realized that *façonnage* techniques might enable him or her to better control the overall volume of the core. From the bifaces themselves, we know that this knapper was able to conceive of fairly complex three-dimensional volumes, and from the refits at Boxgrove we know that these knappers had enough working memory capacity to monitor *façonnage* for useable flakes. White and Ashton's (2003) proposal is therefore in keeping with other things we know about *Homo heidelbergensis* cognition. But we think that "innovative conceptual leap" may be overstating the case. First, the *façonnage* and *debitage* techniques were all part of the procedural repertoire of these stone knappers. It seems unlikely that the cognitive underpinnings of the two were so separate from one another that integrating the two required the kind of conscious inventiveness White and Ashton ascribe. Second, the subsequent developments in prepared core techniques unfold over tens of thousands of years – hardly a rate that requires active innovation. However, White and Ashton are correct to a degree. It would appear the *Homo heidelbergensis* had a working memory capacity that exceeded that of *Homo erectus*, a capacity that freed technical cognition from the tight grip of rote-procedural long-term memory. But we suspect that *Homo heidelbergensis* had no "theories" or "concepts" of stone knapping, and no conscious experimentation. *Homo heidelbergensis* was simply able to control more information, and this increased capacity had both a long-term component (more procedures) and a working memory component, which in turn included developments in the visuospatial sketchpad and attention.

Symbolic thinking

Thus far in our presentation we have given only brief attention to language and symbol use despite their importance in modern human cognition. Much of modern life is experienced through language and symbols. Some philosophers even aver that much of modern cognition consists of inner speech, a kind of internal conversation using words and grammar as a way of thinking and problem-solving (Carruthers, 2002). Any account of the evolution of human cognition must address directly, sooner or later, the evolution of language and symbol use. We have delayed to this point because we see no compelling evidence for either language or symbol use prior to *Homo heidelbergensis*. Yes, some features of *Homo erectus* anatomy suggest that it had greater reliance on vocal communication than modern apes (see chapter 7), but nothing else about *Homo erectus* would seem to require it. The situation is more promising for *Homo heidelbergensis*. First, brain size for *Homo heidelbergensis* was in the modern range (Kabwe had a cranial capacity of 1,280 cc, for example). Second, some features of *Homo heidelbergensis* cognition were also modern – spatial cognition in particular. Finally, the archeological record provides evidence for non-utilitarian behavior in the guise of pigment use. From the latter two lines of evidence, it is possible to build an argument for symbol use. Language itself is more intractable, and we will treat it separately.

A sign is something that stands for something else (Casson, 1981). Semioticians, the scholars who study signs, distinguish between three kinds of signs: icons, indexes, and symbols. An icon stands for its referent through its physical resemblance – a drawing of a giraffe can stand for a giraffe. An index relies on an association – smoke is an index of fire, a hoof print is an index of the animal that made it. The link between a symbol and its referent, however, is arbitrary. There is no resemblance, and no natural association; someone must decide that "G-I-R-A-F-F-E" stands for giraffe. Because semioticians consider all three to be signs, there is an understandable tendency even for scholars to lump them together and assume a close linkage, both cognitively and evolutionarily. But this is dangerous and misleading. Are the cognitive requirements of an index the same as those of a symbol? In order to make a coherent argument about the evolution of symbolic thinking it is important to be as clear as possible about which kinds of signs one is studying. Our approach at this point will be to focus on the index because it was in the form of indexes that signs first appeared in the hominin repertoire.

The evidence of pigment use at Twin Rivers in Zambia, which dates back to about 300,000 ago (Barham, 2002), at first may strike the reader as mundane – just lumps of hematite and specularite, a few of which had been scraped or ground. Yet, as Barham notes, their presence required several actions by the hominins: first, they selected particular colors; second, they carried the bits of pigment several kilometers; third, they made powder out of the pigment. Why? The utilitarian explanations of hide processing, or hafting, or personal hygiene, appear to be ruled out by the clear selectivity for the different colors. There is no reason to select a variety of colors if the most abundant and local would do the job. Color itself appears to have been the reason for pigments. We do not know what they were coloring. It could have been objects or bodies. But that they attended to color is itself a provocative piece of information. There are a range of possible interpretations, from the emergence of an "aesthetic" sense, to full-blown symbolic marking in which colors stood for some arbitrary set of referents. The only way to choose, absent any specific contextual information, is to compare this activity to the other information we have about *Homo heidelbergensis*. And this brings us back to handaxes.

Homo heidelbergensis invested more effort in handaxe production than was necessary for its mechanical function (Machin, 2006). This suggests that appearance itself was often an important consideration. We have already explored the possibility, proposed by Kohn and Mithen (1999), that handaxe shape had a role in sexual selection – those who produced more attractive handaxes were better prospects for mating. And we have seen that, as odd as the proposal may sound, it does a better job of explaining handaxe variability than more mundane mechanical explanations. Of course, the sexual selection argument is a kind of indexical argument. Nice handaxes "stood for" good mating potential. Moreover, any tool is a natural index of its use. By simply displaying a handaxe, and especially by gesturing with one, it would have been possible to evoke its use, even if no actual work were done. And recall that handaxes almost certainly existed *as tools* in the minds of *Homo erectus*, not just procedures. This indexical argument has been developed by Byers (Byers, 1994) who sees such indexical use (he prefers the term "warrant") as an important bridge between the here-and-now communication of apes and the symbolic reference of modern language. A handaxe used as an index could evoke its future use, or past use, or use in another place. In other words, one variety of sign use may have been in operation since the advent of *Homo erectus*. But something about it changed with *Homo heidelbergensis*. Not only was the spatial thinking better, and technical thinking better, but *Homo heidelbergensis* produced a greater variety of shapes. Perhaps what had been pre-attentive (a strictly procedural memory as in a well-practiced motor movement habit) in *Homo erectus* had become attentive or conscious for *Homo heidelbergensis* and, thus, also subject to declarative memory. The indexical role of handaxes, and other aspects of material culture, had become explicit. *Homo heidelbergensis* may have been consciously endowing his products with meaning.

The Boxgrove landscape evidence provides a provocative hint that *Homo heidelbergensis* may have responded to the natural indexicality of stone tools. Pope and Roberts (2005) suggest that the handaxes discarded around the water hole acted to mark the value of the locale.

Individuals at the site were more likely to drop bifaces at locations that had proved themselves productive and had been routinely visited than at single episode butchery sites. There is also another possibility, which remains to be explored further, that the very presence of large quantities of tools in a restricted area created a feedback mechanism, either by triggering occupation activity or increased tool discard rates. (Pope and Roberts, 2005: 89)

If true, *Homo heidelbergensis* was exploiting the natural ability of tools to index their uses. Their landscape had meaning, but not the kind of symbolic meaning we might attach. Instead, tools on the landscape "stood for" the activities that the landscape afforded, structuring the landscape in terms of practical habits and procedures.

The pigment use at Twin Rivers fits easily into this indexical model for *Homo heidelbergensis* sign use. But what could the natural indexicality of pigment have been? Chris Knight (2009) and others have long argued that red ochre could be an index for menstrual blood, and that *Homo heidelbergensis* females used it as a way to manipulate social relations. Barham (2002) is more cautious and points to the range of colors selected by the Twin Rivers hominins as suggesting a variety of possible referents. For our purposes the specific meaning is not necessary (and is probably beyond our reach). What is significant is the probable semiotic role, attested by both the tools and the pigments. This indexical role for tools and colors continues into modern times, and remains an important component of symbolic culture. The irony is that a red Ferrari carries semiotic load not as a true symbol (arbitrary reference), but primarily from its indexical value. This component of symbolic culture appears to be much older than the arbitrary reference of true symbols. Perhaps Byers is correct in seeing indexical usage as a key bridge into true symbolic systems.

The variety of pigments selected at Twin Rivers and the variety of handaxe shapes produced at contemporary sites such as Kalambo Falls, suggest that a greater range of indexical referents were at play than would have been the case with *Homo erectus*. This is slim evidence, but it is nonetheless real, and is not easy to account for using practical, utilitarian explanations. We believe it is congruent with the cognitive developments we have already documented for *Homo heidelbergensis*. In particular, it fits with evidence for the larger working memory capacity indicated by biface reduction and prepared core strategies. Semiotic reference is an added consideration that must have been held in attention. Some other cognitive abilities are also required. One is shared attention. In order for the indexicality of a tool or a color to function as communication, it is necessary that two or more actors share their attention. Such shared attention is not only one feature of theory of mind; it is also a prerequisite for teaching. Here the prepared core technology provides independent support. Whereas it is possible to learn *façonnage* reduction by simple observation, it may not be possible to learn prepared core *debitage* without instruction. At a minimum, a teacher must direct a novice's attention to specific steps in the procedure. Linguistic instruction may not have been required, but shared attention was. Finally, the archeological evidence tempts us to conclude that the indexical use of objects had become explicit; *Homo heidelbergensis* may have actively exploited the indexical potential of tools and colors. This would account for the greater variability of products compared to those of *Homo erectus*. It would also explain why technologies began to change, albeit very slowly. If *Homo heidelbergensis* had explicit knowledge of what they were doing, must they not have had language?

Language

Language is more than symbol use. If *Homo heidelbergensis* was truly linguistic, it must also have used words and grammar. Neither preserves directly in the archeological or fossil records. Any argument about *Homo heidelbergensis* linguistic capacity must therefore be based on circumstantial evidence. For *Homo heidelbergensis* this circumstantial evidence is more compelling than it was for *Homo erectus*, but there is still considerable room for doubt, especially in regard to grammar.

The anatomical evidence suggests that *Homo heidelbergensis* had modern vocal abilities, and perhaps language. The endocast of the Kabwe *Homo heidelbergensis* cranium is well within the modern range in terms of size (1,280 cc), demonstrates a modern pattern of left occipital and right frontal petalias, and the left ventral premotor cortex (Broca's area) is enlarged relative to the right (Holloway et al., 2004). Kabwe's basicranium is more angled than that of *Homo erectus*, a feature that has been linked to lengthening of the pharynx. Finally, the diameter of the hypoglossal canal is in the modern range. This is the passage in cranial base through which pass the nerves that enervate the tongue. An enlarged canal suggests greater control of the tongue; Kabwe, at least, had a modern speech anatomy (Kay et al., 1998; but see also DeGusta et al., 1999). A confounding problem for more general interpretations is that not all *Homo heidelbergensis* fossils express all of these features. Indeed, the African *Homo heidelbergensis* appear, on average, more modern than the European variety, especially in regard to the cranial base (leading some paleoanthropologists to place the African forms into a separate species, *Homo helmei*). However, the suite of characters suggests that speech was a component of *Homo heidelbergensis* behavior. The case for grammatical language is weaker, and rests on Broca's area and overall brain shape and size, neither of which actually requires the presence of language. Arguments for grammar have most often invoked stone tools.

Grammars produce sequences of words, and tool use produces sequences of action. Archeologists and non-archeologists alike have suggested that the complex action sequences of stone knapping share something in common with grammar, and might therefore be used as evidence for language. The abundance of tools in the archeological record makes this an attractive idea, but it is probably groundless. The action sequences of tool use are very different from the syntactical sequences of grammar. They are acquired differently, and deployed differently (Wynn, 1991). A child acquires the rules of grammar almost effortlessly, as long as he or she is raised in a linguistic environment. A child learns tool use laboriously, and even if exposed to regular models will not acquire the skills until he or she has repeated the actions over and over. Tool use relies on procedural memories, and procedural sequences are learned through association and chaining. The only inherited component to this is the procedural memory capacity itself. A child inherits something much more specific when it comes to grammar. Coded in his or her genes is a cognitive structure that guides the child to a narrow range of possible grammatical rules. Experience fills in the details, but genes provide the template. When using his or her grammar an individual can generate an infinite number of meaningful sentences, and this productivity is almost effortless. A skilled artisan can also be productive, but only after years of practice. Expertise can yield impressive results, but even an expert's range of solutions pales in comparison to the range of sentences that an average speaker of any language can produce. The difference is stark. Yes, sequential tool use can reveal some interesting and important things about the evolution of cognition. It cannot, however, reveal anything about grammar.

A more fruitful approach to linking tool use to language may be through a study of instruction. Most tool use can be learned through observation and practice, but perhaps there are complex technologies that require verbal instruction. This argument has been developed by archeologist Stanley

Ambrose (Ambrose, 2001) in the context of prepared core technologies. He argues that understanding the complex decision points in prepared core reduction could not be learned by observation alone. Someone needed to explain it, and explanation requires language. We are sympathetic with the first half of his argument (complexity), but do not see how instruction would require grammatical language. Shared attention, and perhaps words, would be sufficient. In sum, the archeological record of *Homo heidelbergensis* is more complex in many senses than that of *Homo erectus*, but this complexity, sequential and otherwise, does not provide clear evidence for the use of grammatical language.

The most compelling reason for suspecting that *Homo heidelbergensis* had some form of grammatical language derives not from the paleoanthropological record, but from the nature of language itself. It is such a sophisticated system of communication, with not only grammar and words, but also rules of phonology and morphology, modes of speech, social conventions, prosody, etc., that it must have evolved over an extended period of time, with many discreet steps. In this we agree with Pinker (1997a, b). Because *Homo heidelbergensis* was a relatively recent hominin, in an evolutionary sense, it seems likely that some, perhaps even most, of the features of language were in place.

Conclusion: Puzzles and Pictures

Homo heidelbergensis lived much closer to our time than the first *Homo erectus*. For this reason we have more fossils and more archeological sites on which to base an interpretation of cognition. This increase in quantity and also quality of evidence make *Homo heidelbergensis* appear more modern. On the other hand, 400,000 years was still a long time ago, and much has vanished from the paleoanthropological record. As we shall see in later chapters, the fossil and archeological record from 30,000 years ago is much richer than that for *Homo heidelbergensis*. Much, but not all, of this richness reflects better preservation. Bednarik (1994) refers to a "taphonomic threshold," placed sometime around 100,000 years ago. Fossil and archeological remains older than this threshold are poorly preserved. They are especially bereft of organic remains such as wood, thin bone, and pigments placed in open exposed areas.

After the threshold, preservation is better, especially in protected, uneroded sites. The threshold is simply a function of time and the natural processes that constantly alter remains. It biases the record in favor of stone and hard body parts of animals. Equal care must be given to avoid underestimating early material. There is also a definite European bias in the remains. Most of the best *Homo heidelbergensis* sites are European (Atapuerca, Bilzingsleben, Boxgrove, Lazaret, Schöningen, etc.) not because Europe was the center of evolution, but because far more research has taken place in Europe than in Africa or Asia.

Following is a list of cognitive developments, derived from the archeological record, that we believe distinguished *Homo heidelbergensis* from *Homo erectus*:

- Spatial cognition with allocentric perception and coordination of spatial quantity and shape recognition.
- Technical cognition with longer, more hierarchically organized procedural routines.
- Shared attention, required for technical learning.
- Ability to maintain two goals simultaneously (suggests a possible increase in working memory capacity).
- Attentive use of indexical signaling.

This is a conservative list, guided by the constraints of including only minimum necessary competencies. Nevertheless, it does mark a change over what had characterized *Homo erectus* cognition for almost 1 million years, a change that presages modern abilities.

The Jigsaw Puzzle

Our understanding of the *Homo heidelbergensis* mind remains a jigsaw puzzle, most of whose pieces are missing. We are not in a position to construct a comprehensive picture of the life world of these hominins; indeed, to fill in the gaps we must fall back on theories of cognition, and any selection of a theory of cognition depends on personal and scholarly history as much as the evidence.

From the theoretical stance of cognitive neuroscience, the *Homo heidelbergensis* puzzle presents a mixed picture. Some of the pieces appear modern, and would not be out of place in a modern scene: spatial cognition and the procedural component of technical cognition are the best examples. Other pieces are not modern: the lack of active innovation in technical cognition, and the use of indexes but not depictive images, are good examples. There are many missing pieces whose absence may be real, or simply a matter of archeological invisibility: grammar is the most frustrating example. *Homo heidelbergensis* was certainly very different from an ape, and from *Homo erectus*, but it was not modern. Some of the developments bear on our central concern, the evolution of working memory capacity.

For the first time, there is compelling evidence for working memory itself. The knapper at Boxgrove who set aside the nice, large, flakes while making a handaxe clearly was able to keep two goals in mind. It is hard to compare his or her working memory capacity to earlier hominins because we do not have an equally well-preserved reduction sequence. Nevertheless, there are other hints of an expansion of working memory. Prepared core-reduction sequences require some response inhibition when maximizing the size of future flakes by producing smaller, otherwise useless, preparatory flakes. Investing handaxes with conscious indexical load, if true, would also require that the craftsmen kept more things in attention as they knapped. But even though there are hints of greater working memory capacity, it was clearly not yet on a par with modern executive functions. There is no evidence yet for the complex contingency planning, and long-range spatial and temporal planning, that characterize the modern world.

What emerges most clearly from the *Homo heidelbergensis* puzzle is the importance of long-term procedural memory routines. This is expressed in technical expertise, where the procedures necessary for *debitage* strategies required longer and more hierarchically complex procedural memories than the antecedent *façonnage* strategies. It is also consistent with what little we know about *Homo heidelbergensis* subsistence, which included hunting, with spears, of large gregarious mammals. Although successful tactical hunting would not have required modern planning abilities, it would have required a repertoire of alternative procedures that could be accessed quickly as circumstances demanded. Animal behavior is predictable, on a general level, because one can anticipate a range of responses in the presence of predation, but the specific response will vary for every episode. The quickest way for the predator to respond would be through pre-attentive, procedural, muscle memories. In true carnivores these are at least partly hard-wired (watch a kitten stalk a beetle), but they are not hard-wired for hominins, who must learn them mostly through practice and repetition. This adaptive strategy was first evident for *Homo erectus*; *Homo heidelbergensis* developed it to a much higher degree.

An increase in the number and complexity of procedural routines fits nicely with the evidence for the increase in brain size that began about 500,000 years ago. The brains of *Homo heidelbergensis* were bigger than those of *Homo erectus*, and much of this increase was in the parietal lobes, the region of the brain containing the motor strip, spatial processing, and many long-term memories. *Homo heidelbergensis* brains were larger than *Homo erectus* brains, and the *Homo heidelbergensis* cognitive strategy was an enhanced version of the *Homo erectus* strategy.

This expert strategy is still with us. It powers our impressive abilities in sport, musical performance, craftsmanship, tool use (including driving!), and many games, including video games. These activities are all based on pattern recognition and rapid access to procedures held in long-term memory. They are a very effective way to respond to the variability of the physical and social world. But they are not inherently innovative. For invention to occur, the actor must be able to call up, analyze, and reflect upon his or her responses, and this is the domain of active attention, working memory, and executive functions. *Homo heidelbergensis* had only minimal capacity in this domain.

10

The Rise and Fall of Neandertal

Sometime between 30,000 and 24,000 years ago, somewhere on the Iberian peninsula, the last Neandertal died. As an evolutionary event, this extinction was neither unique nor particularly remarkable. Undoubtedly, many local populations of hominins had disappeared without issue during the course of our 5+ million years on the planet, including many populations of the genus *Homo*. But Neandertals hold a unique place in our preconceptions about human evolution; we would bet that every educated adult carries some image of a Neandertal in his or her head, an image that is more than likely based on misinterpretations that are over a century old. Many see the Neandertal as the archetypal cave man: dressed in animal skins, carrying a club or crude spear, with a dazed, puzzled, or brutal look on his face, Neandertals stalk our imagined past. They were similar enough to us to evoke recognition, but different enough to evoke mystery, amusement, or even fear. This image derives more from European folk traditions of doppelgängers, trolls, and village idiots than from solid science. Historically, Neandertals were the first fossil humans ever to be recognized by science, and it is therefore not surprising that they acquired instant celebrity and notoriety; it is also not surprising that they quickly acquired a suite of not-quite-human, savage characteristics. The tenor of the times in the late nineteenth century, with the European scramble for Africa, the British Raj in India, White Man's Burden – the belief that it was Europe's obligation to colonize other countries for their own benefit – and faith in universal progress, almost required such a characterization. It is an image against which paleoanthropologists continue to struggle. And it has polarized our interpretations. Reaction against this public image of Neandertals has led many paleoanthropologists to downplay or even deny differences between Neandertals and modern humans, and emphasize their undoubted humanness. Paleoanthropologists who argue for Neandertal distinctiveness risk being labeled as prejudiced or even racist (we have had this last accusation leveled at us by an anonymous reviewer). Sensibilities are especially heightened when Neandertal cognition is the focus of inquiry. Any attempt to characterize the Neandertal mind risks misunderstanding. Nevertheless, it is important that we make the attempt. Neandertals represented the zenith of a cognitive strategy that had evolved in Europe for several hundred thousand years. Neandertals were very successful, so much so that in the first encounter between Neandertals and anatomically modern humans, Neandertals prevailed. But 60,000 years later they lost out, largely, we contend, because of a small, but significant advantage carried in the modern human mind.

Grades and Clades

Thus far in our presentation we have treated the various hominin taxa as evolutionary grades – groups of related populations that shared the same basic phenotype and adaptation. Certainly, not all populations of *Homo erectus* or *Homo heidelbergensis* were direct ancestors of ours; indeed relatively few, perhaps only one in each case. Yet all shared the same basic adaptation and cognitive abilities. In an attempt to document general evolutionary trends, it was appropriate to lump them. It was not until the comparatively recent evolutionary past that the resolution of the fossil and archeological record became detailed enough for paleoanthropologists to be more comfortable with identifying clades – biologically coherent groups whose specific fates can be traced in the macro-evolutionary record (they are also monophyletic, which means that there is only one member). Neandertals and modern humans represent two such clades. For several hundred thousand years, they had relatively separate evolutionary paths, and for much of that time occupied the same evolutionary grade. But modern humans eventually acquired characteristics that Neandertals did not acquire, and vice versa, and one of these differences was to have profound long-term consequences.

Description

Neandertals were true Europeans. They evolved in Europe from a European population of *Homo heidelbergensis*, and developed characteristics that adapted them to European conditions, including severe climatic fluctuations associated with multiple advances and retreats of the northern European glacial ice sheet. Earlier hominins, such as *Homo erectus*, abandoned Europe during glacial cycles, but Neandertals and their immediate ancestors stayed and adapted, except perhaps for the brief periods of extreme cold. Many of the derived features of their anatomies reflect this local adaptation. At the outset it is important to note that when taken individually most Neandertal characteristics fall within the range of variability of *Homo sapiens*, modern and ancient (Wolpoff et al., 2004; Trinkaus, 2006); it is the combination of features that allows us to distinguish them.

By modern human standards, Neandertals were relatively short, stocky, and powerfully built. Average stature was about 160 cm or 5ft. 6in. (165 cm for males (N=8) and 156 for females (N=5)). This is very similar to earlier *Homo heidelbergenesis* (and also to western Europeans in 1915!). A male weighed perhaps 80 kg (about 176 lbs), making them about 20 percent heavier than modern humans of the same height (body mass can be estimated from diameter of the trunk, which is reflected in the distance between the two wings of the pelvis). They had a rounded, barrel-like trunk. The areas on the bones where muscles attached are pronounced and well developed, indicating that Neandertals were heavily muscled. Their forearms and lower legs were relatively short compared to their upper limbs, their radii were slightly bowed (the radius and ulna are bones of the forearm), and the position of the bicep attachment on the ulna was slightly further forward than true for the average modern human. This is a classic build for upper-body strength; one would not want to arm wrestle a Neandertal, or compete in a weightlifting competition! These features were true of females as well as males, and indeed appeared early in ontogeny. They were part of the genetic make-up of the population, and not simply the result of heavy exercise during life, though there is good evidence for this as well. This build is also a good example of Bergmann's and Allen's rules of body proportion: cold-adapted mammals have compact bodies (Bergmanns's rule) and shorter limbs (Allen's rule) to maximize heat retention (and reduce heat loss) (Arsuaga, 2002; Hublin, 1998, 2007; Trinkaus, 2006).

The Neandertal skull was a combination of ancestral characteristics, cold adaptations, and derived features perhaps attributable to genetic drift. The ancestral characteristics include a long cranium, a large face with brow ridges, and large teeth. Cold-adapted features include a large nose (for heat exchange during breathing), and expanded frontal sinuses. The derived

features of Neandertals are mostly ones that have no clear adaptive significance, such as an oval depression on the surface of the occipital bone
(suprainiac fossa), but which are common on Neandertal skulls.

All in all, Neandertals were a distinctive, and relatively distinct, population of archaic humans. But what is perhaps most telling about their
anatomy is the retention of many old, ancestral characteristics, especially
in the shape of the skull (Trinkaus, 2006). Neandertals looked very much
like their *Homo heidelbergensis* ancestors, and even their *Homo erectus* deep
ancestors. This old anatomy had been altered by cold adaptations, and a
variety of odd characteristics likely to have been the result of isolation as
a small population; but the overall plan was an old one, a point made long
ago by Krantz (1980). The one feature that would seem to be a dramatic
exception to this pattern was brain size.

Neandertal Brains

Neandertals had large brains: the mean cranial capacity was 1,427 cc (N=28),
with a range of 1,250 cc–1,700 cc (Holloway et al., 2004). As an absolute
measure, this exceeds the modern human average (about 1,350 cc), but
whether or not there was a significant difference in EQ is clouded by
Neandertals' obvious muscularity, and the decrease in body mass that
has occurred in modern populations over the last 10,000 years (based on
skeletal remains, not twenty-first-century McDonald's-fed teenagers . . .).
Nevertheless, even a conservative interpretation must conclude that
Neandertals were at least as encephalized as modern humans. If size were
the only issue of relevance, our consideration of Neandertal brains would
end here, and we could consider them neurologically indistinguishable
from ourselves. But size is not the only consideration; Neandertal brains
differed in shape from modern human brains. And here again we encounter
an ancestral condition. The overall proportions were very similar to *Homo
erectus*; it was just bigger. There is no evidence for relative expansion of
some regions or lobes over others, at least in comparison to earlier *Homo*.
As we will see in the next chapter, modern *Homo sapiens*' brain shape included
expansion of the parietal lobes and deviated significantly from the pattern
established in *Homo erectus*. But Neandertal brains appear to have been
larger *erectus* brains, a paleoneurological fact that may help us make sense
of the archeological evidence.

Neandertal Archeology

On the temporal scale of hominin evolution, Neandertals lived comparatively close to the present. As a consequence, many more of their activity sites have survived to be found by archeologists. This advantage has been amplified by Neandertals' practice of using caves and rock shelters, where their archeological remains are well preserved, and by their occupation of western Europe, one of the most thoroughly researched regions of the archeological world. We therefore know much more about what Neandertals were doing than about any other pre-modern human group.

Subsistence

Many sites attest to the skill and effectiveness of Neandertal hunters. At the site of Mauran near the French Pyrenees, they repeatedly used a narrow tongue of land lying between two river escarpments to funnel and concentrate herds of bison, which they killed and butchered. At La Borde to the north, they repeatedly used a collapsed limestone cavern as a trap for wild cattle, and at Cotte de St. Brelade on the Isle of Jersey (off the north-western coast of France), they drove mammoth and rhinoceros over a cliff. Bison, aurochs, and mammoth are formidable prey, especially when they are in groups, yet Neandertals repeatedly visited these places, presumably because local landscape features provided them with an advantage. This was not simple, opportunistic hunting. Neandertals knew the "lay of the land" in their territories, and they used it to their advantage (Mellars, 1996). But when it came to the actual killing, Neandertals relied on brawn as much as brains. Their primary weapon was a stone-tipped thrusting spear. Archeologists have recovered only one actual spear (from Lehringen in Germany), but they have recovered many of the stone spearheads. The patterns of breakage, and wear on the edges of these triangular flakes, indicate that these points had been hafted on the ends of shafts, and often broken in use (Shea, 1993). Injury patterns on Neandertals themselves attest to close-in killing. Healed upper-body and head injuries are common on Neandertal skeletons, and the kinds of injuries mimic those received today by rodeo athletes (Berger and Trinkaus, 1995). Neandertals were clearly having close encounters with large, dangerous beasts.

The proportion of the Neandertal diet that came from meat is hard to determine. The archeological record is heavily biased toward animal remains and away from plants. Nevertheless, most paleoanthropologists believe that hunting large animals was a very important part of Neandertal subsistence systems. For much of their tenure, Neandertals lived in a Europe that was colder and drier than today. In such a habitat, edible plants would have been rarer than in modern Europe and large herd mammals more common. Also, Neandertal caloric requirements would have been high. They were large, active mammals in a cold world. The most concentrated source of calories would have been game. Both Neandertal bodies and technology appear to have been geared to this resource, and not to plants.

There has been much debate among archeologists concerning the nature of Neandertal hunting. Some have seen them as little more than opportunistic scavengers; others as strategic hunters little different from the modern humans who succeeded them. Over the last 20 years, the evidence has tended to favor the latter interpretation. Much hinges on whether or not Neandertals specialized on single species and had year-long plans of exploitation. Sites such as Mauran, La Bordes, and Cotte de St. Brelade are dominated by single species. This does not require, however, that Neandertal hunting singled out these species as the focus of a hunting strategy. Similarly, evidence suggests that Neandertals may have used these sites only in particular seasons (e.g., late summer/fall at Mauran), which one could construe as reflecting a tightly scheduled foraging strategy. But, as always, we must invoke Occam's razor. Mauran may contain only late summer bison remains because that was the season in which that herd of bison naturally used that particular locale, and Neandertal hunters often found them there. The archeological remains do not require that Neandertals planned these hunts a year in advance, only that Neandertals had an effective technique to use when they did encounter them. This was tactical hunting, of an effective and brutal kind, but it did not require a tightly scheduled seasonal strategy. Archeologists also know a bit about Neandertal patterns of movement within their territories, as we will discuss shortly.

Technology

Neandertals' technology continued trends established by European *Homo heidelbergensis*. Lithic technology emphasized a variety of different edge types produced on flakes. There were steep-edged "scraping" tools, flakes with coarse serrations (denticulates), points, and many others (see figure 10.1). Sometimes the points were bifacially trimmed "leaf" points (Blattspitzen

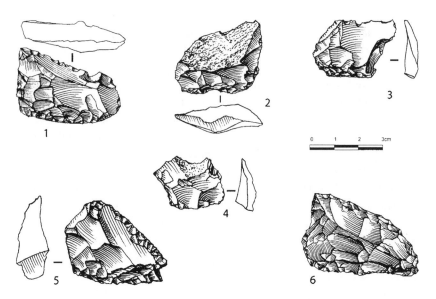

Figure 10.1   Neandertal flake tools from a reindeer hunting camp

Source: Sandrine, Meignen, Beauval, Vandermeersch, and Maureille, 2006. © 2006 Elsevier Inc.

in German), but just as often the Neandertals used unmodified triangular-shaped flakes produced by a special core preparation technique. Neandertals continued to make handaxes, but they were less common; presumably many of their functions had been taken on by flaked tools with more specialized edges. All in all Neandertals' stone tools present a greater variety of edge types than those of *Homo heidelbergensis*, suggesting that their approach to tools had become a bit more task-specific. It looks as if a certain job elicited a fairly specific response by way of flake size and the shape of the edge. The range of lithic technical responses was larger than that of *Homo heidelbergensis*. But in another respect their technical repertoire remained limited: Neandertals only rarely made tools out of wood, or bone, or antler. Of course, these materials preserve much less well archeologically, but many Neandertal sites do preserve bone well, and even at these sites tools of bone are virtually non-existent. Neandertals must have used wood for their spears, so they were not ignorant or incapable of exploiting these materials. They just appear not to have used them for hand tools.

Neandertals rarely traveled far for their raw materials. Most of the stone tools found in Neandertal sites were made on local rock types available within a few kilometers of the site. Some raw materials are much better for stone knapping than others, but Neandertals appear not to have had a systematic system for accessing and exploiting the best sources. Archeologists have found occasional lumps of high-quality flint whose source was up to 100 km away, but these are rare. Invariably, they are heavily reduced; Neandertals produced as many flakes as possible from these cores before abandoning them (Geneste, 1988; Feblot-Augustins, 1999). They apparently had no reliable way to acquire the raw material itself; the journey was too far, perhaps the kind of trip that an individual might have made only once or twice in his or her lifetime. This raw material evidence is actually quite important to our understanding. Neandertal lives were local. They rarely traveled far from their home territories and had no long-range social networks on which they could rely (Mellars, 1996; Gamble, 1999).

As with *Homo heidelbergensis*, our most reliable picture of Neandertal technology comes from the refitted cores that preserve the actual sequences that Neandertals used in stone knapping. The best understood of these techniques is known as Levallois, and it has come to be a hallmark of Neandertal technology. It is also one of the more difficult stone-knapping techniques to master, and as such provides an interesting glimpse into the Neandertal mind.

Levallois is a prepared core technique in which a knapper prepares the entire volume of the core in order to control the size and shape of a few large flakes (Boeda et al., 1990, 1994; Chazan, 1997). The knapper first shaped the core, using trimming flakes, into an inverted "tortoise" shape whose "top" was a shallow convex surface, and whose bottom a deeper convexity that carried the greater mass of stone (archeologists say that the core was asymmetric); see figure 10.2. The knapper then prepared a specific location on the "under" side edge to act as a striking platform – the point where the knapping blow would fall. The shape of the top convexity, and the shape and angle of the striking platform, determined the way force was transmitted through the core. If done properly, the knapper could strip off a thin flake that covered most of the upper convex surface. There were several variations on this theme. In one of them, the knapper trimmed the upper convexity in such a way that he or she could produce a triangular flake that could then be hafted onto a spear without further modification. After striking one (or in some varieties two or more) Levallois flakes, the knapper could re-prepare the core for another flake.

One refitted Levallois core from the site of Maastricht-Belvedere (in the Netherlands) reveals much about the thought processes of the knapper.

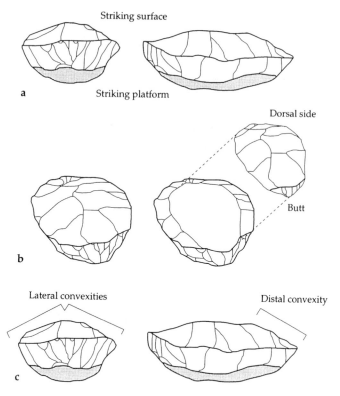

Figure 10.2   An idealized Levallois core identifying the major features that controlled the management of the core mass

Source: Chazan, 1997. © 1997 Elsevier Inc.

It is known a "Marjorie's" core after the person who made the initial refit, but the detailed description was done by Nathan Schlanger (1996) in a *tour de force* of archeological analysis. The refitted core is made of only 38 total flakes (figure 10.3), nine of which were the large targeted Levallois flakes. The knapper produced these flakes in seven phases, each phase consisting of preparation of the top convexity, preparation of the platform, and striking off of the final products. The first thing the knapper did in each phase was to search the top of the core for a convexity to act as the terminus of the intended flake, that is, the convex surface opposite the striking platform. He or she then trimmed the sides of the convexity, prepared the platform, and struck off one or two large flakes. For the next phase he or she invariably

Figure 10.3 The refitted Levallois core from Masstricht-Belvédére known as "Marjorie's core"; note especially the asymmetric profile of the core, which attests the knapper's ability to control the core mass

Source: Based on Roebroeks, 1988

rotated the core 90° so that what had been a lateral convexity could now act as the distal convexity (figure 10.4).

The knapper clearly looked ahead to the consequences that his or her action would have on future reduction phases. The knapper also adjusted the technique as the core size diminished; even though the core became successively smaller, the resulting Levallois flakes remained large. Some archeologists have suggested that Levallois was a wasteful technique, and hence not sophisticated. Marjorie's core belies that claim. After initial preparation, the entire reduction sequence consisted of only 38 flakes. Compare this to the 1,500+ flakes for the Boxgrove biface reduction described in the last chapter. The knapper of Marjorie's core managed the volume of the core from the beginning to the end, using a minimum number of gestures and efficient use of time and material.

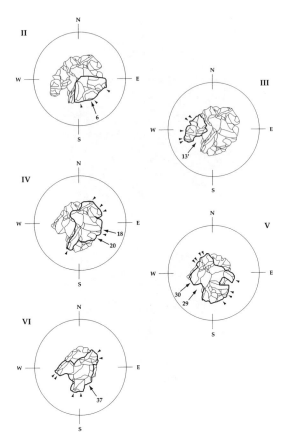

Figure 10.4   Five phases in the reduction of Marjorie's core; note that the final, "Levallois," flake removal(s) in each phase (numbered arrows) was/were oriented 90° from the final flake removal of the previous and subsequent phases, once again attesting the knapper's overall management of the knapping process

Source: Schlanger, 1996. © 1996 Cambridge University Press

Symbolism and social life

Even early in the study of Neandertals, paleoanthropologists knew one piece of behavior that made Neandertals appear very human – they occasionally buried their dead. This is one of the reasons that we have such a good record of Neandertal postcranial skeletons. If a body is intentionally buried soon after death, it will not be ravaged by scavengers nor have its bones scattered by water. But burial is prone to over- and under-interpretation. Unfortunately, there remain serious problems to accepting many, perhaps even all, Neandertal burials as being the result of intentional interment (Gargett, 1999); and the few convincing examples are very late in the time range. But the existence of even a few Neandertal burials is provocative. It has led many serious, and not so serious, scholars to posit that Neandertals had a rich symbolic and religious life, with a concept of the supernatural and an afterlife. This is almost certainly unwarranted. There are many reasons to bury a corpse, only some of which involve the supernatural. Neandertal burial is the first of two Paleolithic "Rorshach blots" – the interpretation of which may tell us more about the paleoanthropologist than about Neandertals (the second blot is cave painting). Neandertals were not actually the first hominins to mess about with corpses. At Atapuerca in Spain about 400,000 years ago, *Homo heidelbergensis* dragged over 30 bodies into a deep cave and dropped them into a shaft – it is known as Sima de los Huesos, the pit of bones (de Castro and Nicolos, 1997). We do not know why, but it cannot be explained by natural causes, and was unrelated to the day-to-day challenges of survival in Middle Pleistocene Spain. Archeologists often hide behind the "non-utilitarian" label when describing such activities, implying a lack of practicality that made it superfluous to *Homo heidelbergensis'* real lives. But this sells short both *Homo heidelbergensis* and Neandertals. They had reasons for the way they treated corpses, and the effort they invested in dragging corpses and/or digging graves suggests that it was anything but superfluous. We do not know what their reasons were, but the very act of having reasons is itself an important piece of evidence. However, when these reasons can vary from the pragmatic (corpses stink) to the esoteric (preparation for an experience after death), the cognitive interpretations can also vary widely.

Evidence for Neandertal symbolism is as enigmatic as it was for *Homo heidelbergensis*. Once again pigment use is the most convincing example. At over 40 sites, Neandertals left evidence of processing mineral pigments, most often manganese dioxide, which produces a black powder when ground. The evidence consists of lumps of the mineral with flat facets produced by scraping or grinding (d'Errico et al., 2003). And, again, we do not know their purpose; the most parsimonious explanation is that Neandertals colored something with the pigments (though black is not quite a color), although recent experimental and archeological work by Wadley (March 2008, personal communication) has shown that Middle

Stone Age people in Africa (who were not Neandertals) combined such mineral pigments with sand and plant resins to make effective adhesives for the hafting of spears. Neandertal sites have also produced objects with markings that resemble engraved lines. Most of these "engravings" resulted from natural processes or damage during excavation (d'Errico et al., 2003; Nowell and d'Errico, 2007) and need not concern us. But a few are anthropogenic. The most widely accepted example is a pebble from the Hungarian site of Tata. This round pebble has a natural crack extending across the diameter. A Neandertal scratched a second diameter line perpendicular to this crack. Other Neandertal examples of engravings are as enigmatic; they are also very rare and found in complete isolation from one another. There is no reason to conclude that Neandertals had a regular tradition of engraving.

Archeologists know a bit more about Neandertal social life, based primarily on spatial distributions of remains within sites. Neandertal residential groups appear to have been relatively small by standards of modern hunters and gatherers. The occupation debris in Neandertal sites usually covers much less total area than that of later modern humans. There are also fewer hearths. It is very difficult to attach a specific size to this evidence, but a conservative guess would place Neandertal groups in the 30- to 50-person range, much smaller than the 150-person estimates for penecontemporaneous *Homo sapiens*. Neandertal cave sites often yield a wide range of artifact sizes and edge types, as well as a variety of faunal remains. They appear to have been true home bases to which Neandertals returned on a regular basis. There is even evidence that they occasionally leveled their living surfaces to make them more comfortable (and in the process played havoc with the archeologists' stratigraphy!). Neandertals apparently practiced a radiating pattern of foraging, traveling out and back in their search for food (Mellars, 1996; Gamble, 1999; D. Lieberman, 1998). Their residential sites were the center of this pattern. However, the nature of the hearths and distribution of refuse appear not as tightly organized into specific activity areas as those of later modern humans. And, more provocatively, Neandertal hearths are less "structured." More often than not Neandertal hearths are diffuse scatters of ash; there are a few exceptions but Neandertals rarely dug fire pits, or lined their hearths with stone (Bar-Yosef, 2002; Speth, 2006). This suggests that Neandertal hearths were practical fires used for the task at hand, and may not have been the focus of Neandertal social life, as they are for modern humans. The image of an elder tending the fire as he or she told stories to entertain or enlighten the young, is not an image we can associate with the more casual fires of Neandertals.

We assume that Neandertals had some form of speech. The topic of Neandertal speech is one of the more contentious in an already contentious field, and scholars venture into this minefield at their peril. Unlike African *Homo heidelbergensis*, the Neandertal basicranium was not modern in shape. In this respect, it resembled its predecessor, European *Homo heidelbergensis*. This anatomical difference may indicate that Neandertal throats were shaped differently from ours, and that they had a different range of vocal sounds (P. Lieberman, 1984, 1989), although more recent simulations by Boë et al. (2002) suggest that the Neandertal's vocal tract could potentially produce all vowel sounds of modern human speech. Even if the former assertion was true, it would not obviate speech. In the previous chapter we averred that *Homo heidelbergensis* probably had some form of symbolic speech and, given the complexity of modern grammatical language, probably had some form of grammar, albeit simpler than ours. We have no reason to deny Neandertals a similar ability, or even one slightly enhanced. Indeed, a symbol-based protolanguage similar to one long posited by linguist Derek Bickerton (1990) would fit the overall Neandertal zeitgeist very nicely. But the anatomical and archeological evidence do not tell us this directly, and for the time being any attempt to describe Neandertal speech (or language) is informed guesswork.

Age and gender divisions of economic labor

Kuhn and Stiner (2006) recently came to the provocative conclusion that Neandertals lacked the division of economic labor by age and gender and that the latter is a salient feature of the recent human condition and that it emerged relatively late in human evolutionary history. Their review of anthropological evidence suggests that Neandertals may have had more narrowly focused economies with women and juvenile activities more closely aligned with adult males. See figure 10.5: what we think this cartoon suggests, although not explicitly referenced to Neandertals, is that women and children also participated in the hunting of large animals, even if only in support roles, and they, along with juveniles, appear to have not been actively hunting alternatives to large game, like birds, fish, and small animals.

"Why do we always have to eat out?"

Figure 10.5   An example of the proposed lack of age and gender divisions of economic labor in Neandertals. © The New Yorker Collection 2007 Michael Maslin from cartoonbank.com. All Rights Reserved

Neandertal Cognition

The archeological and fossil evidence indicate that Neandertal cognition continued the pattern established by *Homo heidelbergensis*, but accentuated or enhanced many of the component abilities. There appears to have been no significant change in brain shape accompanying the evolution of Neandertals, but there was an increase in overall size. Similarly, few striking behavioral novelties accompanied Neandertals, at least not until very late in their tenure on the European continent. However, they do appear to have been more adept than *Homo heidelbergensis* in many of their shared behaviors. The simplest generalization about the evidence for Neandertal cognition is that it represented an increase in raw information storage.

Neandertals could learn, store, and retrieve from long-term memory more task-relevant information and procedures than earlier *Homo heidelbergensis.*

Spatial cognition

We earlier argued that *Homo heidelbergensis* demonstrated a modern Euclidean conception of space. There is no evidence that Neandertals had an enhanced version of this ability (though this might be hard for us to recognize because our cognition is not enhanced!). However, the greater detail of our knowledge of Neandertal daily life allows us to revisit Silverman's argument for the role of hunting in the evolution spatial cognition. If hunting selected for space constancy, as Choi and Silverman (2003) have proposed, presumably the very adept Neandertal hunters would provide convincing evidence. They do not. We have no reason to conclude that Neandertals used intercept strategies that required the plotting and following of novel routes, or traveled on long-range expeditions requiring novel routes home. The best way to describe Neandertal movement in space is by using radiating or star-shaped patterns – moving out from home bases and back again along established paths and tracks (Gamble, 1999). Over millennia and lifetimes, Neandertals appear to have learned their territories and their opportunities intimately, including the locations of every stream, rock, and thicket, and every path between. This required spatial memory, but not the ability to imagine novel paths.

Technical cognition

In the domain of technical cognition we see a clear enhancement of abilities. The reader will recall the following facts about Neandertal technology:

1. The prepared core techniques used by Neandertals (e.g., Marjorie's core) provide evidence for longer chains of action, with more hierarchically organized sub-routines than the *façonnage* and *debitage* strategies of *Homo heidelbergensis.* Neandertals relied on a greater variety of prepared core techniques.
2. Each prepared core technique included a large number of procedural options, and knappers regularly shifted from one to another while reducing a single core.

3. Neandertal flake tools present a larger variety of edge types, and contexts (e.g., associated fauna, location in the site) suggesting that there were fairly specific functions for each of the edge types.

4. Neandertals hafted stone tools onto spears, and perhaps other artifacts as well.

5. The lithic production technologies are truly impressive. In their organization and complexity they rival the procedures and products of modern craft production. Elsewhere (Wynn and Coolidge, 2004) we have compared Levallois *debitage* to the procedures followed by a modern blacksmith and found them comparable (with one important difference we will detail later). At the level of technical activity Neandertals were as adept as modern humans. This in turn points to the cognitive ability that still underpins most of modern technical activity – the strategy of expertise.

Much of Neandertal technical activity could have been guided by procedural cognition – chains of action learned by repetition and held in long-term motor and procedural memory. Association, chaining of actions into sequences, with each component eliciting the next, all enabled via perceptual cues, are the cognitive bases for most technical activity. This is why apprenticeship remains the primary strategy for learning technical procedures. But expertise is more than rote routines. It also requires the flexibility to respond to changing conditions. One could respond to change by inventing something new, but this is something experts almost never do. It is quicker, and more reliable, to fall back on an alternative procedure. The more alternative procedures one can learn, hold in long-term memory, and have available, the better the response will be. This appears to be precisely the approach Neandertals took to technology. Their corpus of procedural knowledge far exceeded that of *Homo heidelbergensis*, and may even have exceeded our own.

Neandertals did develop at least one new feature of technology – hafting – and this feature has inspired many claims for being a kind of cognitive Rubicon (Ambrose, 2001). The common-sense interpretation sees this multi-component tool, made of a variety of disparate materials, as requiring a leap in Neandertals' understanding of the nature of transferring force, and the ways in which heretofore different tools could be combined (see examples of these tools in figures 10.6 and 10.7). But this interpretation assumes that Neandertals understood this technology the way that we do – always a dangerous approach in cognitive archeology. Did hafting require

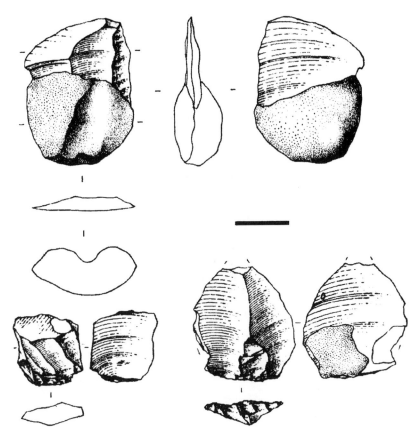

Figure 10.6 Neandertal flake tools with hafting tar still attached (stippled area in drawing; the bar is 2 cm)

Source: Mazza et al., 2006. © 2006 Elsevier Ltd

any cognitive ability above and beyond the already formidable procedural abilities known for Neandertals? We think not. Yes, it did require new knowledge, and new procedures. Someone, presumably a Neandertal, was the first to haft a point, and it would be very informative to know how this invention occurred. It might tell us something provocative. But we do not know how this technology developed, and given the virtual dearth of other Neandertal inventions, we cannot conclude that invention was a normal component of Neandertal technology. Learning how to haft, and hafting itself, are well within the domain of expert technical cognition.

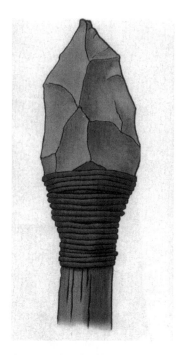

Figure 10.7   Drawing of a Neandertal hafted spear
Source: Wynn and Coolidge, 2008. © 2008 Sigma Xi, The Scientific Research Society, Inc.

Symbolism

The evidence for Neandertal symbol use is qualitatively no different from that of *Homo heidelbergenesis*. There is, however, a bit more of it. Ochres and manganese dioxide are common in Neandertal sites. Part of this increase in quantity no doubt reflects archeological serendipity: the caves and rock-shelters frequented by Neandertals present a concentrated signature of activity, and the preservation tends to be good. But some of this increase in the quantity of pigments may reflect a greater role in Neandertal life. The proposed pragmatic explanations (hafting; anti-louse agent, etc.) do not adequately account for the selectivity (see chapter 9) and a semiotic explanation continues to be more likely, with an indexical role being the most parsimonious interpretation. We simply do not know how color played out in Neandertal daily life. The cognitive prerequisites remain relatively simple, and there is no good reason to argue for a cognitive development over that of *Homo heidelbergenesis*. Similarly, Neandertal archeology provides more examples of scratched and engraved bones and stones, but they were still very rare – isolated cases separated from one another by hundreds of kilometers and thousands of years. They are hardly the signature of an established symbolic tradition. The simplest explanation is that they were the output of single Neandertals at single moments in time. The cognitive requirements consist only of the motor skill to do the task, and a spatial understanding that had already been in place for several hundred thousand years (Hodgson, 2000).

Language

Language remains the most salient unknown of Neandertal life. Anatomical evidence indicates that Neandertal faces were not rotated under their crania to the degree true of modern humans, and this may imply that the length of their pharynxes differed as well, though the relationship is far from clear. This feature, combined with their large noses, suggests that Neandertal vocalization probably sounded different from ours, but not by much. This does not, however, mean that Neandertals lacked spoken language. In the last chapter, we argued that *Homo heidelbergenesis* must have had some form of language, if only because language rests on such a complex cognitive foundation that it must have evolved in several stages. By the same reasoning, Neandertals must also have had language. The only difference we can suggest between *Homo heidelbergenesis* and Neandertals is that the evidence for expanded long-term memory in Neandertal technology may imply a similar expansion in raw lexical capacity. Neandertals may well have had more words and more stock phrases producing larger linguistic capacity. Our account is consonant with that of braver scholars such as Bickerton (1990) and Mithen (1996, 2006) who propose models of proto-language. Beyond this we are reluctant to venture.

Social cognition

The richness of Neandertal archeology, compared to that of *Homo heidelbergenesis*, reveals some of the features of the Neandertal social world, and the resulting picture is one of small, local groups, who rarely if ever traveled beyond the confines of their own river valleys. In his 1999 book,

The Palaeolithic Societies of Europe, Clive Gamble describes Neandertals as living within a "landscape of habit," a characterization that fits nicely with everything else we know of Neandertal life. Neandertal social networks were small; indeed, the term network may be inappropriate. There is no reason to conclude that Neandertal social life extended beyond the boundaries of their face-to-face social interactions. They knew everyone in their local groups intimately. As primates, it is almost certain that either young men or young women must have left their natal group to join another local group, but there is little direct evidence for this – unless it is the rare pieces of high-quality exotic material, carried along perhaps to diffuse aggression in the new group. Beyond this, there is no reason to posit permanent social bonds beyond the face-to-face group. And the face-to-face relations of a small group rely on the experiential and repetitious resources of long-term memory. There is no need to track the hypothetical actions of distant kin, real or fictive. Everyone is within the range of direct action, if not today then yesterday, or the day after tomorrow. It appears that long-term procedural memory and behavioral habit were the cognitive resources of Neandertal social life.

This account of Neandertal social life makes sense of the evidence for symbolism. The Neandertal social world did not require the ornaments and art that enable a social "release from proximity," to use Gamble's apt phrase. Neandertals did not need to control information that signaled varying statuses to distant people who bore only a tenuous social connection to themselves. All distant people were equally strangers, and all could be treated as such regardless of what they wore, or painted on themselves, or presented as tokens of some presumptive social link. If, as Kuhn and Stiner (2006) suggested, Neandertals even lacked age- and gender-based divisions of labor, then their social lives were considerably less diverse than those of modern humans, lacking in particular much of the negotiation, disputation, and enforcement found with modern economic roles (e.g., Shea, 2006). Here again there is the hint that Neandertals did not control the same variety of information typical of modern humans, which in turn would have required a different capacity to make decisions, plan, and organize activities in line with short- and long-term goals.

Theory of mind and shared attention

One of the more useful features of modern social cognition is theory of mind, i.e., understanding and predicting the emotional states of others.

Modern humans are very good at imagining the mental states of others. What about Neandertals? Given their large brains, and modern technical cognition, might we not posit that Neandertals were fully capable of imagining the mental states of other Neandertals? As we saw in earlier chapters, even though theory of mind is relatively easy to describe – we all know what it means to imagine someone else's thoughts – it is much harder to investigate in a rigorous way. And if it is difficult to test in living subjects, how much harder it must be to test in Neandertals; after all, we cannot give them a false-belief test. Nevertheless, as tempting as it may be simply to assume that Neandertals had theory of mind based on brain size, technology, and symbol use, to do so would be to abandon a rigorous approach to cognition. One of the basic components of theory of mind – shared attention – does in fact leave some signatures, and these point to subtle, but perhaps significant, differences between Neandertals and the modern humans that followed.

Neandertals almost certainly relied on shared attention to teach and learn complex core reduction strategies. Understanding how a master knapper made efficient use of core volume, while at the same time setting up future sub-routines, would almost require that the master direct the novice's attention to specific features of the task. This might have been via vocalization, but other techniques are possible. What is key here is that the master and the novice must come to attend to the same features, and know that they share this attention. This strikes us as an antecedent of full theory of mind. But in this case it is small scale and local; there is no reason why the novice needed to imagine the master's theory of stone knapping, but only that he or she use the shared attention to construct his or her own theory of knapping.

One neural basis for the shared attention in stone knapping may be the mirror neuron system, a group of neurons that are activated when a primate both performs an action and observes an action in another. It is thought that the mirror neuron system, in both human and non-human primates, is involved in understanding the intentions of others, including grasping objects and other goals and in imitating others and later being able to perform similar procedural memories (e.g., sequences of physical actions like stone knapping). In macaques, the mirror neuron system involves frontal and parietal cortices, and in humans it additionally involves the intraparietal sulcus (see figure 2.2, chapter 2, the region superior to Broadmann's area 7), for example, as discussed by Hamilton and Grafton (2006). It is possible, therefore, that the shared attention in stone knapping required the mirror neuron system, which might be considered an anteced- ent of theory of mind, but it probably did not require expert stone knappers and their apprentices to understand and appreciate the emotional states and higher-order intentions of each other as in full theory of mind.

Other aspects of Neandertal archeology suggest that they may have lacked group shared attention and large-scale shared attention. Neandertals made and used fire, and organized their living sites in such a way that refuse was thrown to the peripheries. Also, certain heavy jobs such as large-scale butchery were performed away from living areas (Speth, 2006). But there is also something unstructured about Neandertal living sites. The hearths are more often than not diffuse patches of ash, suggesting ephemeral (short-lived) fires without intense burning. Neandertals occa- sionally scooped out a depression for the fire, but only rarely lined the pit with stone, or built the hearth in any significant way. And the hearths were not predictably in the center of the living area; they were in fact rather haphazardly placed. Psychologist Matt Rossano (2006) has suggested that Neandertal groups did not use fires as the focus of activities of shared attention. In other words, Neandertals appear not to have sat around their fires for storytelling, or ritual, keeping the fire intense, and using it as the metaphorical center of the social group. Such shared group attention is the basis for the modern ritual life. If Neandertal did not, or could not, maintain sustained group attention for purely social purposes, then their lives were very different from our own. This lacuna in Neandertal social life has implications for symbolism and language. Without shared group attention, there would be no occasion for complex narrative structures and abstract symbols, i.e., no reason for the more complex and subtle features of modern narrative language.

Executive functions and working memory

The archeological evidence suggests that Neandertals possessed several enhanced cognitive abilities when compared to *Homo heidelbergensis*. Foremost among them was an enhanced capacity in procedural long- term memory, which empowered greater complexity in lithic technology, hunting tactics, and an ability to adapt to the harsh cold of European glacial climates. The success of this cognitive repertoire cannot be denied. However, the archeological signature of Neandertal cognition has always struck archeologists as more than a little foreign:

There may certainly have been some changes in mental capacity and composition from Neandertal to fully modern human forms (corresponding to many excavators' intuitive feeling that there is "something" intangibly different about Neandertal behavior). However, at the level of biological capacities, these appear to be very subtle; neither the relative change in brain size nor morphology indicates that this was a very significant change. Neandertals may not have been quite capable of doing nuclear physics or calculus; however, it is a travesty of the available data to argue that they did not have the full complement of basic human faculties or act in recognizably modern fashions. (Hayden, 1993: 137)

The Neandertal cognitive strategy appears not to have included a significant enhancement of working memory capacity; the archeologically visible components of modern executive functions are nowhere to be found in the archeological signature of Neandertals. Neandertal life did not include plans of action that extended far into the future or over great distances. Neandertal life appears to have been local in both time and space. We have no evidence that Neandertals scheduled their foraging over periods of years (as we do for modern humans) or even over one year. Yes, they could and did respond to seasonal and climatic changes, but these were tactical responses based on a large corpus of available knowledge. Similarly, their technology was local in time and space. They relied almost exclusively on local sources of raw material, available within a few kilometers of the sites where they produced their tools. Exotic raw materials are rare in Neandertal sites and do not indicate that Neandertals were able to access it systematically. They did not plan long-range expeditions in order to acquire high-quality raw material, nor do they appear to have traded for it. More telling, Neandertal technology was a "maintainable" technology. The tools did not require a heavy investment of time for production and maintenance. A Levallois point took a fraction of an hour to produce – unlike the tens of hours for many modern human tools – and if it broke during use it could be replaced relatively easily. Neandertal hunters could fix their tools when they failed. But there is no evidence of tools designed to work remotely (e.g., traps) or tools designed to withstand possible mishaps in use (e.g., projectiles with replaceable foreshafts). Neandertals did not anticipate the ways in which their tools might fail, and plan accordingly. It appears that they just did not plan much beyond the immediate future.

There is no evidence for abstract thinking, and little evidence for innovation. Abstract thinking results from an ability to hold several ideas in active attention, compare them, and draw generalities. This is the same ability that powers analogical and metaphorical thinking – using one set of ideas to think about another. There is nothing in the Neandertal archeological record that even suggests that they could do this. There are no images or figurines of mythological beasts, no calculating devices, no astronomical alignments of stones, no evidence for storytelling around hearths. With a sole exception, they produced no personal ornaments, and there are alternative explanations to the exception (Coolidge and Wynn, 2004). There is no reason to think that they could "step back" from their daily routines and ponder the meaning of their own existence. There is also no reason to think that Neandertals actively innovated. There is no evidence for experimenting with new techniques, and no evidence for the rapid technical changes that occur when people set out to invent a new solution. Occasionally, Neandertals did acquire new techniques, but it happened at such a slow rate (once every several thousand years) that active innovation is precluded. Active innovation requires either thought experiment – working through new possibilities in one's imagination, and then trying them out – or an ability to monitor rote procedures as they are performed, and conceive of alternative procedures. Both innovative techniques require working memory capacity beyond that necessary to activate and deploy technical routines. That Neandertals never did this is a good prima facie argument that their working memory capacity was not as large as that of modern artisans.

The Neandertal Role in Human Evolution

The role of Neandertals in human evolution is unresolved, even though paleoanthropologists know a great deal more about them than we did even 20 years ago. The idea, once widely held, that Neandertals marked a stage in human evolution immediately preceding fully modern anatomy is now effectively defunct. Recovery of ancient mitochondrial and nuclear DNA suggests that Neandertal and modern human DNA is at least 99.5 percent identical, but that the groups had separate evolutionary histories for perhaps half-a-million years (Serre et al., 2007; Green et al., 2006; Noonan et al., 2006). What remains unresolved is the degree to which Neandertals contributed to modern gene pools. Neandertals could well have existed as a relatively distinct population for 500,000 years without becoming a separate species. If so, then Neandertals would have been able to reproduce with modern humans, and gene flow between the two would have been possible, even likely, when groups of each came into regular contact. Indeed, most paleoanthropologists acknowledge that some admixture of genes between Neandertals and modern humans was likely. If true, one would expect there to be at least a few Neandertal genes in the modern European gene pool. Serre et al. could not completely rule out the possibility of at least some DNA admixture between Neandertals and modern humans, but they could rule out any major DNA admixture. Green et al. (2006) even go so far as to suggest that what admixture did occur was from modern males to Neandertal females (based on X chromosome divergence). However, it would be a mistake to consider modern Europeans to be a direct lineal descendant population of Neandertals. The consensus among those researching ancient DNA is that the majority of the modern gene pool is of recent African origin. And within this gene pool, we suggest, were the alleles that enhanced working memory capacity.

From a cognitive perspective, Neandertals represent a fascinating parallel to us. They were very successful in overcoming the challenges of a hostile world, used complex technical procedures, were brutal and effective hunters, and relied on the close emotional bonds of family – extending to the care of their dead. There is even evidence that they cared for their infirm; some Neandertals survived serious bone breaks that would have required a period of convalescence during which they could not have been effective foragers. However, some anthropologists have noted there are no cases where broken legs have healed (Berger and Trinkaus, 1995), which may imply that Neandertals were also brutally pragmatic. A Neandertal may have been able to go on a hunt with a broken arm, but not with a broken leg. Neandertals appear to have been masters of their local universe. The apparent lack of abstraction or innovation is not as dire as one might suppose. Most of our own solutions to problems also rely on learned routines and procedures. Few of us invent new tools or new ways of doing things; long-term procedural memory is our primary strategy in many domains of everyday life. Neandertals may even have been better at this strategy than modern humans. When Neandertals and anatomically modern humans encountered one another in the Levant 80,000 years ago, it was the modern humans who retreated back into their African homeland. But 40,000 years ago the encounter had a different outcome. Within 15,000 years Neandertals had vanished as a distinct population. There is no evidence for violent interactions between the two; indeed, their coexistence in parts of Europe for thousands of years argues against systematic conflict or genocide. Nevertheless, *Homo sapiens* survived and Neandertals did not. Perhaps *Homo sapiens* were simply better able to adapt in the presence of such direct competition. We suspect that the flexibility of Neandertals' expert cognition was not quite as successful as the executive functions of *Homo sapiens* in adjusting to changing environments and the changing response of a competing variety of *Homo*. And, in the end, the *Homo sapiens* way of life and thinking survived, and the Neandertal way of life came to an end.

11

The Second Major Leap in Cognition: Enhanced Working Memory and the Evolution of Modern Thinking

Who's Who

At the outset of this chapter, let us review the key players and the current anthropological thinking about our origins. Sometime between 8 and 7 million years ago the common ancestor of humans and chimpanzees speciated into two distinct evolutionary taxa, or clades; one eventually evolved into modern chimpanzees and bonobos, the other into humans. We began the discussion of our origins even later, about 3.6 million years ago with *Australopithecus afarensis.* These early hominins were bipedal apes; they had acquired a novel way of moving about, bipedalism, but their brains were little different from those of other African apes. The first hominin that paleo-anthropologists assign to the genus *Homo* appeared about 2.5 million years ago, and this hominin did have a larger brain. It was also probably the maker of the earliest stone tools. The evolutionary fate of these first *Homo* is not well understood. They might have been ancestors of ours or, if not, an as yet unidentified relative might have been. In many respects this East African early *Homo* resembled an *Australopithecus*. It was a small bipedal ape that almost certainly spent considerable time in trees, including sleeping. But its adaptive niche included a greater reliance on meat acquired through scavenging, and this dietary shift removed selection against large brains. This initially modest dietary change led to a significant grade shift in hominin evolution. This transition included a full commitment to terrestrial life (both sleeping and waking) and introduced a suite of necessary adaptations that resulted in the evolution of *Homo erectus* by 1.8 million years ago. *Homo erectus,* who some consider to have been the first true *Homo* species, then made a dramatic geographic expansion into Asia and southern Europe. In Africa and Europe, over the next 1 million years or so, *Homo erectus* evolved into *Homo heidelbergensis*, whom we discussed in chapter 9. Thus, *Homo heidelbergensis* lived in both Africa and Europe about 500,000 to 400,000 years ago. In Europe, *Homo heidelbergensis* then evolved in relative isolation into Neandertals. In Africa, *Homo heidelbergensis* evolved into what ultimately became modern *Homo sapiens*.

We Are All Africans

The fossil record and the genetics of modern populations point to the same significant fact: all living humans descend from a small population that lived in Africa in the relatively recent past. Studies of mitochondrial DNA (MtDNA) and Y-chromosomes reveal that modern populations in Africa have the greatest amount of genetic variability. MtDNA varieties found in other populations are present in African populations, but there are African variants that are found nowhere outside of the continent. The most parsimonious explanation for this pattern is that modern humans evolved in Africa, after which groups from this original population migrated out of Africa to colonize the rest of the habitable world. Most paleoanthropologists now agree that some gene flow occurred between these modern humans and local archaic populations, but that the latter contributed relatively little to the modern gene pool (Green et al., 2006).

Modern humans differed anatomically from their Neandertal contemporaries, a difference that was the result of several hundred thousand years of separate evolution. Some of these differences represent derived characters that evolved separately for each group, and some represent different ancestral characters retained from *Homo heidelbergensis* and *Homo erectus*. Some of the differences in derived features result from different adaptations (e.g., some of the cold-adapted features of Neandertals), but some are likely the result of genetic drift. It is well to keep in mind that Neandertals and the first anatomically modern humans were very similar to one another. Indeed, there are very few individual characteristics true of Neandertals that never occur in modern populations, and vice versa (Trinkaus, 2006). It is the combination of features, the "package" if you will, that sets the groups apart. However, among those traits that are potentially definitive ("autapomorphic" in cladistic terms), an interesting pattern emerges.

Of 75 physical traits, Trinkaus found about 25 percent were shared by Neandertals and modern humans, 25 percent were unique to Neandertals, and 50 percent were unique to modern humans. Thus, Trinkaus concluded that it is not Neandertals who are unusual, special, or derived. "It is we." (p. 607).

There is a large and arcane literature in paleoanthropology concerning Neandertal and anatomically modern human anatomy, much of which is tangential to our concerns. Instead of presenting a comprehensive account of anatomically modern humans' physical differences, we choose to focus on those trends in the modern line that have clear implications for cognition. The two most telling are the trend toward a more lightly built postcranial skeleton, and the trend toward parietal expansion of the cranium. Modern humans were (and are) less robust than their *Homo heidelbergensis* ancestors, and much less robust than Neandertals. The bones themselves had a thinner external osseous layer, and the points where muscles attached were less pronounced. This gracility extended to the face. Modern humans had smaller teeth, smaller jaws with more pronounced chins, and smaller upper faces, including noses and brow ridges. Like their *Homo heidelbergensis* ancestors, their faces were rotated underneath the cranium, a feature that may have had implications for their vocal tract. The overall gracility of modern skeletons probably reflects a difference in the levels of stress placed on the body. This is unlikely to be the result of genetic drift and suggests a change in the basic adaptive niche. Similar to the trend in the Neandertals, anatomically modern humans evolved a larger cranial capacity. But whereas the Neandertal increase simply expanded the *Homo heidelbergensis* cranium, the modern trend also included a change in shape. Modern human crania are higher (paleoanthropologists sometimes use the term "vaulting"), the forehead rises more vertically behind the brow, and the point of maximum breadth is high on the sides. As we will discuss soon, this change in shape reflects a change in the proportions of the brain and has important implications for cognitive evolution.

The package of modern features took several hundred thousand years to evolve. The earliest fossils presenting a significant number of modern features are, not surprisingly, African and date to between 150,000 and 200,000 years ago. The earliest fossil (about 190,000 years ago) is a partial cranium from Omo Kibish in Ethiopia that has "parietal bosses," the rounding high on the sides of the cranium that mark the point of maximum breadth (Shea et al., 2007). The younger Herto crania (about 160,000 years ago), also from Ethiopia, are more complete (White et al., 2003). They, too, have the parietal bossing, but their faces are not as gracile as is typical for modern Africans. The Herto crania also present a curious pattern of damage with some implications for the beginnings of modern behavior. One was defleshed with a stone tool, and all three, as we noted earlier, have polished surfaces that suggest that they had been carried around in bags. Later still are remains from Qafzeh and Skuhl in Israel (about 100,000 years ago). They resemble Herto in having robust faces along with high, vaulted crania. These are the earliest modern humans "out of Africa." They appear to have moved into the Near East along with an expansion of African fauna that accompanied the last interglacial period (about 128,000 years ago). When the climate deteriorated, they apparently retreated into Africa along with the African fauna. Interestingly, this retreat also coincided with the arrival of Neandertals into the Near East, who moved in from the north.

This first possible encounter between anatomically modern humans and Neandertals was followed by the disappearance of moderns in the Near East. Perhaps they simply accompanied the fauna as it shifted south, or perhaps they could not compete with Neandertals who were, if you recall, formidable hunters. There is nothing here to suggest modern superiority; quite the contrary. It is a quasi-historical episode that highlights one of the most interesting features of these early modern humans: despite their modern anatomy, their behavior was indistinguishable from that of their more archaic counterparts.

The Archeology of Modern Humans

All scholarly disciplines have topics that evoke passionate debate. Scholars argue back and forth for years, often decades, until evidence and theory finally settle on one widely (though perhaps not universally) held interpretation. For Paleolithic archeology, the topic that currently evokes the greatest passion is the emergence of modern behavior. This topic took on special significance once it became clear that the first anatomically modern humans left an archeological record indistinguishable in all important respects from that of Neandertals. These people were anatomically, but not behaviorally, modern. As in most debates there are two basic positions, with many hybrids lying between. On the one hand are archeologists who consider modernity to have evolved very quickly – they often use the term revolution – in the relatively recent past. Advocates of this position differ as to a specific date, but most would place this revolution at about 50,000 years ago (Klein, 2000). On the other hand, there are those archeologists who argue that modernity evolved gradually over the course of tens, or even hundreds of thousands of years (McBrearty and Brooks, 2000). These are strikingly different interpretations of the same archeological evidence. The differences hinge on what data are deemed significant, how these data are interpreted, and on preconceptions about the mechanism of change.

This may seem at first to be an issue of only parochial concern to archeologists. However, it actually bears heavily on how paleoanthropologists have viewed the evolution of the modern mind, and as such has a direct bearing on the central topic of this book. The roots of the disagreement between the "revolutionary" and "gradualist" views lie in the history of Paleolithic archeology itself, and in a peculiarity in the geography of human evolution.

The European Upper Paleolithic

Africa may be the home of all modern people, but Europe is the historic home of archeology, including the archeology of human evolution. Beginning in the nineteenth century, European archeologists excavated in the mouths of caves in deposits that contained stone tools, animal bone, and occasionally even human remains. One stratigraphic pattern presented itself again and again. The upper layers yielded a rich variety of remains: a diverse set of stone tools made on long, narrow flakes (termed *blades*), spear and harpoon heads carved out of bone and antler, beads and pendants made of shell and ivory, carved figurines of humans and animals, and even hybrid human-animal figurines (termed *therianthropes*). Examples of these are shown in figure 11.1.

Stratified immediately below these "Upper Paleolithic" remains was a very different archeological assemblage: a less diverse set of stone tools made on flakes (often Levallois), but not tools of bone or antler, no beads or pendants, and no figurines. It was this lower "Middle Paleolithic" industry that was always found in the layers with Neandertal remains (see figure 10.1, chapter 10).

The stark contrast between Upper Paleolithic and Middle Paleolithic was accentuated with the discovery and authentication of the justly famous Paleolithic painted caves found in southern France and northern Spain. The

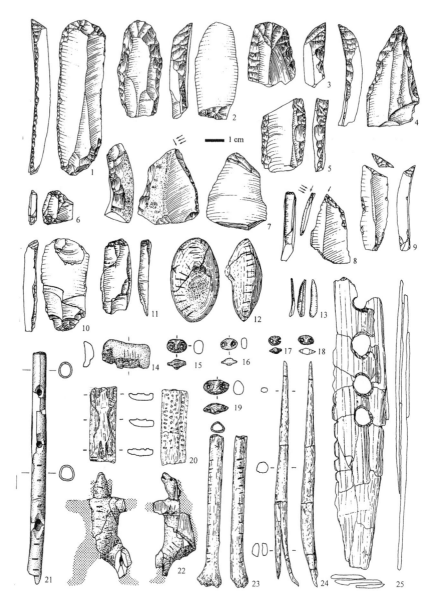

Figure 11.1   Early Upper Palaeolithic artifacts from Geißenklösterle, Germany; in addition to stone tools, there are bone points (24), ivory figurines (22), ivory beads (16), notched bones (23), and even a flute (21)

Source: Conard and Bolus, 2003. © 2003 Elsevier Science Ltd

few artifacts found in association with these spectacular paintings of animals were Upper Paleolithic in style. For the nineteenth-century archeologists, the picture was clear. Modern humans, carrying Upper Paleolithic technology, had invaded western Europe and rapidly replaced the Neandertals. These people, called Cro-Magnons for the name of the cave where their artifacts were found in southern France, were thought to be smarter and even more handsome (at least that has been the stereotype) than Neandertals, and it was they who were founders of European culture. This culture was termed *Aurignacian*, named after a small French village where the artifacts of Cro-Magnon were found. This script became instantly popular, and rapidly entered the domain of literature and cinema. The Cro-Magnons became an embodiment of the noble savage ideal: tall (actually about 170 cm or about 5 ft 9 in.), beautiful, bravely hunting dangerous beasts in order to provide for wife and children, celebrating their primitive deities, and controlling supernatural forces through paintings and carvings of animals. The Upper Paleolithic acquired the status of a Golden Age in human evolution: masters of the natural world who lived before the drudgery of farming and civilization. This image was so powerful that it came to dominate not just popular views of the Stone Age, but also scholarly views. Echoes can still be found in modern textbooks. But the long-term effects were unfortunate. The European replacement scenario became the model for modern human origins – abrupt and spectacular – and archeologists all over the world looked to find the same pattern on their own continents. Not surprisingly, they often did, whether or not the evidence warranted this interpretation. But this was the result of applying a Eurocentric perspective onto local archeological remains, a shoehorning process that often misrepresented indigenous developments. An early attempt to break away from this bias was that of Goodwin and van Riet Lowe in South Africa (1929), and it is the African perspective that continues to challenge facile conclusions drawn from European evidence (McBrearty and Brooks, 2000).

The implications of the European replacement scenario for cognitive evolution have been equally profound; indeed, it still colors the way paleoanthropologists reconstruct the evolution of the human mind. Two implications have been especially influential. First, because the most evocative products of the European Upper Paleolithic have been the painted caves and carved figurines, paleoanthropologists have come to place an inordinate emphasis on symbolism, to the degree that other candidates for components of modern cognition have been entirely ignored. Second, paleoanthropologists have come to see modern behavior as a package of activities somehow linked via this symbolic ability. But they rarely make the links explicit. When pressed, paleoanthropologists have fallen back on ad hoc justifications, such as the argument that bead production required syntactical language. Such ad hoc justifications have little real persuasive power. The argument is the wrong way around. It assumes that beads are the mark of the modern mind, and then searches for a cognitive reason; but it does not examine the basis for the assumption itself. There is a better way: start with known features of modern cognition and search for evidence of them in the paleoanthropological record.

A Small but Significant Difference

We propose that the Aurignacian culture, with its innovative set of tools made from a variety of materials, cave paintings, carved figurines of humans, animals, and therianthropes, personal ornaments of beads made from shells and ivory, and ritualized burials, developed because of an additive genetic mutation or epigenetic event that affected the neural organization of the brain. We were not the first to propose a neural mutation as the basis for modern thinking (e.g., Mithen, 1996; Klein and Edgar, 2002), although none of our predecessors in this regard specified the nature of the mutation or its specific cognitive effects. We were also not the first to propose that working memory capacity may somehow underlie modern cognition (Russell, 1996). It is important to note that there is far from a universal consensus that a dramatic cultural revolution occurred at the beginning of the Upper Paleolithic; even some European specialists prefer to see modern human cognition as a long, gradual process, and they see no need to invoke a neural mutation because they view the Aurignacian as simply the outcome of a slow, gradual cultural development (e.g., White, 2001).

A Heritable Event Leads to
Enhanced Working Memory

It is important to remember that humans are largely the product of genetic mutations and epigenetic events coupled with natural selection, from our very beginnings as single-celled organisms to the highly complex living beings we are today. Some of these genetic changes have been horrific and end life instantly or slowly. Many have been neutral and appear not to have any known consequences, and a few have given our ancient lineage a special adaptive significance. It is also important to remind our readers that language and other cognitive abilities, such as thinking, reasoning, and decision-making have millions of years of prehistory. We are therefore not speaking about a single genetic event that somehow gifted speech to *Homo sapiens* while Neandertals remained mute. We are proposing an *additive* genetic mutation or epigenetic change that acted upon a pre-existing ancient storehouse of cognitive abilities that did, nevertheless, result in dramatic behavioral advantages. We call this consequence *enhanced working memory*. As we noted in chapter 3, we built upon Baddeley's working memory model that posited a central executive with its host of executive functions, two sub-systems, phonological storage for the processing of sounds and language, the visuospatial sketchpad for the processing of visual information, and an episodic buffer that integrates and stores this integrated information long enough for the central executive to manipulate it consonant with short- and long-term goals.

The genetic hypothesis was recently strengthened in a genetic haploid typing study by Evans et al. (2005). By sequencing a gene *Microcephalin* (MCPH1) that regulates brain size, where mutations in this gene are known to cause microcephaly, they found that a genetic variant of MCPH1 increased rapidly in modern humans about 37,000 years ago (95 percent confidence interval = 14,000 years ago to 60,000 years ago). They also concluded that the gene variant appeared quickly, making it unlikely that the gene appeared through simple neutral drift. Interestingly, they could not conclude that the gene was necessarily selected through its direct effect upon neural substrate, although that remains an intriguing possibility. Equally intriguing, however, is the possibility that there was some extraordinarily advantageous phenotypic consequence of the gene upon cognition, language, or personality. Indeed, as previously noted, we believe that an additive genetic mutation similar to MCPH1 did have a phenotypic affect upon working memory capacity, and that the gene was naturally selected for and spread rapidly because of the extraordinary consequence of enhanced working memory for cognition and language.

Working memory and working memory capacity

When we refer to enhanced working memory, we are referring to an enlargement or increase in working memory capacity. Remember, working memory is simply a construct that refers to a general cognitive ability that appears to underlie or even empower a host of well-known behaviors, including attention, intelligence (general, crystal, and fluid intelligence), language acquisition and vocabulary learning, language comprehension, reading, general learning and memory processes, response inhibition, processing and thinking strategies, and theory of mind (understanding the intentions of others). It is probably not controversial to associate these abilities with modern behavior, but it is a hodgepodge of a list. How could all of these behaviors be enabled by one additive mutation, or even a few? It is necessary that we be more specific as to the possible nature of this mutation.

Phonological storage capacity and recursion

It is possible that the mutation had an additive effect on the capacity of the phonological store. Ian Tattersall, curator of the division of anthropology at the American Museum of Natural History in New York, has proposed that language was somehow the critical key to modern thinking. As we noted in chapter 3, Baddeley and his colleagues (Baddeley and Logie, 1999; Baddeley, Gathercole, and Papagno, 1998) proposed that phonological storage capacity "might reasonably be considered" to form a critical bottleneck for language production and comprehension. Recent empirical studies support this contention (e.g., Gathercole, Pickering, Ambridge, and Wearing, 2004). It is especially provocative that phonological storage capacity is significantly related to general intelligence and fluid intelligence, although to a lesser extent than some other measures of working memory capacity. Adults who have greater phonological storage capacity have also been found to do better on verbal tests of intelligence and score higher on measures of verbal fluency; they also do better on retroactive and proactive interference tasks (Kane and Engle, 2002). In children who are matched on non-verbal intelligence measures, those with greater phonological storage capacity had a larger vocabulary, produced longer utterances, and demonstrated a greater range of syntactic construction (Adams and Gathercole, 2000). Taken on the whole, these findings tend to support Baddeley's tentative contention that phonological storage capacity may have evolved primarily for the acquisition of language, and this evidence lends support for his bottleneck hypothesis. Also, critical to this hypothesis would be that phonological storage capacity must be shown to be a heritable trait, and modern twin studies have shown that phonological storage capacity is a highly heritable, additive genetic trait (Ando, Ono, and Wright, 2002; Rijsdijk, Vernon, and Boomsma, 2002).

If phonological storage capacity did play some role in modern thinking because of its relationship to language, what might be the specific nature of its role? Many linguists have touted recursion as the key to modern language (Hauser et al., 2002; Reuland, 2005). Recursion is the grammatical rule that produces certain kinds of embedding: "I know that Harry knows Hermione" is a recursive phrase; "Harry knows Hermione" is a phrase that is the object of "I know." It is embedded. "I know that Harry knows that Hermione uses magic" adds another level of embedding. One could theoretically continue this embedding forever, using the same rule. Note that the embedding produced by "that" does not change, but the load on attention surely does. One must somehow keep all of the "thats" and their entailed relations in mind in order to understand the sentence. This is why we cannot practically continue embedding forever; we simply lose track of the relationships. Of course, attention capacity is the *sine qua non* of working memory. The role of working memory is actually a bit more complex than simple attention. The phonological storage subsystem of working memory is the place where utterances are formed and held until spoken or understood, and it includes a subvocal rehearsal mechanism that keeps sequences of words activated. But it may not itself make sense of the embedding relationships, which likely taps into the central executive. However it is done, working memory plays an important role in deploying and receiving the words and syntax of language. Any enhancement of working memory capacity would have increased the potential complexity of utterances, and increased the capacity of the system to carry information. Aboitiz, Garcia, Bosman, and Brunetti (2006) have noted that phonological storage capacity represents a short-term memory ensemble that also allows more complex memories. They also hypothesized that phonological storage capacity allows multiple items to be combinatorially manipulated, and they noted that this process would demand significant working memory resources, which we believe is the equivalent of our enhanced working memory.

If recursion is a key to modern language and modern thinking, and fully recursive abilities do require greater working memory capacity, then what is it about recursion that allows it to accomplish its magic? Hauser et al. did not specifically address the natural selection advantages of recursion, other than noting that it may have evolved for reasons other than language and offering a vague statement that recursion offers "limitless expressive power." But we think that the evolutionary advantage of recursion is fairly simple and straightforward: it enables longer, and more complex utterances, and longer and more complex utterances make for more complex plans and interactions. How exactly would expanded phonological storage capacity allow creative, flexible thinking? We postulate that enhanced working memory, by way of expanded phonological storage capacity, may have allowed the speaker to "hold in mind" a much greater number of options, and, as such, given the speaker a greater range of behavioral flexibility and even creativity. We previously hypothesized (Coolidge and Wynn, 2005) that reflection upon a greater number of options allows the organism not only a choice among those options, perhaps based on previous successes or failures of each option, but also to choose a future option or actively create an alternative plan of action. We also noted in chapter 3 that the evolution of culture may have been aided by "thought experiments." Shepard (1997), Dawkins (1989), and others have proposed that simulating future outcomes in one's mind not only increases the probability of choosing a successful strategy but also saves one from the inherent dangers of actual trial and error. Remembering to institute a plan of action has been called *prospective memory*, while creating alternatives for future actions has been called *constructive episodic simulation* (e.g., Schacter and Addis, 2007).

To summarize our argument thus far, recursion is said to be the hallmark of modern language. There is empirical evidence that recursion not only requires greater working memory capacity but also greater phonological storage capacity. One possibility, then, is that an additive genetic neural mutation or epigenetic event enhanced phonological storage capacity. The sequela of the latter change may have allowed recursive and canonical utterances. For an example of a recursive declarative statement, see figure 11.2.

Other possibilities

But there are other possibilities. An increase in phonological storage capacity could have aided cross-modal thinking. Hermer-Velasquez and Spelke (1996) found that young, pre-linguistic children rely highly on geometric information when disoriented in a room. It seems they are not capable of integrating geometrical and non-geometrical information when searching for a hidden object. Success in the task is not dependent on IQ, age, or

"I said I'm sorry."

Figure 11.2   An example of a recursive statement. © The New Yorker Collection 2005 Mick Stevens from cartoonbank.com. All Rights Reserved

vocabulary size. The only successful predictor was the conjoint use of spatial vocabulary with non-geometric information in a single thought or memory (e.g., it's to the right of the blue one). Hermer-Velasquez, Spelke, and Katsnelson (1999) were also able to replicate this finding in adults in a related but different task.

Recently, Baddeley (2007) has acknowledged that words held in the phonological store may enhance the processing potential of the central executive itself, an interpretation that jives well with Hermer's and Spelke's results. As a whole, these findings support Carruthers's (2002) contention that language serves as the vehicle of inter-modular (verbal-visuospatial) thinking, and we contend that increased phonological storage may have allowed the "tagging" of visuospatial information, making it easier to memorize, recall, and communicate this information with others. Gathercole et al. (2000) found that increases in memory capacity as children grow older may be due to increased rates of rehearsal (articulatory processing). In younger children (less than 7 years), where spontaneous rehearsal is rare, the phonological loop may consist only of the phonological store. Older children not only rely on articulation as a storage mechanism but they also recode visual inputs into a phonological form through the articulatory processor.

However, granting the phonological store the power of cross-modal thinking does muddy Baddeley's otherwise elegant model. Cross-modal integration is supposed to be the province of the central executive via simultaneous storage in the episodic buffer. So, a second hypothesis is that the additive mutation or epigenetic event enhanced not the phonological store, but the episodic buffer. In essence, this would be an enhancement of the amount, variety, or even the complexity of information that could be held in attention for processing.

Speech acts

There is yet another possibility: that it may not necessarily be recursion or the length of an utterance, per se, that were evolutionarily advantageous, but their effect upon the nature of speech acts or the pragmatics of speech. A speech act refers to the act that is done or performed by speaking (e.g., Adams, 2002). There is far from a general consensus on a single taxonomy; speech-act analyses typically measure exclamatives (shouts of pain, pleasure, or surprise), imperatives (commands), declaratives (statements of fact, greetings, denials), interrogatives (questions or requests), and subjunctives (expresses subjective statements, such as wishes, possibilities, and statements that are contrary to facts). It should also be noted that numerous subsequent and rival systems have emerged for the analysis of speech acts (see Adams, 2002; Cruse, 2000; Levinson, 2000). Interestingly, the first four of these speech acts can be expressed by simple or even single morphemic structures: exclamations (ouch!), imperatives (move!), declaratives (nice!), and interrogatives (where?), and, thus, recursion does not appear to be a necessary condition for those speech acts. However, the subjunctive mode of speech, "what if" thinking, does appear to require recursion or, at the very least, longer canonical utterances. The conundrum here is that subjunctive grammatical constructions (e.g., "Were I king") may act to reduce the load on phonological storage, but we suspect that such grammatical short cuts could only have arisen if a subjunctive mode of expression was already in place and important to communication. Thus, recursion may have allowed the formation and release of subjunctive thinking but recursion, in turn, required expanded phonological storage capacity and greater working memory capacity.

The episodic buffer and episodic memory

There is much less empirical knowledge about Baddeley's most recent (2000; 2007) addition to his model than there is for the central executive and its two main subsystems. However, Baddeley's concept of episodic buffer has many similarities to cognitive psychologist Endel Tulving's construct of episodic memory, and the overlap between the two concepts invites an evolutionary hypothesis that links them. As we discussed in chapter 3, in 1972 Tulving proposed that there should be two subtypes of *declarative memories*, the traditional *semantic memories* for facts and simple details, and *episodic memories*, defined by Tulving as a coherent, story-like reminiscence for an event in time and place. We think another important feature of episodic memories is that the more "memorable" of these memories very often have a strong emotional valence attached to them. In fact, we think that the emotional valence itself is what causes the memory to be learned so easily and to persist so well over time (but that is another story). Episodic memory has also been labeled *personal memory* or *autobiographical memory*. We also noted earlier that an episodic memory will, of course, include semantic details, but its recall and subjective experience will be psychologically and neurologically different from the recall of the semantic components alone. We reiterate what we stated in chapter 3. Tulving's concept of episodic memory is replete with *short-term* memory implications, as well as long-term memory traces, even if he did not explicitly state as such. We think that Tulving's concept of episodic memory is heavily reliant on Baddeley's episodic buffer. This is entirely in keeping with Baddeley's understanding of the episodic buffer, which he considers to be the primary route through which the central executive accesses long-term memories (Baddeley, 2007). It is in the episodic buffer that the elements of an episodic memory are assembled in attention, drawing on long-term memory traces, images from the visuospatial memory, and descriptive scripts actualized in the phonological store.

So how could the episodic buffer be relevant to our evolutionary concept of enhanced working memory? There is a strong adaptive value in the ability to simulate the future, with potential consequences for innovation and creativity. In this second proposed scenario for the nature of enhanced working memory (besides increased phonological storage capacity), perhaps, the additive genetic mutation or epigenetic event affected the episodic buffer. Also in chapter 3, we noted that Tulving (2002) proposed that the ability to simulate and contemplate future scenarios has been the driving force in the evolution of episodic memory. Through the recall of episodic memories, humans become mentally aware that time is subjective, and by way of recall of the past and anticipation of the future, they can travel through time. Tulving used the term *autonoesis* to refer to the ability, unique to humans, of a special kind of consciousness that allows individuals to become aware of the subjective time in which past events have happened and in which future events might occur or be anticipated to occur. As noted previously, this anticipation and simulation of future events has been labeled constructive episodic simulation.

In summary, our proposed additive genetic mutation or epigenetic event may have affected the episodic buffer, giving an awareness of the subjectivity of time and permitting the realization that one can travel through time. It may have also allowed the simulation of various future events that draws upon past events and flexibly rearranges particular elements of the past to simulate the future. And, as we noted earlier in this chapter, our present approach is to start with known features of modern cognition and search for evidence of them in the paleoanthropological record, rather than the reverse. In this regard, we offer what we think is a strong case for autonoetic thinking in the Upper Paleolithic.

The Archeology of Executive Functions and Enhanced Working Memory

We could simply conclude at this point that enhanced working memory accompanied the evolution of anatomically modern humans, reasoning that if overall brain size and shape were modern, cognition must have been modern as well. There are two sound reasons for eschewing this simple solution. First, the parietal hypertrophy that produced modern brain shape cannot be easily linked to enhanced working memory; yes, brain imaging and neuropsychology indicate that working memory relies on a neural network with extensions to parietal and temporal lobes, but it is not at all clear how this could account for parietal expansion. Second, the archeological signature produced by the first anatomically modern humans bears no hallmarks of enhanced working memory; indeed, it is largely indistinguishable from that of Neandertals (though there are a few provocative bits we will discuss later). So, even though the first anatomically modern humans looked modern, they did not behave in a modern fashion.

Similarly, we could simply conclude, following numerous precedents, that the complex of traits associated with the European Upper Paleolithic was the signature of enhanced working memory, and that an understanding of the Upper Paleolithic would yield an understanding of the evolution of modern cognition. But this is also too simple, and again for two reasons. First, the traits that define the Upper Paleolithic were not defined with explicit attention to cognition, let alone working memory. As we have seen, the complex of Upper Paleolithic traits is largely a historical accident. They bear no necessary relation to cognition whatsoever. Second, the individual elements of the Upper Paleolithic did not in fact evolve as a package, a fact clearly demonstrated by the African archeological record, and a variety of separate evolutionary accounts will probably be necessary to explain them all.

We advocate a more explicit archeological approach. This entails several steps. First, it is necessary to identify specific human activities that require modern working memory. Second, one must then define specific archeological attributes that reliably document the presence of these activities in the prehistoric record. Third, one must apply a strict standard of parsimony when searching the archeological record for these attributes. If a simpler set of activities can explain the archeological signature, these must be given priority. Yes, this runs a real risk of under-assessing prehistoric ability, but it is the only logical way to proceed. Finally, we must risk being pedantic and emphasize an important point: the archeological record does not preserve working memory per se. It does, however, preserve some of the actions organized by executive functions, which, as we have argued, are largely enabled by working memory.

When we take an explicitly archeological approach a picture of the evolution of modern cognition emerges that does not match up well with the traditional story, and in which modern cognition enters only very late.

Technology

Documenting modern executive functions and working memory through technology is unexpectedly frustrating. Tool-making and tool-using are arguably the domains of human activity that leave the clearest archeological signatures; archeologists have literally millions of ceramic pots, some dating back 10,000 years, and millions of stone tools, some dating back 2,600,000 years. Moreover, many people in the modern world would rank technological accomplishments at the apogee of human achievement – iPhones, hybrid automobiles, the Internet, etc., would appear to mark the triumph of the modern mind. Yet the plain fact of the matter is that the vast majority of tool-related activities (but luckily not all) fail to tap into the powerful forces of executive functions and enhanced working memory. Instead, they tap into a different and much older cognitive ability, that of procedural memory and expert cognition. Perhaps the clearest way to appreciate the accuracy of this assertion is to examine how people learn technical activities. One does not learn tool use by reading books, or via the effortful reflection of working memory. One learns tool use and tool-making through apprenticeships – through observation, repetition, and failure. Tool use and tool-making rely, quite literally, on hands-on learning, even in today's modern technologies (Keller and Keller, 1996). This is the only way to acquire the necessary motor and procedural memories that are the essence of technical expertise. Yes, there are engineers who design new technologies, and in doing so use their executive functions, but even here the process relies heavily on well-learned algorithms and long-established procedures. When working memory reflects upon the content of procedures, true innovation can result, but it is remarkable how unusual innovation was in human history. It is one of the things we can look for in the archeological record but, as we shall see, innovation has only very, very recently become a force in human technology. The vast majority of tools from the long history of technology document only the evolution of procedural cognition and expertise. The "only" in the previous sentence is of course misleading. The "expert" strategy was at the core of early hominin cognitive and evolutionary success. It is ours still, and powers many of our most cherished achievements in sport, music, and art; we should not underestimate its importance in modern life. But it does not often engage the resources of executive functions and working memory.

Luckily, technology is not entirely mute. Some tools and technology do implicate executive functions and working memory, mostly via their role in contingency and long-range planning. One obvious example that has at least modest antiquity is the alloying of metals, which requires the combining, at high temperature, of two or more metals, each of which must be acquired from a different source, and brought together at one place. It is the organization of raw material supply that implicates executive functions. Bronze is the earliest example. Copper Age smiths in southeastern Europe began adding tin and arsenic to their smelted copper about 5,000 years ago, and the requirements of bronze smelting led to the

Figure 11.3 A fish weir, based on ethnographic examples from the north-west coast of North America; such facilities require long-range planning and delayed gratification, both features of modern executive functions

establishment and maintenance of trading networks that stretched across the European continent. The system clearly implicates executive functions and enhanced working memory, and indeed there are many other technical signatures of executive functions in the late Neolithic that corroborate such an assessment. But then, few scholars would balk at granting modern cognitive abilities to people who lived only 5,000 years ago.

Earlier technical evidence for executive functions is best seen in the evidence for facilities, a term that anthropologists apply to fixed structures used to capture energy or perform tasks (Oswalt, 1976). If a tool, or set of tools, was designed to work remotely in time or space, especially in the absence of an active human operator, then this would be good evidence for the long-range planning of executive functions. The best archeological examples are traps and fish weirs (a kind of dam used to funnel fish; see figure 11.3). Because most of these are made of perishable materials such as wood and fiber, they do not preserve well. There are good examples

Figure 11.4   Inuit harpoon set; sets of interrelated gear require extensive downtime to produce and maintain; Bleed has termed systems "reliable" weapons; they are a mark of modern executive functions

that date back to the European Mesolithic (*c.*9,000 years ago) and the North American Archaic period (a bit more recent). In the Middle East hunters used long, converging lines of boulders, known as desert kites, to funnel gazelle into killing zones. The oldest of these date back to perhaps 12,000 years ago.

It is harder to extend executive function-based technologies earlier than this. The best possible example is the use of harpoons. A harpoon is a projectile with a detachable head that is attached by a line to a float or to the original shaft. It is a complex set of separate tools that works together as a system for capturing prey. They imply executive functions because they must be produced well in advance, and carefully maintained. Prehistoric Inuit developed the best-known examples, which were used for hunting seals (see figure 11.4). Archeologists can trace them back at least 4,000 years in arctic sites. But there are much earlier examples. Late Upper Paleolithic hunters in France and Spain also made harpoons, carving the barbed heads out of antler, and launching the projectiles with spear throwers. These date back perhaps 17,000 years (see figure 11.5).

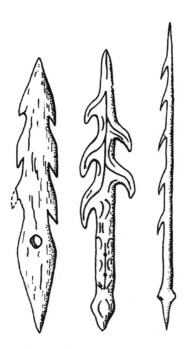

Figure 11.5   Late Upper Paleolithic (*c.*17,000 BP) barbed harpoon heads that were probably components in reliable tool sets

Earlier than this, there are no technologies that would have required modern executive functions and enhanced working memory. Yes, there were projectiles, some as old as 400,000 if the Schöningen spears were thrown, but the simple use or even manufacture of a projectile does not require long-range contingency planning.

Our final technological signature is innovation itself. The active invention of new tools and technologies relies heavily on the kinds of thought experiment and analogical reasoning that are the stuff of executive functions (Shepard, 1997), and in fact is largely responsible for or modern engineering successes. The problem is identifying active innovation in prehistory; active innovation via executive function problem-solving is not the only source of new technologies or procedures. Serendipitous discovery and recognition – the accidental production of useful mistakes – is another source of new procedures, and one that would tap into the kinds of procedural knowledge that were paramount for most of human evolution. This is the most likely source for the few inventions that did occur over the mind-numbingly vast ages of the Lower and Middle Paleolithics. Distinguishing this source of novelty from the active innovation of executive functions may well be impossible. Our only possible avenue is in rates of change. If we can recognize a significant change in the rate at which new technologies appeared this would be provocative evidence for the advent of active innovation.

Once again there is abundant evidence for rapid change over the last 5,000 years; it is the earlier evidence that is harder to document. One good example occurred on the Plains of North America about 11,500 years ago. Stone Age hunters invented a projectile system that included spear throwers, spear shafts with detachable foreshafts, and a sophisticated stone projectile point known as Clovis. These hunters then adjusted this technology, producing a rapidly changing set of newer projectile styles, a sequence in which few styles survived for more than a generation or two. What makes this example even more compelling is that these "Paleoindian" hunters were among the earliest inhabitants of a previously unoccupied continent, making it impossible to attribute the rapid innovation rate to a large population. Again, earlier examples are not as convincing. In the European Upper Paleolithic, bone and antler projectile styles, including overall shape and method of attachment, did change much more rapidly than earlier Neandertal tools, but the scale is over thousands of years, not the hundreds of the Paleoindian example. Toward the end of the Upper Paleolithic, the pace of change did pick up, but interpretation is clouded by an increase in population that resulted from demographic concentration caused by the Late Glacial Maximum. Here, again, we can confidently find evidence back perhaps 12,000 years, and less confidently back 30,000 years.

This late technological signature for executive functions is one of the surprises of the archeological record. Given our modern obsession with technological solutions, one might expect that tools were always on the forefront of human evolution. But the archeological evidence suggests otherwise.

Subsistence

The evidence for what people ate and how they acquired it parallels that of technology. The vast majority of modern people live by agriculture in all of its guises, and all agriculture relies on executive functions. Agriculturalists (including pastoralists) manage their food supply, which requires the contingency planning and response inhibition of executive functions. It would not do to eat one's seed corn, or eat one's milk cow, even in times of want. Effective agriculture entails plans of action, often ritualized, that extend years in advance – crop rotations, transhumance, irrigation, and so on. It seems uncontroversial to grant executive functions to all prehistoric agri-culturalists, which again extends the record back about 10,000 years.

What is not as obvious is that the few hunters and gatherers surviving today also manage their food supply. Their most common technique is scheduling – timing the exploitation of a plant or animal in a way that maximizes its usefulness without detracting from its future availability. Hunters and gatherers also manipulate environments to their advantage. Groups of native Australians regularly burn off sections of landscape in order to elicit a second green-up of grass, which in turn attracts herbivores. But they do not randomly set range fires; instead, they carefully select tracts of land to burn, and rotate the chosen patches over a cycle of years (Lewis, 1982). This kind of hunting and gathering relies on the same planning abilities as agriculture, and indeed is arguably a prerequisite (and antecedent) for the origin of agriculture itself.

Archeological evidence for this kind of managed foraging is, then, a potential marker for modern executive functions. And all over the world there is evidence for this kind of managed foraging, going back at least 10,000 years. An especially good archeological example is that of Abu Hureyra, a village on the Euphrates River in Syria (Moore et al., 2000). Here, 12,000 years ago, prehistoric people hunted gazelle, and gathered a wide range of plants, including many wild grasses. By shifting the focus of their foraging on a seasonal basis they were able to live in the same place year-round. But an even better indicator of managed foraging was their response to crisis. About 11,000 years ago the climate suddenly cooled and became drier, and many of the grasses on which they depended shifted away from the vicinity of the site. The people's response was to begin cul-tivating one of them, rye. Here we not only have the management abilities associated with executive functions; we also have innovation, a signature of enhanced working memory.

Extending managed foraging back further in time is problematic. Not all forms of hunting and gathering qualify. We have good archeological evidence for specialized slaughter of single species of animal going back tens of thousands of years, but unless we can demonstrate that this hunt-ing was a component of a managed system, with year-round scheduled resource acquisition, we can explain such specializing more parsimoniously via tactical hunting. There are, nevertheless, a few examples older than 12,000 years that may qualify as managed. The first were the Late Upper Paleolithic reindeer hunters of northern Spain and southern France. Faunal remains from archeological sites indicate that these people used a form of mass killing in the autumn, probably during the seasonal migrations of herds, and a different tactic of selective hunting of individual animals during summer (Straus, 1996). This suggests a tightly scheduled cycle, and perhaps even an eye toward herd maintenance, and extends our examples back to 18,000 years ago. And, perhaps not coincidentally, these are the same people who manufactured the harpoons discussed earlier. A more provocative case comes from Niah Cave in Borneo. Pollen evidence indicates extensive burning (pollen of species that invade after burns), more burning than one would expect naturally in this tropical environment. Perhaps the Niah hunters used scheduled burning, much as modern Australians do. Dates for Niah are not very precise, but this burning occurred sometime between 42,000 and 28,000 years ago (Barker et al., 2007).

The range of dates for managed foraging is remarkably similar to those for modern technology: strong evidence back to 12,000 years or so, and then a very rapid fade as we look farther back in time. This may be a coincidence, or it may reflect the nature of preservation. But it may also reflect the very recent acquisition of modern executive functions and working memory, and their deployment in technology and foraging.

Colonization

People colonized Australia at least 40,000 years ago (Thorne et al., 1999; Bowler and Magee, 2000), an event that required them to sail over the horizon in boats, with spouses and dogs (and rats as tag-alongs) (Davidson and Noble, 1992). Indeed, it is very tempting to cite this achievement as the earliest evidence for enhanced working memory, much as Klein, Davidson, and Noble, and others have used it as evidence for symbolic language and modern behavior in general. There are several cognitive challenges inherent in over-the-horizon colonization. First is the knowledge that the target was even there. Either the potential colonists stumbled across the knowledge serendipitously while doing something else (e.g., fishing from boats, which itself has interesting implications) or by reasoning from indexical indications (birds, smoke columns). As it is probable that the latter ability had been in place since *Homo erectus*, the answer to "how did they know?" does not include executive functions as a requirement. Second, such colonization was a group effort that must have included both sexes. This would have required some form of communication, and indeed Davidson and Noble have used the colonization of the Sahul (Australia and New Guinea) as evidence for modern language. But communication of intent may just be possible without modern language. Moreover, group effort was almost certainly a component of earlier hominin activities (e.g., hunting), and here again would not require modern executive functions. Third, colonization would have required planning over distance and time, in very much the same vane as managed foraging, and this would appear to have required modern executive functions.

However, we must admit to lingering doubt. Our hesitation in trumpeting this colonization event as the earliest evidence for enhanced working memory stems from our ignorance of just how the colonization occurred. It is just possible that such a feat could have been achieved through the application of expertise, or, perhaps even more likely, expertise "gone wrong," as when a short-range inter-island sea voyage was blown far off course. If we had good evidence for systematic over-the-horizon colonization, in the guise of voyages to multiple sea islands, then an ascription of the modern executive functions would be easily supportable. However, such evidence does not emerge until after 30,000 with evidence for the settling of islands off the New Guinea coast (e.g., the island of Buka) (Rabett and Barker, 2007).

Abstract images and algorithmic devices

Earlier, we discussed how evidence for the use of symbols does not also constitute evidence for modern executive functions or working memory; indeed, simple symbolism has a pedigree going back at least to the pigment use at Twin Rivers, some 300,000 years ago. There are, however, certain kinds of symbols that do imply the use of an enhanced working memory capacity: symbols, usually images, that represent abstract or autonoetic concepts.

Figure 11.6 is a drawing of arguably the most provocative artifact produced in the course of the European Upper Paleolithic, the Hohlenstein-Stadel figurine. It is the image of lion-headed person, carved out of mammoth ivory, 30 cm in height (about 12 inches). It is about 32,000 years old (Hahn, 1986). The artisan of this figurine either shared in, or conceived

Figure 11.6   The Hohlenstein-Stadel figurine; this evocative mammoth ivory carving is evidence for abstract thinking in which two very different concepts, in this case lion and person, are merged in attention

independently, an abstract concept that combined the characteristics of a human with those of a dangerous beast, and this merging must have first occurred in someone's working memory. We know from the evolutionary psychological and cognitive anthropological literature that humans have a powerful, relatively encapsulated, ability to recognize, distinguish, and classify living organisms, an ability often termed "folk biology" (Medin and Atran, 2004). All humans classify animals and plants in a similar way, and the perceptual sensitivity to living things appears in very young infants. Our ability to detect and classify organisms rapidly, even pre-attentively, has an obvious evolutionary utility, and is undoubtedly very old. Abstract beasts are not part of it. To imagine the Hohlenstein-Stadel Löwenmensch (German for *lion-man*) someone had to access the category of lion from folk biology, hold it in attention, and combine it with an equally old and encapsulated category, that of person. This is analogical reasoning, and it is the stuff of modern, enhanced working memory and executive functions. Note that it is not the image, per se, but the abstract concept behind it that argues for modern executive functions and working memory. A simple figurine of a lion, or a human, would not carry such weight.

Conard (Conard and Bolus, 2003) has reported the discovery of three other figurines carved from mammoth ivory at Hohle Fels Cave in the Swabian Jura of south-western Germany, which also provides evidence for such figurative art more than 30,000 years ago. One of the figurines is similar to the Hohlenstein-Stadel *Löwenmensch*, although less than one-tenth its height (about 2.6 cm or barely 1 inch). Conard suggested that this second *Löwenmensch* lends support to the hypothesis that Aurignacian people may have practiced shamanism, and he argued it should be considered strong evidence for fully symbolic communication and cultural modernity. These Löwenmensch firmly establish modern executive functions and working memory at 32,000 years ago. But there are earlier carved objects about which claims of modernity have also been made, so perhaps 32,000 years ago is too cautious.

Similarly provocative evidence comes from burial at the Russian site of Sungir, which dates back to about 27,000 years ago. One of the graves contained two individuals, a young female about 8 to 10 years old, and a young male about 12 to 14 years old. They were buried simultaneously in a double grave. The two children were placed head to head, and both were covered with beaded ornaments. The boy was covered with 4,903 beads in strands. Around his waist was a belt decorated with 250 canine teeth of polar foxes. His chest was adorned with an ivory animal-shaped pendant. He had an ivory pin near his throat, presumably a closure device for clothing. Near his left shoulder, there was an ivory sculpture of a mammoth. Also, on his left side, there was a polished human femur that was packed with red ochre. On his right side, there was a large mammoth ivory spear, with a carved ivory disk nearby. The girl was buried with 5,274 beads of similar size to the boy's. She also had a beaded cap and ivory pin near her throat, but no fox teeth and no pendant on her chest. On each of her sides, there were smaller mammoth ivory spears, and two antler batons decorated with drilled dots. Like the boy, her grave also contained three ivory disks with a center hole and lattice patterns.

There are a number of implications of the Sungir burials. Producing the 10,177 beads adorning the two children would itself have taken thousands of hours. The burials have important implications for social complexity, but this is not the most interesting implication when it comes to working memory. Instead, one of the grave goods has significant implications for the use of the episodic buffer and autonoesis. Perhaps you will be surprised that it is not the impressive array of beads that we find compelling; it is the ivory spears.

Mammoth ivory makes lousy spears for hunting. It is far too soft and fragile, particularly for piercing tough animal hides. These spears were almost certainly ornamental, especially the girl's, because they were apparently fashioned to be appropriately smaller than the boy's and more appropriate to her smaller stature. They were not designed for real hunting or protection; instead they were designed for hunting or protection in the afterlife. Burial goods, in general, are thought to be indicative of some awareness of a life or experience after death. To us, these ornamental Sungir spears suggests an autonoetic awareness, that is, a recognition that life after death might be phenomenologically different from one's present life experience. In other words, if the makers of the spears viewed life after death as the same experience as life in their present state, then the spears would have been more likely to be of hard stone and fire-hardened woods. Indeed, the Schöningen hunting spears of 400,000 years ago had tips that were fire-hardened. Thus, we see the Sungir burials as highly suggestive of autonoetic awareness and completely consonant with our concept of enhanced working memory.

Autonoetic thinking may also have some unintended consequences. Suddendorf and Corballis (2007) noted that episodic memories and mental time travel can induce a new kind of "mental stress," that is, the anticipation of negative future outcomes, including death anxiety. Indeed, with burgeoning episodic memory capabilities, we might recall sorrowful past events, inducing depression and anticipate negative future outcomes, inducing anxiety. The subjective awareness and feelings associated with these experiences and constructions might even serve as the inchoate beginnings of psychopathology. Given the great prevalence of these two disorders in present-day psychopathology, depression and anxiety have been labeled the common colds of the variety of mental disturbances (e.g., Davidson, Neale, and Kring, 2004).

Corroboration of the timing of abstract and autonoetic concepts comes from a set of seemingly enigmatic objects excavated from other Upper Paleolithic sites. These are rods or plaques of bone, usually only a few inches in maximum dimension, on which Upper Paleolithic people carved or engraved sets of lines and dots (figure 11.7). In the 1970s and 1980s, Alexander Marshack made a controversial argument that these were lunar calendars, based largely on microscopic examination of the marks themselves. More recently, Francesco d'Errico has also made a detailed

Figure 11.7 The Lartet plaque (*c.*28,000 BP); in this case the notches and lines were produced by different tools at different times; archeologists believe that such objects were devices used to keep track of something, and were the first calculating devices

examination and has reached a similar, if less romantic, conclusion. These scholars were able to demonstrate that the dots and slashes were produced by different engraving tools, probably at different times. D'Errico concluded that the Upper Paleolithic people used them as "external memory devices," that is, they were recording something. We clearly do not know what they were recording; it could have been game, or menstrual cycles, or even, as Marshack initially proposed, days. *What* they were recording is not important for us; *that* they were recording something is.

The cognitive implications of such recording devices are very revealing. First, the marks themselves are a kind of arbitrary, symbolic representation of a thing or event. At a minimum they represent a kind of one-to-one correspondence that is the basis for numeracy. But, as interesting as these are, they are not the most revealing cognitive ability. The use of such a recording device is the use of an algorithm. Algorithms are sets of rules (e.g., arithmetic) that help us solve problems, and one way they do this is by easing the load on working memory. Instead of reasoning through arithmetic relations every time one uses numbers, one can simply hold a rule, e.g., the commutative rule, in attention, freeing up the remaining working memory capacity to handle content. And if the algorithm is an external device, say an abacus, then even more working memory capacity is freed (with an abacus, much of the work of computation is actually shifted to expert cognition). But some working memory capacity is still required to maintain the rules, or the device, in attention, so algorithmic devices such as the Lartet plaque both require and enhance working memory capacity. Such mechanical aids are common in the modern world, but the very earliest we see them is with the Upper Paleolithic of Europe; the Lartet plaque is at most 28,000 years old.

The Wrench in the Monkey Works

Earlier, we reviewed the extensive and growing literature that stresses the important role of the frontal lobes and prefrontal cortices for the functions of the central executive and episodic buffer. Indeed, a near myth has been perpetuated that frontal lobes have been solely responsible for the creation of the modern mind (e.g., Goldberg, 2002). Part of this myth involves the notion that frontal lobe enlargement and widening have been unique to *Homo sapiens*. Semendeferi et al. (2001) have shown through neuroimaging that human frontal lobe cortices are not larger than many other great apes, at least in terms of relative size of the frontal cortices to non-frontal cortices. It may be surmised, however, that relative size may not be as important as the interconnectivity of human frontal lobes to cortical areas and subcortical structures and the unique cytoarchitecture of the human frontal lobes with regard to other primates. Note that the neuroimaging methods of Semendeferi et al. would not detect these two latter characteristics of human frontal lobes.

It would certainly be a boon to our hypothesis of the critical role of frontal and prefrontal cortices to working memory functions and capacity if there was evidence for some unique allometric trajectory for the frontal lobes of Upper Paleolithic *Homo sapiens*, especially when compared to Neandertals. However, a metaphoric wrench was thrown into the monkey works of our hypothesis by the work of Italian paleoneurologist Emiliano Bruner. He and his colleagues (Bruner, 2004; Bruner, Manzi, and Arsuaga, 2003) performed two- and three-dimensional allometric analyses of the fossil crania of a wide variety of hominins including *Homo erectus*, Neandertals, and anatomically modern humans. Their statistical analyses demonstrated a frontal lobe stasis particularly between Neandertals and modern *Homo sapiens*. Certainly, the evolution of the entire genus *Homo* has been associated with greater cranial capacity, increasing encephalization, and frontal widening; however, Bruner proposed two different allometric trajectories in the evolution of these types of human brains. One trajectory suggests that, as cranial capacity increased, the parietal areas underwent a shortening and flattening. Occipital lobes, in general, have shown a steady reduction in the evolution of humans, and a change from a posterior location behind the parietal lobes to a more advanced location inferior to the parietal lobes. The allometric trajectory that best distinguished anatomically modern *Homo sapiens* and Neandertals was a tendency towards klinorhynchy or globularity in modern humans. Bruner (2004) speculated that the sequela of globularity was probably greater interconnectivity between the major lobes of the brain and an expansion of the parietal lobes. Bruner also cited the work of Konrad Lorenz (1973), who saw spatial orientation and the potential to create an "imagined space" within the central nervous system as the basis for all conceptual thinking and language. Bruner further speculated that considering the role of the parietal lobes in visuospatial integration and their role in making this information accessible to language, and, thus, to the recognition and communication of the external environment, this parietal lobe expansion may be directly related to the evolution of such an inner reality.

Bruner's (in press) most recent analysis of the specific nature of the parietal lobe hypertrophy in modern human brains may be even more provocative. In his preliminary analysis of just three endocasts – *Homo erectus* (*sensu latu*), dating to about 500,000 years ago, Neandertal (from La Chapelle-aux-Saints), and *Homo sapiens* (from northern Italy, dating to about 8,000 years ago) – he found that the volumetric changes were the greatest for the superior regions of parietal lobes in *Homo sapiens*, particularly the area superior to the supramarginal and angular gyri, that is, the upper parietal lobe, intraparietal sulcus, and the upper convolutions of the lower parietal lobe. The center of this enlargement appeared to him particularly evident in the intraparietal sulcus (see figure 2.2, chapter 2, the region superior to Broadmann's area 7). The intraparietal sulcus is particularly of interest because it has been found to be important in both symbolic numerical processing (Cantlon, Brannon, Carter, and

Pelphrey, 2006) and interpreting the actions, intentions, and goals of others (e.g., Hamilton and Grafton, 2006).

There are caveats to Bruner's research. First, Bruner's work should be cross-validated with a bigger sample and a wider range of fossil hominins. However, one interesting aspect of Bruner's past and present work is that it may even provide evidence that it is the older of the two working memory subsystems, the visuospatial sketchpad that has been crucial to the development of modern thinking, or it may have served as a kind of bottleneck to modern thinking. Furthermore, it is still important to note that working memory is a multi-component system, and, as such, it may be futile to try to isolate a component as singularly critical. Nonetheless, we think the working memory will continue to be highly heuristic in the explication of ancient and modern thinking.

Blombos Cave and the Enigma of Early Anatomically Modern Humans

The archeological evidence for modern working memory capacity presents us with a surprisingly shallow time depth; indeed, nothing convincing (cognitively valid and archeologically credible) clearly antedates the 32,000 years ago date for the Hohlenstein-Stadel and Hohle Fels figurines. This date partially reflects the serendipity of discovery. However, several lines of evidence – technology, subsistence, abstract symbols – have yielded dates that are roughly comparable. The parsimonious interpretation is that modern executive functions did not emerge much earlier than 32,000 years ago. This is at least 150,000 years after the earliest anatomically modern humans, one of whose derived features was a non-allometric expansion of the parietal cortex. Must we conclude that this expansion, beyond what one would expect from an overall increase in size, had no behavioral consequences? The answer, we believe, lies not in working memory per se, but in another cognitive domain, that of concept formation.

Blombos Cave is a 77,000-year-old site on the southern coast of South Africa. Here Christopher Henshilwood has excavated a range of artifacts that have effectively debunked the primacy of Europe, and which he has used to argue for the presence of fully modern behavior at this early date. The crucial artifacts are a set of bone points, two engraved bones, a piece of ochre with an engraved pattern, and shell beads. At first consideration, these would seem to rival the products of Upper Paleolithic people who lived 45,000 years later; art and ornaments are hallmarks of the Upper Paleolithic. But recall that the hallmarks of the Upper Paleolithic were not defined with cognition in mind. Recall also that engravings and ornaments do not require modern working memory capacity. If the engravings included sequential marking with different tools at different times, they would qualify as algorithmic devices, but they do not. Simple geometric engraving engages motor procedures, and visual-spatial guidance, but does not require enhanced working memory (Hodgson, 2000; Hodgson and Helvenston, 2006). The shell beads are perhaps the most provocative. See figure 11.8. D'Errico has suggested that the beads must have marked social status, were therefore symbols, and a signature of the modern mind.

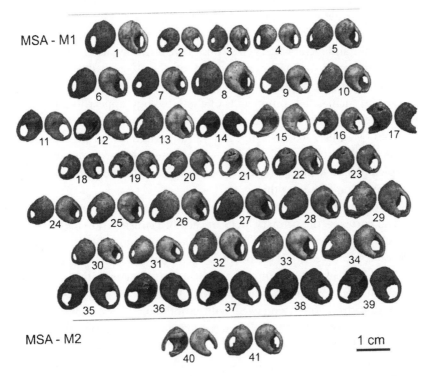

Figure 11.8 Beads from 77,000-year-old levels of Blombos Cave, South Africa; these are the earliest examples of human ornaments yet discovered; even though they have interesting and provocative implications for social roles and theory of mind, they need not have required enhanced working memory

Source: F d'Errico, Henshilwood, Vanhaeren, and van Niekerk, 2005. © 2004 Elsevier Ltd

We concur with part of this chain of inference. The beads *do* suggest something modern, but not yet modern working memory capacity; instead, they suggest the use of artifacts to mark social categories.

In the modern world personal ornaments fulfill two primary functions: personal advertisement (wealth, attractiveness) and social marking. Intentionally and unintentionally, they mark who we are and with whom we belong. The latter is useful because we live in groups that are too large to engage everyone on a one-to-one basis. When our social reach extended only to kin and the range of people we encountered on a regular basis (Dunbar numbers these at a maximum of about 150 (Dunbar, 1993, 2005)), we could establish and maintain social relationships through individual contact, largely through speech. We could recognize all of the significant people in our lives, and deal with each as an individual. But if our social universe, our network if you will, grows larger than 150 we must begin to deal with some of them as categories: bankers, Montagues and Capulets, Republicans and Democrats, and so on. There is then an advantage to have indexes or symbols that mark category identity – gang signs, flags, uniforms, etc. From a cognitive perspective, categories have a complex basis. Some categories, such as the components of a folk biology, appear to arise from hard-wired biases in the visual recognition system, and are evolutionarily very old (Mandler, 2004; Martin, 2007). But beyond a very basic us/them, friend/foe, kin/stranger dichotomy, social categories are unlikely to be completely hard-wired. They must be created and learned, and of course social marking facilitates this.

Current neuropsychology and neuroimaging evidence points to the parietal cortex as the primary locus of category construction and concept formation (Medin and Atran, 2004). It is the region where the brain integrates multiple sensory modalities into comprehensive models of the world (Lou et al., 2004). Once created these are not reflective, attentive, ideas put together in working memory. Instead they are pre-attentive social categories, often endowed with emotional salience, and eliciting visceral responses. The ability to interpret correctly the actions, intentions, and goals of others, a form of theory of mind, may also be considered an important step in successful social interactions, including evaluations of unlikely or unpredicted actions of others. Properly interpreting the actions, intentions, and goals of others is obviously useful in planning our own actions and forming our own goals. Again, the epicenter for these latter abilities appears to be the intraparietal sulcus (e.g., Hamilton and Grafton, 2006). Because cognitive science is a long way from unraveling the workings of the parietal cortex, we are left with only a provocative coincidence. Early anatomically modern humans had an expanded parietal cortex, and the presence of beads indicates they also had expanded social networks. We suggest that there was a link via the neurology of concept formation.

But do not such concepts implicate the same cognitive abilities as the Hohlenstein-Stadel and Hohle Fels cave figurines, made 45,000 years later? Is it not pig-headed to withhold ascribing modern minds to the people who lived at Blombos 77,000 years ago? We think not. The kinds of social categories implied by the Blombos beads (I belong to group A, as opposed to group B, with whom we exchange spouses; group C with whom we fight; group D who are occasional but unreliable allies, etc.) are not abstract, and do not combine elements from distinct categories. Neither are they "superordinate" categories – categories of categories – which too might implicate executive functions (the tally marks on the Lartet plaque might be). So, although the Blombos beads imply category formation processes, they did not, we believe, require executive functions and enhanced working memory.

Why Doesn't Symbol Use Imply a Modern Mind?

Symbol use is the most commonly cited "cognitive" marker of modernity, so it is important for us to delineate further why we think the personal ornaments at Blombos Cave are not strong evidence for fully modern thinking or fully modern language. We shall employ two well-known psychological constructs, classical conditioning and operant conditioning. Classical conditioning was first described by Russian physiologist Ivan Pavlov. Pavlov found that certain stimuli (any form of physical energy) were innately linked to certain responses, without any former learning or training. This pairing has been stated as an "unconditioned stimulus elicits an unconditioned response." For example, we do not have to learn that a very hot object is painful and we should remove our hand away from the hot object. We reflexively move our hands away from very hot things. Pavlov noticed in dogs, for example, that the mere sight of food (the unconditioned stimulus) made dogs salivate (the unconditioned response). Importantly, however, if a neutral stimulus – that is, a stimulus that when presented does not seem to elicit any particularly unique response – is repeatedly paired with an unconditioned stimulus, eventually the neutral stimulus will come to elicit a response similar to the unconditioned response. Thus, when Pavlov paired the sight of food with a bell, the bell came to elicit salivation (the conditioned response).

American psychologist John Watson and, later, American psychologist B. F. Skinner were credited with developing the construct of operant conditioning. At its simplest, operant conditioning proposes that reinforcement increases the likelihood of a behavior. In the most deflating of examples, imagine a word like *apple* printed on a disk, and the disk when pressed earns a monkey or ape a real apple. It does not mean that the animal has learned to read. It also does not mean that the animal knows that the word *apple* symbolizes an apple. The animal has been operantly conditioned. Because apples generally serve as reinforcers to hungry monkeys or apes, the likelihood of an event (pressing the disk with the word *apple* on it) has been increased because apples, like other foods, are unconditioned stimuli.

Therefore, the shell ornaments at Blombos could *symbolize* wealth and social status or a host of other complex cognitive constructs but they are not *sine qua non* evidence for cognitive complexity, and, therefore, are not strong evidence for fully modern thinking or modern syntactical language. Planaria (a relatively simple flatworm without a noticeable brain) can be classically and operantly conditioned. The shell-wearing inhabitants of Blombos Cave 77,000 years ago *could* have had many features of modern thinking and modern language, but they also could have found it socially reinforcing to wear shell necklaces because others like them wore shell necklaces. However, there is no need to invoke higher-order explanations if simpler mechanisms are available. Symbolization can be a much more cognitively complex process, as in the case of language and its written representations, but the basic process of symbolization can occur in organisms without brains.

Could We Be Wrong?

"Just so stories" are narrative musings about the causes of some interesting natural fact (the archetype is "How the Leopard Got Its Spots" from Kipling's *Just So Stories*). Any ambitious evolutionary hypothesis risks being labeled as such by skeptics, largely because historical sciences are not experimental and not subject to the forms of falsification used in experimental disciplines. However, historical sciences do make predictions about what one can expect to find in the data, and what one should not find in the data. If paleontologists ever did find hominin fossils side-by-side with Jurassic dinosaurs, the major narrative of vertebrate evolution would have to be rejected or massively revised. Our hypothesis concerning the evolution of working memory capacity in human evolution is, of course, much smaller in scale, and remains a hypothesis (the major features of the vertebrate narrative have achieved the status of theory). But it, too, makes predictions about what paleoanthropologists should, and should not find, in the archeological data. It can be falsified, and we could be wrong, even very wrong. Indeed, falsification could occur at any of the three steps in the reasoning:

1. Cognitive scientists could demonstrate that "executive functions" and/or "working memory" are unreliable, or invalid, constructs that do not describe a real, coherent, cognitive ability. Alternatively, if comparative psychologists demonstrate that chimpanzees (or gorillas, or macaques) have a working memory capacity that is no different from that of humans, then our hypothesis would be falsified.
2. Experiments (by archeologists or cognitive scientists) could demonstrate that executive functions are not, in fact, required for the patterns that we emphasize. For example, if experiments could somehow demonstrate that enhanced working memory is not necessary to imagine a therianthrope, then this piece of our argument would be falsified.
3. The archeological record itself could falsify our account. If archeologists discover that *Homo erectus* constructed and used remotely operated traps, then that piece of our argument would be falsified (indeed, this bit of evidence might require us to reject the entire hypothesis).

We are confident that the major outlines of our hypothesis are sound: that the evolution of working memory capacity was an important component in human cognitive evolution, and that a final enhancement occurred relatively late. We are less confident about some of the details, primarily because the serendipity of archeological recovery may still hold some surprises (a therianthrope at Blombos Cave, maybe?).

Summary

The paleoanthropological evidence suggests that the evolution of derived features of modern human cognition included two distinct steps away from the archaic pattern established by *Homo heidelbergensis* and perfected by Neandertals.

Step 1

The advent of anatomically modern humans was marked by a distinct, non-allometric expansion of the parietal cortex, a development that also changed the overall appearance of the cranium. This change had occurred by 200,000 years ago and was increasingly accompanied by gracilization of the face and postcranial skeleton. Behavioral sequelae of this change are not obvious in the archeological record, at least not initially. The 160,000-year-old Herto crania provide one tantalizing clue. The skulls had been defleshed and carried around in a bag. Why? We only have living peoples to inform our speculations, and 160,000 years is a long time to extend ethnographic analogy. But it is our only source. Among modern people such an activity would almost certainly be a kind of social marking – leadership ("I carry the skull of the previous leader"), prowess ("I am a fierce character"), role ("I commune with ancestors"), etc. Obviously we do not know, but it smacks of some kind of social marking and a message intended for other people. About 80,000 years later the Blombos beads provide a convincing example of just this kind of social marking. It would not surprise us if more such examples, dating to the intervening millennia, eventually turn up when Africa becomes better known. Such multi-sensory mental models would be consistent with parietal expansion. Again, these need not have been abstract concepts, and indeed may have been largely pre-attentive categories, perhaps with lexical labels, that made up the social world of the anatomically modern human. They were more sophisticated than the mental models of *Homo heidelbergensis* and Neandertals, which, if you recall, relied heavily on well-learned expert procedural cognition. The mental models of anatomically modern humans would have provided a more subtle parsing of the social and natural world. This was not a better way of thinking life (indeed Neandertals' expertise may have trumped anatomically modern humans' mental models, initially), but it was certainly different.

Step 2

Later in human evolution anatomically modern humans evolved an enhanced working memory capacity that powered executive function ability. These enabled complex contingency planning (e.g., managed foraging), abstract reasoning with superordinate categories (e.g., Hohlenstein-Stadel), and innovation. These abilities are evidenced in the archeological record only very late, indeed not until 32,000 years ago, and this is a puzzle. Sometime after 70,000 years ago modern humans began to leave Africa, and in the astonishingly short time, in an evolutionary sense, of 30,000 years had reached all corners of the Old World, including Australia. Did the earliest of these wanderers have enhanced working memory and modern executive functions? We would like to think so, but thus far there is no convincing evidence. There is the real possibility that alleles for enhanced working memory evolved later, and then spread rapidly via the long-range social networks hinted at in the Blombos beads. Whichever of these scenarios turns out to have been true, modern people with modern minds had taken over the known world by 30,000 years ago, and the rest is, well, history.

Glossary

adaptive niche: what an organism does in its habitat to be successful; includes any feature of anatomy or behavior that adjusts an organism to its local circumstances (diet, locomotion, predator avoidance, etc.).

additive genetic inheritance (aka polygenic inheritance): a form of heritable transmission in which more than one gene controls a phenotype (as opposed to classic single-gene inheritance in which the combined action of two alleles (dominant and or recessive) of a single gene controls phenotype). It is thought that most complex behavior, such as intelligence, executive functions, etc., are controlled to some degree by additive genetic influence.

algorithmic device: any artifact, such as an abacus or calendar, that is an aid to making calculations.

Allen's rule: in evolutionary science, the tendency for mammals living in cold habitats to have relatively short limbs and mammals in hot habitats to have relatively long limbs. These proportions result from natural selection optimizing limb length for heat retention or cooling.

allocentric: characterized by perception of an object or scene from another perspective or viewpoint rather than from one's own.

allometric: a relationship is allometric if there is a predictable correlation between two related measures (e.g., one can predict brain size from body size and vice versa). If however, one of the measures,

	say parietal volume, is larger (or smaller) than one would predict from the other measure (e.g., neocortex volume), then it has grown non-allometrically, and it requires an explanation beyond simple growth.
altricial:	less mature than expected for ontogenetic age (opposite of precocious); often used to describe the helplessness of newborn human infants.
amygdala:	a bilateral almond-shaped structure located on the anterior portions of the hippocampus; thought to be critical to fear reactions and conditioning.
anagenesis:	evolutionary change within a single lineage without speciation.
analogy:	in evolutionary science, any similarity between two organisms that is a result of similar adaptations to similar adaptive niches (e.g., the wing of a bird, and the wing of a bat). The more formal term in evolution for such a similarity is *homoplasy*.
anatomically modern human (AMH):	refers to *Homo sapiens* who lived within the last 200,000 years or so and who were indistinguishable skeletally from modern humans. Anatomical modernity appeared in the fossil record before evidence for behavioral modernity appeared in the archeological record, so there were populations that were anatomically modern, but not behaviorally modern.
ancestral:	a homology inherited from an ancestor that lived prior to the last common ancestor of the organisms in question (e.g., neocortex when primates are compared to one another).
angular gyrus:	located in the inferior portion of the parietal lobes (and posterior and inferior to the supra-marginal gyrus); appears to have an important function in phonological storage, that is, the ability to take speech sounds or written words and turn them into internal speech and in metaphor production and comprehension.
anterograde amnesia:	refers to the inability to recall recent events, usually after a trauma.

anthropogenic: caused or made by humans.

anthropoid: sub-order of primates that includes the monkeys, apes, and hominins.

aphasia: a speech or language disorder.

apoptosis: pronounced *a-poe-toe-sis*, is a programmed form of cell death that begins within the cell as opposed to destruction of the cell from a force or puncture to the outside of the cell wall.

apraxia: an inability to conduct intentional motor movements, usually resulting from damage to the parietal lobes.

arboreal: having to do with trees, as in living in them, or adapting to life in trees.

archeology: the scientific study of people through the material traces they have left behind (artifacts, garbage, landscape modifications, and so on).

Ardipithecus: genus of Pliocene hominin that lived in East Africa between 4.5 million and 4 million years ago. Fragmentary remains indicate that it was probably bipedal but retained many ape-like features in its teeth.

Aurignacian: term used to refer to the archeological remains left by the first anatomically modern humans to enter Europe beginning about 42,000 years ago; characterized by blade technology, tools of bone and antler, personal ornaments, and art (figurines).

Australopithecus: genus of bipedal hominin that lived in Africa between 4 million years and 2 million years ago.

Australopithecus afarensis: a species of australopithecine that was a possible ancestor of modern humans, whose earliest remains date to about 3.6 million years ago. Lucy, who dates to about 3.2 million years ago, is the most famous example. These australopithecines were fully bipedal but retained some features of climbing anatomy, suggesting that they spent significant time in trees. They have not been found in association with stone tools, and were clearly sexually dimorphic. Cranial capacity was about 400 cc, within the range of modern chimpanzees.

autonoesis:	an awareness of subjective time in which past events occurred, or future events will occur; mental time travel.
axon:	a part of a neuron that transfers a signal from the cell body to the synapses of other neurons.
basicranium:	of, or relating to, the base of the skull.
basal ganglia:	a collection of subcortical neurons whose clearest function appears to be the control of movement. The group includes the substantia nigra, responsible for the manufacture of dopamine and implicated as a cause of Parkinson's disease. Recently, the basal ganglia have been found to have a role in controlling actively maintained task-relevant information in the prefrontal cortex.
Berekhat Ram figurine:	recovered from a site in the Golan Heights, Israel, that dates to about 400,000 years ago. It is a small lump of lava (< 3 cm) that has a number of grooves scratched by a stone tool. To some it resembles the figure of a woman; to others it resembles a lump of lava. (Note: Ram is part of the name of a place, not an animal).
Bergmann's rule:	in evolutionary science, the tendency for mammals living in cold habitats to have compact bodies and mammals in hot habitats to have relatively elongated bodies. These proportions result from natural selection optimizing body build for heat retention or cooling.
biface:	in lithic technology, a core tool produced by bifacial trimming along all or most of the margin; often bilaterally symmetrical.
bilateral:	(literally *two sides*), usually used in reference to the brain, implying that the same structure appears in both hemispheres.
bipedal:	habitual locomotion using only the hind legs (walking on two feet).
blade:	in lithic technology, any flake that is twice as long as it is wide. A specific technique of blade manufacture, the prismatic core technique, has often been associated with the first modern humans who lived in Europe.

Blombos Cave: a 77,000-year-old site on the southern coast of South Africa that has yielded arguably the earliest evidence of personal ornaments and shell bead necklaces, as well as engraved objects and bone tools.

Bodo: a *Homo erectus*-like skull from Ethiopia, dating to about 600,000 years ago, found with defleshing marks.

bonobo: one of the four species of great ape, sometimes termed pygmy chimpanzees. They are smaller than but closely related to the larger common chimpanzee.

Boxgrove: a large prehistoric landscape on the southern coast of England that dates to the time of *Homo heidelbergensis*, 400,000 years ago. Archeological remains include evidence for hunting, butchery, and stone tool production, and well-preserved remains of many single episodes of activity.

brachial index: ratio of the length of the forearm to the length of the upper arm.

brain stem: the upper end of the spinal cord that contains the pons, reticular formation, and the medulla oblongata. The brain stem has connections to the thalamus, hypothalamus, cortex, and cerebellum. It regulates basic automatic functions such as heart rate, breathing, blood pressure, sleep, eating, and sex and also alertness, attention, and motivation.

Broca, Paul: French neuroanatomist who in the 1800s identified areas of the left hemisphere associated with language.

Broca's aphasia: a brain disorder where understanding is preserved but intentional speech is impaired.

Broca's area: a brain region in the left frontal lobes associated with the production and motor control of speech.

Brodmann, Korbinian: German neuroanatomist who in 1909 defined the 52 regions still used in descriptions of the brain.

burin: in lithic technology, a chisel-edged flake.

canonical utterance: synonymous with recursion, that is, embedding a phrase within a phrase.

central executive: a component in the working memory model whose functions include attention, active-inhibition, decision-making, planning, sequencing, temporal tagging, and the updating and maintenance of information from the other sub-systems. In neuropsychology, the functions of the central executive are synonymous with the executive functions of the frontal lobes.

central sulcus: an indentation that demarcates the frontal lobes from the parietal lobes, and, in one of the oldest brain theories, demarcates the motor cortex (anterior to the central sulcus) from the somato-sensory cortex (posterior to the central sulcus).

cerebellum: (literally meaning *little brain*) is one of the oldest evolutionary brain structures. Its most prominent role is the integration of sensory perception and motor output, and the control of fine motor movements. It may play a minor role in thinking and cognitive processes.

***chaîne opératoire*:** (French) literally, operational chain; the sequence of actions involved in the completion of a task, including major subdivisions and decision points.

cingulate cortex (or cingulate gyrus): a region located in the frontal lobes, inferior to the prefrontal cortex and running anterior to posterior in the middle portions of the inferior cortex. The anterior portion of the cingulate cortex appears to be responsible for one's choice of what to attend to in the external and internal environments.

clade: any group of related organisms (usually species) that are all descended from a single common ancestor (i.e., a single branch of the evolutionary tree).

classical conditioning: a form of learning, originally identified by Russian physiologist Ivan Pavlov, which demonstrates that previous neutral or novel stimuli can come to elicit conditioned responses if paired repeatedly with a stimulus (unconditioned stimulus) that innately yields a particular response (unconditioned response).

cleaver: a biface with a bit (untrimmed transverse edge on one end).

cognitive archeology: a branch of archeology that studies the evolution of human cognition and draws upon a wide variety of disciplines and evidence including psychology, neuropsychology, developmental psychology, paleoanthropology, animal cognition, and material artifacts from the archeological record.

commissure: brain tissue which transmits information between brain regions.

commissurotomy: an operation which severs tissue which transmits information between brain regions. The most common form severs the corpus callosum in epileptic patients in order to eliminate or reduce seizures.

confabulation: usually exhibited during neuropsychological testing, where patients provide imaginative answers or excuses to mask memory errors. It is not known to what extent confusion plays a role in the mixing of imagination and memory or what other motivations may be involved.

constructive episodic simulation: a cognitive ability that flexibly draws on past experiences and recombines these elements of previous experiences to simulate possible future events.

***contra coup* effect:** a blow to one side of the head propels the brain inside the skull to hit the opposite side of the skull (away from the injury site) and, many times, the *contra coup* site exhibits greater dysfunction than the actual site where the skull was initially injured.

contralateral: literally *opposite side*. A term in neuropsychology often used to indicate a connection from one hemisphere to the opposite side of the body, as in a contralateral neural connection from the left hemisphere to the right ear.

core:	in lithic technology, a core is any mass of stone from which flakes are removed.
corm:	the enlarged, fleshy, bulb-like base of the stem of a plant.
corpus callosum:	the major connective tissue which transmits information between the two cerebral hemispheres.
cortex:	(**1**) (plural *cortices*) in brain anatomy, it refers to the relatively thin, upper six layers of the surface of the brain, although it is also used to refer to whole brain (except for subcortical structures such as the limbic system and brain stem). A synonym is neocortex; (**2**) in lithic technology, it refers to the external, weathered surface of a stone.
cranial capacity:	a measure of the volume of the cranium; slightly larger than true brain size, but a reliable surrogate for brain size when studying fossils.
cranium (neurocranium or braincase):	(plural *crania*) the part of the skull that surrounds the brain.
Cro-Magnon:	term used for the earliest modern humans in Europe. The name came from skeletal remains found by geologist Louis Lartet in 1868 in the Cro-Magnon rock-shelter at Les Eyzies, France.
cross-modal integration:	the ability of the mind to coordinate distinct neural networks, as when an artisan coordinates the shape-recognition network (primarily temporal lobe) with the spatial network (primarily parietal lobe) in conceiving and executing a figurine.
crystal intelligence:	a form of intelligence that is highly dependent on learning, schooling, and verbal knowledge (as opposed to fluid intelligence which is the ability to solve new problems and is less dependent on prior knowledge).
cytoarchitecture:	how cells are organized into larger arrangements.
debitage:	(French) in lithic technology, any technique in which the emphasis is on the production of flakes.
declarative memory:	a memory for words and their meaning. Two types of declarative memories are commonly listed,

semantic memory, for the recall of facts and lists of words, and episodic memory, for the recall of personal experiences, often recalled like a story with time, place, and feeling characteristics.

dendrite: the branching part of a neuron that receives signals from other cells and sends this information to the cell body.

denticulates: in lithic technology, flakes with a coarse serrated edge (denticulate: toothed).

derived: a characteristic that evolved after the last common ancestor of the groups under consideration (e.g., bipedalism for hominins when comparing apes to one another).

dichotic listening: a neuropsychological research paradigm in which different words or sounds are played to each ear at the same time, and the participant is asked to repeat what he or she heard. The paradigm can be used to determine language lateralization among other questions.

digit-span task: classic test of short-term memory in which participant is asked to repeat back increasingly longer sequences of digits.

Dmanisi: site in the Republic of Georgia that has yielded remains of *Homo* as old as 1.8 million years, causing havoc to long-cherished arguments for an African origin to the genus.

doppelgänger: (German) the ghostly double of a living person.

dorsolateral prefrontal cortex: a region in the frontal lobes associated with classic executive functions such as selective attention in spite of interference, organizing tasks in space and time, selective inhibition, response preparation, goal-attainment, planning, and flexibility.

dura (dura mater): is the tough outer layer of the three-layered meninges, which is the outer protective membrane covering the brain.

EEG: electroencephalograph, an amplifier used to measure brain waves (producing a graphic record, the electroencephalogram).

encephalization: increasing brain size.

encephalization quotient (EQ): a measure of how much larger (or smaller) a brain is than predicted by the regression of brain size to body size of all placental mammals.

endocast: natural or artificial cast of a brain made from the impressions the brain produced on the internal table of the cranium. Endocasts preserve overall brain shape, but are poor in detail.

enhanced working memory: refers to the specific hypothesis by Coolidge and Wynn that modern human thinking was created by a genetic mutation or epigenetic event with additive effects that led to a revolution in culture (such as highly ritualized burials, personal ornaments, cave art, therianthropic figurines, etc.). It is thought that the heritable event is an enlargement in general working memory capacity, such that a larger number of thoughts or ideas could be held in mind despite interference.

environment of evolutionary adaptedness (EEA): in evolutionary psychology, the hypothetical physical and social environment that selected for modern cognitive abilities.

epigenetic: non-traditional forms of genetic transmission; epigenetic processes may involve RNA, chromatin, "junk" DNA, interactions among DNA strands, and still as yet unrecognized methods of heritability and any other non-DNA linked forms of inheritance.

epilepsy: a brain syndrome characterized by abnormal electrical discharges of the brain.

epiphyseal: a part of a bone originally separated by cartilage becoming fused as bone over time.

episodic buffer: the memory component of the central executive in the working memory model where phonological and visuospatial information are integrated with long-term memory traces and acted upon by the central executive.

episodic memory: a coherent, story-like reminiscence for an event, often with a time, place, and feeling signature, initially proposed by Tulving. Episodic memory has also been labeled personal memory or autobiographical memory.

evolutionary psychology: research discipline that emphasizes the role of natural selection in configuring and maintaining brain structures, cognitive abilities, and behavioral differences among individuals.

equifinality: in lithic technology, it implies that many different procedures can produce the same end product.

Euclidean conception of space: an implicit understanding that space is structured as a set of permanent (absolute) positions definable in three dimensions.

exaptation: change in function in which a phenotype that evolved for one purpose takes on a new function (e.g., feathers evolved initially for thermoregulation and were later exapted for flight).

executive functions of the frontal lobes: a metaphor to describe abilities of the human frontal lobes that resemble those of an executive, that is, making decisions, planning, and developing alternative plans when original plans fail.

expensive tissue hypothesis: hypothesis that argues that encephalization must be "paid for" in an evolutionary sense by reduction in some other expensive tissue, usually gut length, which in turn requires a shift in diet to higher-quality foods.

extractive foraging: any foraging in which animals must gain access to hidden or embedded food (e.g., chimpanzees using hammers to crack open nuts).

facilities: archeological term for fixed structures, such as traps, designed to operate on a large scale or remotely.

façonnage: (French) in lithic technology, any technique in which the emphasis is on the shaping of a core tool.

fissure: a major split or gap between two adjacent regions of the brain. A minor gap or split is called a *sulcus*. The largest fissure in the brain is the one that divides the two cerebral hemispheres.

flake: in lithic technology, the sharp piece that is struck from a core.

FLK: an abbreviation for Frieda Leakey Korongo, an early Pleistocene hominin site in the Olduvai

Gorge, Tanzania. Korongo is the Swahili word for a gully or arroyo. Frieda Leakey was the first wife of famed paleoanthropologist Louis Leakey.

fluid intelligence: a form of intelligence that involves the ability to solve new problems.

female philopatry: feature of social organization in which females of a social group are related genetically, and males leave at adolescence to join another group.

folivory: leaf-eating.

frontal lobotomy: an operation which severs connections within each frontal lobe of the brain. The operation leaves the patient less violent, less anxious, and permanently and profoundly apathetic.

frugivory: fruit-eating.

fusiform gyrus: an area of the inferior temporal lobe gyrus that appears to be responsible for facial recognition in humans and other non-human primates.

gene: a unit of inheritance, also definable as a segment of DNA that controls expression of a trait.

general intelligence: the broadest form of intelligence, consisting of both verbal knowledge (crystal intelligence) and novel problem-solving abilities (fluid intelligence). Synonymous with IQ (intelligence quotient), which originally was the ratio of one's behavioral or mental intelligence to one's chronological intelligence multiplied by 100.

genetic drift: a mechanism of evolutionary change in which a characteristic increases or decreases in frequency by chance rather than natural selection. This process is especially important in the evolutionary fate of small populations.

glenoid: shoulder joint.

gracile: characterized by a delicate or lightly built anatomy, usually in comparison to a more heavily built related (robust) form (e.g., *Australopithecus* vs. *Paranthropus*, or modern humans vs. Neandertals).

grade: group of organisms, usually related, that have a similar organization and phenotype but that

grammar: in language, the rules for combining symbols into meaningful utterances.

Gran Dolina, Spain: a cave in the Atapeurca region of Spain where hominin fossils have been found dating to between 1 million and 780,000 years ago.

grandmother hypothesis: argument that hominin females were able to reduce birth intervals and care for altricial infants because their mothers helped by foraging for their daughters and granddaughters (also an argument for the evolution of postmenopausal females).

gray matter: refers to the color of the surface of the cortex in dead brains, and therefore the term is synonymous with the cortex or surface of the brain. In living brains, the surface is reddish.

great apes: a group of primates that includes gorillas, orangutans, chimpanzees, and bonobos (pygmy chimpanzees). Great apes do not constitute a coherent clade unless humans are also included. However, they do represent an evolutionary grade, with similar phenotypes and behaviors.

hafting: affixing one tool to another, as in joining a spear point or axe head to a shaft.

hammerstone: in lithic technology, a hard, usually roundish, stone held in the hand and used to strike flakes from cores.

handaxe: in lithic technology, a biface with lateral edges that converge to a tip; characteristic of Mode 2 technologies, but also made throughout the Middle Paleolithic.

hemifield vision: a derived feature of primate vision in which the right side of each retina records the left visual field (and the left, the right).

hemispherectomy: removal of an entire hemisphere of the brain.

Herto: site in Ethiopia dating to about 160,000 years ago that has yielded the remains of three crania with many anatomically modern features, and which

	appear to have been defleshed and carried around in bags.
hippocampus:	is a bilateral horseshoe-shaped structure whose first known purpose was the memorization of spatial locations in both humans and animals. In humans, the hippocampus also appears responsible for the transformation of short-term declarative memories into long-term storage.
Holocene:	a geological epoch beginning about 12,000 years ago and continuing into the present.
hominid:	shorthand term for member of the family *Hominidae*. Until the cladistic reassessment of primate taxonomy 25 years ago, this family included only humans and fossil ancestors and relatives of humans. Now that the family *Hominidae* includes the African apes, the term hominid has come to be potentially confusing. Some still use it to refer only to fossil humans, even though this is formally incorrect.
Hominidae:	(1) in classic Linnaean taxonomy, the family to which humans belong; (2) in modern cladistic classification, the family of great apes, including hominins.
hominin:	any member of the tribe *Hominini*, which includes humans, human ancestors, and several other closely related, bipedal forms.
hominoid:	a member of the superfamily *Hominoidea*, which encompasses all living apes and humans, human ancestors and relatives, and ape ancestors.
Homo erectus:	(translation *upright man*) species of fully bipedal hominin that first appeared in the fossil record about 1.8 million years ago in Africa. It was considerably larger than earlier hominins, had a cranial capacity ranging from 800 cc to 1,100 cc, and had an adaptive niche that allowed it to invade many different habitats in Africa, Asia, and Europe.
Homo erectus sensu lato:	(widest sense) implies a very broad range of fossils that have general *Homo erectus* traits.

***Homo erectus sensu stricto*:**	(strictest sense) implies a more narrow range of characteristics associated with *Homo erectus* fossils from Asia.
***Homo ergaster*:**	early African *Homo erectus sensu lato*; a species created to differentiate African *Homo erectus* fossils from European or Asian ones.
***Homo floresiensis*:**	a small species of *Homo* dating to about 18,000 years ago found on the Indonesian island of Flores, whose anatomical features resemble the first *Homo erectus* who colonized the region over 1 million years earlier.
***Homo habilis*:**	(translation *handy man*) late Pliocene/early Pleistocene hominins assigned to the genus *Homo*, having larger brains than the australopithecines (about 630 cc); associated with the first stone tools, and archeological evidence for an adaptive niche that included some scavenging. Postcranial anatomy indicates that it spent time in trees, but was bipedal when on the ground. Fossils of *habilis* date from about 2.4 million to 1.4 million years ago. Its evolutionary relationship to later and contemporary forms of *Homo* is doubtful.
***Homo heidelbergensis*:**	probable common ancestor of Neandertals and modern humans that lived from about 600,000 years ago to about 250,000 years ago in Europe and Africa. It had a cranial capacity of about 1,100 cc to 1,300 cc, thus overlapping with that of modern humans (1,350 cc).
***Homo helmei*:**	some paleoanthropologists place the African forms of *Homo heidelbergensis* into the separate species *helmei* because they appear, on average, more modern than the European variety, especially in regard to the cranial base.
***Homo rudolfensis*:**	an early form of *Homo* roughly contemporary with *habilis*; similar to *habilis* in brain size, but different enough in facial shape to lead some paleoanthropologists to place it in a separate species.
homology:	in evolutionary science, any similarity between two taxa that was inherited from a common ancestor (e.g., human hand and wing of a bat).

homoplasy:
in evolutionary science, any similarity between two taxa that is a result of similar adaptations to similar adaptive niches (e.g., the wing of a bird, and the wing of a bat).

homunculus:
an archaic idea that appeared in some medical theories hundreds of years ago, which proposed that a very small human being was contained in sperm cells. Presently, the issue of a figurative homunculus appeared in criticisms of the working memory model with regards to the central executive component.

hypertrophy:
a greater expansion of a brain area over time compared to other areas.

hypothalamus:
located below the thalamus, it has projections to the prefrontal cortex, amygdala, pituitary gland, and brain stem. It is important to the regulation of the autonomic nervous system, the endocrine and hormonal systems, and the regulation of the body's general homeostasis.

icon:
a variety of sign that stands for its referent by virtue of its visible resemblance to the referent (e.g., on roadside signs where the stylized figure of a stag stands for "deer crossing").

idiopathic:
usually used in reference to a disease and indicates that the cause or origin of the disease is unknown.

index:
a variety of sign that stands for its referent by virtue of its association with the referent (e.g., a hoofprint is an index of deer).

inferior temporal gyrus:
the lowest positioned gyrus of the temporal lobes. It processes language, particularly word and number recognition. One specific area of the inferior temporal gyrus, the fusiform gyrus, appears to be responsible for facial recognition in humans and other primates.

ipsilateral:
(literally *same side*). A term in neuropsychology usually to indicate a neural connection from one hemisphere to the same side of the body, as in an ipsilateral connection from the left hemisphere to the left ear.

Kabwe: an African *Homo heidelbergensis* with a cranial capacity of 1,280 cc, modern cranial base, but a very heavy face.

Keith Richards: a behaviorally modern (*sic*) human who plays lead guitar for the Rolling Stones.

klinorhynchy: refers to the rotation of the facial structures downward, closing the angle between the facial structures and the bones of the braincase (the latter is called the neurocranium). The opposite of klinorhynchy is airorhynchy, characteristic of howler monkeys and orangutans.

knapping: in lithic technology, the process of removing flakes from a core by percussion or pressure.

knuckle-walking: form of quadrapedal locomotion practiced by African apes in which an individual travels on the soles of its hind feet, and the knuckles of its front feet.

Korsakoff's psychosis: severe memory defects (both retrograde and anterograde amnsesia) associated with thiamine deficiencies, usually as a result of chronic alcoholism and poor nutrition.

Lartet plaque: a bone plaque with sequentially engraved dots, associated with the early European Upper Paleolithic, dating to perhaps 28,000 years ago.

Levallois: in lithic technology, a prepared core technique in which the knapper prepares an asymmetric core volume in order to control the size, shape, and thinness of one or several subsequent flakes. It is one of the prepared core techniques typical of Mode 3 technologies, and often associated with Neandertals and early anatomically modern humans.

limbic system: an arbitrary system of locations and structures enclosed by the temporal lobes involved in the processing of emotions and the formation of memories. The limbic system most often includes the hippocampus, amygdala, cingulate cortex, hypothalamus, mammilary bodies, nucleus accumbens, parahippocampal gyrus, orbito-

	frontal cortex, and parts of the basal ganglia, including the striatum, globus pallidus, and substantia nigra. They are all bilateral structures.
lithic technology:	having to do with the production of stone tools.
lobectomy:	removal of a lobe of the brain.
lobotomy:	severing the connections or disrupting the connections between two lobes of the brain or within a lobe.
Lower Paleolithic:	the earliest subdivision of the Paleolithic, dating from the first appearance of lithic technology, roughly 2.5 million years ago, to 200,000 years ago, and characterized by Mode 1 and Mode 2 technologies.
lunate sulcus:	the sulcus marking the boundary between the parietal and occipital lobes. In general, it is more clearly demarcated in great apes and monkeys than in humans. In the evolution of human brains, the lunate sulcus has moved posteriorly, reflecting the relative expansion of parietal lobes, and a relatively diminished role of the primary visual cortex.
Machiavellian hypothesis:	hypothesis that anthropoid encephalization evolved to solve complex social problems.
MRI (magnetic resonance imaging)	a brain-imaging technique that produces electronic images of cells, tissues, and organs. fMRI (functional MRI) can produce images of blood flow to areas of the brain, indicating greater or lesser activity.
male philopatry:	feature of social organization in which males of a social group are related genetically, and females leave at adolescence to join another group.
managed foraging:	a system of hunting and gathering that includes scheduling and/or intentional manipulation of plants, animals, and landscapes. Archeological evidence indicates that it was widespread by 12,000 years ago but had antecedents several thousand years earlier. It is a subsistence system that relies on executive functions and enhanced working memory.

mandible:	lower jaw.
meninges:	three thin layers of membranes covering the brain. They enclose the cerebrospinal fluid, but also mute the impression of detail on the inner table of the cranium, and hence the detail on endocasts.
mentation:	refers to all aspects or forms of thinking, including dreaming, daydreaming, and other thoughts.
Mesolithic:	an archeological period associated with the end of the Pleistocene and early Holocene in Europe; characterized by managed foraging systems and adaptations to European forested habitats.
Microcephalin (MCPH1):	a gene that regulates brain size. Implicated in microcephaly (abnormally small brains) and thought to have caused a change in brain size about 37,000 years ago (see Evans et al., 2005).
Middle Paleolithic:	the middle subdivision of the Paleolithic, dating from roughly 200,000 years ago to roughly 40,000 years ago and found associated with Neandertals and some early anatomically modern humans; characterized by Mode 3 technologies.
Middle Pleistocene:	a geologic period from about 780,000 to about 200,000 years ago; characterized by increasingly dramatic worldwide changes in climate.
Milankovitch cycles:	cycles reflecting the amount of solar radiation falling on the earth's surface that were the primary governing factors for Pleistocene climate change. Named for the Serbian astrophysicist who first identified and championed them 80 years ago.
Miocene:	geologic period from about 23 million to 5 million years ago; a time of the greatest number and variety of apes.
mitochondrial DNA (mtDNA):	double-stranded DNA that resides in the mitochondria of a cell. As most other DNA is found in the cell nucleus, it is thought that mtDNA has a separate evolutionary origin from nuclear DNA. In mammals and most other organisms, mtDNA is inherited only from the mother. In DNA studies of recent human evolution, using either mtDNA or Y-chromosomes, the former can only trace

maternal inheritance patterns and the latter only paternal patterns. Interestingly, they often give slightly discrepant evolutionary time estimates.

Mode 1 technology: the most basic kind of stone tool technology. It includes hammerstones, cores, and flakes removed by direct percussion. The earliest known knapped stone tools dating to about 2.5 million years ago are Mode 1, but the technology was used more or less constantly throughout human evolution.

Mode 2 technology: also known as Acheulean stone tools for the village of St. Acheul, France, where they were first found. They are most often associated with *Homo erectus*, but were not coextensive (*Homo erectus* evolved earlier than the first Mode 2 technologies). The hallmark of Mode 2 technology is the biface, an extensively trimmed core tool that was often bilaterally symmetrical.

Mode 3 technology: a lithic technology that included any of a variety of prepared core or core management techniques; appeared at about the same time as *Homo heidlebergensis* and was the dominant technology for Neandertals and early anatomically modern humans.

moveable art (portable art): artistic objects that can be moved or carried, such as figurines (as opposed to parietal or cave art).

mnemonitive: relating to memory.

Mousterian: a term for the Middle Paleolithic lithic technology associated with Neandertals and some early anatomically modern humans. Named after the site of Le Moustier in France.

muscle atonia: deep relaxation or paralysis of voluntary muscles that occurs during REM sleep.

mutation: chemical alteration of a gene into a new form; a primary source of new genetic variability.

myelin: white fatty substance lining axons that speeds up transmission of nerve impulses.

Nariokotome: site in northern Kenya that yielded the remains of a virtually complete skeleton of a pre-adolescent

Homo erectus male (WT 15000), and thus the name "Nariokotome" is synonymous with this specific *Homo erectus*.

natural selection: mechanism of evolutionary change first described by Charles Darwin. It is based around differential reproduction: certain individuals reproduce more than others thereby passing more of their genes on to the next generation.

Neandertal: also known as *Homo neandertalensis* or *Homo sapiens neandertalensis*. A robust human type that originated in Europe about 250,000 years ago and persisted until after 30,000 years ago. Their average cranial capacity was 1,427 cc with a range of 1,250 cc to 1,700 cc, the largest of any *Homo*.

neuron: a type of cell in the nervous system (including spinal cord and brain) that is designed to transmit signals from one neuron to another, consisting of a cell body, dendrites for receiving signals, and axons for transmitting them.

neuropsychology: the study of brain and behavior relationships.

Occam's razor: a type of logical reasoning that concludes that the explanation based on the fewest assumptions is best.

occipital lobes: sit posteriorly to the parietal lobes and temporal lobes, and their chief function appears to be primary visual recognition and processing. The lunate sulcus demarcates the occipital lobes from the parietal and temporal lobes in great apes and monkeys more clearly than in humans, suggesting a diminished role evolutionarily of the primary visual cortex in the latter.

ochre: any of a number of mineral pigments of varying mineralogical origin, ranging in color from red through oranges and yellows (including hematite, limonite, and specularite), probably used as a coloring agent and as a binding agent for hafting spear heads.

Omo Kibish: site in Ethiopia that yielded the remains of two partial *Homo* crania with many modern characteristics, dating to about 190,000 years ago.

ontogeny:	the developmental sequence of an individual from conception to death.
ontogeny recapitulates phylogeny:	famous dictum coined by German zoologist Ernst Haeckel in 1866 that argues that the developmental sequence of an individual repeats the evolutionary history of its species. Although modern evolutionary science still acknowledges parallels, ontogeny is no longer considered to be a simple repeat of evolutionary development.
optic chiasm:	the location in the front part of the brain where the inner half of the fibers of the left and right optic nerves crossover to the opposite side of the brain.
orbitofrontal prefrontal cortex:	an area in the frontal lobes region, closely connected to the limbic system and associated with the processing of emotions and the regulation and decision-making associated with social behavior and social interactions. The more central part of the orbitofrontal prefrontal cortex (PFC) is called the ventrolateral PFC. The part towards the middle of the brain is called the ventromedial PFC.
Orrorin:	a genus of late Miocene (about 6 million years ago) hominoid with small, thick enameled molars and postcranial features of bipedalism; possibly earliest documented hominin.
osseous:	bone.
Paleolithic:	(literally *old stone*) an archeological stage initially defined as the first division of the Stone Age, and characterized by knapped stone artifacts, and hunting and gathering subsistence; now known to encompass the first 99.5 percent of technological development, dating from about 2.5 million to about 12,000 years ago.
Paleo-Indian:	term for the earliest Americans, thought to have migrated from Asia sometime around 15,000 years ago. They were expert big-game hunters who used a sophisticated system of spear throwers and spears with detachable foreshafts.
paleoneurology:	the study of ancient nervous systems, especially the brain. A closely related discipline is cognitive archeology.

paleontology: the study of fossils.

Paranthropus: a genus of bipedal hominin that lived in Africa between 3 million and 1 million years ago. It was slightly larger that *Australopithecus*, and had specialized dental and cranial features for heavy chewing. It is not thought to be an ancestor of *Homo*.

parietal art: cave art.

parietal bosses: the rounding high on the sides of the cranium in the area of the parietal lobes that mark the point of maximum breadth.

parietal lobes: the left and right parietal lobes are located posteriorly to the frontal lobes, beginning right after the central sulcus. This area includes the somatosensory cortex known to control and integrate our senses, including the senses of feeling, pain, temperature, movement, pressure, texture, shape, vibration, etc. The parietal lobes are critical in the manipulation of objects in visual space (visuospatial processing). Damage to the parietal lobes results in the classic symptom of apraxia.

pastoralist: one who raises or herds livestock.

PBWM: literally *prefrontal cortex, basal ganglia working memory*, a cognitive/neuropsychological model which purports to account for the mechanistic basis of working memory, the central executive, and its executive functions. As the name suggests, the prefrontal cortex is seen as critical in maintaining representations of an individual's perceptions, which are dynamically updated and regulated by reinforcement learning systems that are modifiable and based on chemical neurotransmitters activated by the basal ganglia and the amygdala.

penecontemporaneous: living at about the same time.

percussion flaking: in lithic technology, the process of striking a core with a hammerstone in order to remove flakes.

PET (positron emission tomography): a brain-imaging technique that uses radioactive tracers to identify regions of greater and lesser brain activity.

petalias: protrusions of the right frontal and left occipital lobes relative to their counterparts in the opposite hemisphere are among the most striking anatomical asymmetries in human brains (and recognizable on endocasts perhaps as early as *Australopithecus*).

phenotype: the actual expression of a characteristic (as opposed to *genotype*, which refers to the genes an individual possesses for that characteristic).

phonological storage (phonological loop): a subsystem of the working memory model which has two components, a brief-sound-based storage that fades within about two seconds and an articulatory control processor. The latter processor maintains material in the phonological store by vocal or subvocal rehearsal. It was also assumed that spoken information gains automatic and obligatory access to phonological storage. Baddeley hypothesized that the phonological store evolved principally for the demands and acquisition of language. The neural location of the phonological loop is thought to be the inferior parietal lobe of the speech-dominant hemisphere, particularly the supramarginal and angular gyri.

phylogeny: the evolutionary history of an organism or group of organisms, usually represented as a sequence of divergences in the form of a tree or bush.

planum temporale: the posterior part of the superior temporal gyrus, said to be critical to musical and linguistic abilities. In humans, the left planum temporale is larger than the right, and symmetry in this regard is associated with linguistic problems and other difficulties.

Pleistocene: a geological epoch extending from 1.8 million to 12,000 years ago, characterized by rapidly fluctuating climates and habitats.

Pliocene:	a geological epoch extending from 5 million to 1.8 million years ago, characterized by modern animals, larger mammals, and global climate cooling.
polyadic:	many or multiple interactions, usually used to indicate simultaneous and complex social interactions.
postcranial:	anatomical features below the head (literally behind the head, but in hominins behind was below).
prefrontal cortex:	refers to the entire frontal lobes, with the exception of the motor cortex, with highly specific functions ascribed to them, such as the executive functions. Further divided into dorsolateral prefrontal cortex (PFC), orbitofrontal PFC, and ventrolateral PFC.
prepared core technique:	in lithic technology, any technique in which a core is shaped in order to influence the shape and/or size of a subsequent flake or flakes (e.g., Levallois).
prepotent:	implies that a particular response tends to dominate over other responses, typically without conscious awareness, because of prior learning or practice, genetic predispositions, priming, maturational primacy, recent elicitation, or interactions with other factors such as motivation.
primates:	are the Order within the Class *Mammalia* that encompasses monkeys, apes (including humans), and prosimians. Most living primates are tropical, arboreal, and live in social groups. Derived characteristics for the Order include grasping hands and feet, and reliance on vision. Primates are more encephalized than most other mammals.
priming:	a term in psychology which refers to the activation of parts of specific memory right before the elicitation of the memory.
procedural memory:	the recall of a motor movement or skill like stone knapping or juggling. It is thought that the mastery of a procedural memory often takes

	hundreds of more trials to learn than a declarative memory.
prognathism:	a protruding lower or mid-face in relation to the vertical plane of the eye sockets. It is often mentioned as a characteristic of Neandertals.
prospective memory:	remembering to carry out intended actions or an image or idea of a future action.
protolanguage:	an earlier form of language, presumably with simpler grammar, rules, and vocabulary.
psychology:	the study of behavior both human and animal.
punctuated equilibrium:	within any given taxon, periods of little or no directional change interspersed with brief episodes of rapid change.
Qafzeh:	site in Israel that has yielded the remains of early anatomically modern humans, including a burial with possible grave goods; dates to approximately 92,000 years ago.
recursion:	in language, a grammatical operation that allows the embedding of phrases.
refitting:	analytical technique used by archeologists in which flakes from a prehistoric knapping episode are refit into their original configurations on a core or part of a core; an important technique for discovering *chaines operatoires*.
REM sleep:	(rapid eye movement) is a period of sleep similar to Stage 1 at least cortically, with low-amplitude, high-frequency EEG waves accompanied by bursts of eye movement; the most vivid, story-like dreams occur during REM sleep, although mentation may occur in other stages.
retrograde amnesia:	the forgetting of past events, usually reserved for very distant memories such as those that are many years old.
reverse engineering:	in evolutionary science, identifying the function of an anatomical feature or behavior by determining what it was designed to do.
robust:	characterized by a heavily built anatomy, with thicker bones and evidence of greater muscularity; usually in comparison to a more lightly built

Sahelanthropus:

related form (gracile), e.g., Neandertals compared to modern humans.

a genus of late Miocene hominoid (about 7 million to 6 million years ago) known from a single distorted cranium found in Chad (central Africa). Dental and facial features suggest it may qualify as the earliest known hominin.

Sahul:

a reference to the Pleistocene continent of Australia and New Guinea.

**Schöningen,
Germany:**

a large open-pit coal mine in Germany where several carved wooden spears, dating to about 400,000 years ago, were found associated with the remains of horses.

secondary altriciality:

derived human characteristic in which infants are born much less mature than those of other apes, necessitating rapid brain growth postnatally.

seizure:

an abnormal electrical discharge of the brain that usually interferes with consciousness. It is the chief symptom of epilepsy.

semiotic:

explanations of signs and symbols and their functions.

sexual dimorphism:

any time males and females of a species differ in features of non-reproductive anatomy, including size. In primates, greater sexual dimorphism (males being much larger than females) appears to correlate with greater male–male aggression.

sexual selection:

form of selection that occurs when individuals with certain sexual-display characteristics (size, beauty, etc.) have a reproductive advantage over others; includes situations in which members of one sex preferentially select individuals of opposite sex who possess desirable characteristics (which may well be otherwise counterproductive).

shared attention:

one of the basic components of learning a procedural memory such as stone knapping, which requires a student to pay attention to a teacher and vice versa. It is also thought to be a necessary component of theory of mind but not synonymous or a sufficient condition for it.

Sima de los Huesos: (from Spanish; *pit of bones*) a site in Atapuerca, Spain, where paleoanthropologists have recovered the remains of over 30 *Homo heidelbergensis*, mostly young adults and juveniles, that appear to have been dropped down a shaft deep in a cave; dates to about 400,000 years ago.

slow-wave sleep: stages of sleep (3 and 4) characterized by slow-wave frequencies (.5–3 Hz) that have a high amplitude and, in humans, an absence of mentation. Evolutionarily, it appears to be much older than REM sleep.

somatic marker hypothesis: a neuropsychological theory to explain the interrelationship of the orbitofrontal cortex, anterior cingulate gyrus, and amygdala and their contributions to decision-making, which includes the use of emotional valences to rapidly narrow behavioral options by automatically determining the affective consequences of each action.

somatosensory cortex: area immediately posterior to the central sulcus devoted to receiving and processing neural sensory signals coming in from the body, other than the primary sense organs (eyes, ears), such as signals from the skin, body, and its location and placement in space.

space constancy: refers to the cognitive ability to hold positions, sizes, and distances of objects in constant relation to each other in physical space. In evolutionary psychology, Silverman and colleagues have proposed that this ability is the root of gender differences in spatial cognition and evolved as an adaptation to better wayfinding in hunting.

speech acts: refers to the act that is done or performed by speaking, such as declaring a fact, commanding, exclaiming, asking a question, or posing a hypothetical.

split brain: an operation which severs the corpus callosum in order to eliminate or diminish epileptic seizures.

stasis: a macro-evolutionary term applied to periods of little evolutionary change within a lineage.

striking platform: in lithic technology, the place on the edge of a core where the knapping blow falls.

sulcus: a minor split or gap between two adjacent regions of the brain. A major gap or split is called a fissure.

Sungir: a site in Russia that includes the burial of three modern humans, an adult and two juveniles, dating to about 27,000 years ago. The burials were accompanied by thousands of beads and ornamental ivory spears.

superordinate category: categories of categories, that is, abstract categories whose contents are also categories, united by some arbitrary similarity, like the set of all sets.

superior temporal gyrus: also called Wernicke's area. This region is critical to the understanding of speech.

Supervisory Attentional System (SAS): a cognitive theory, originally proposed by Norman and Shallice, that appears to be synonymous with the attentional functions of Baddeley's central executive, and recently attributed to the anterior cingulate gyrus. It is surmised that the SAS takes control when novel tasks are introduced, when pre-existing habits have to be overridden, or when danger threatens and task-relevant decisions must be made.

suprainiac fossa: an oval depression on the surface of the occipital bone on Neandertal skulls.

supramarginal gyrus: located in the inferior portion of the parietal lobes (and anterior and superior to the angular gyrus), appears to control sensory discriminations, particularly tactile interpretations, and may have a role in phonological storage, learning, and memory.

supraorbital torus: brow ridge; the ridge of bone above the eye sockets of some fossil hominins.

Sylvian fissure: the gap which demarcates the frontal lobes from the temporal lobes. Also called the lateral fissure. This is one of the few features that can be discerned on endocasts.

symbol: a variety of sign that has an arbitrary link to its referent (e.g., the word "deer" standing for deer).

synapse:	the space between axons and dendrites where chemical neurotransmitters are excreted and absorbed for the transmission of nerve impulses.
tactical deception:	use of deception to solve a novel social problem.
Tata pebble:	a round pebble was found in Hungary with a natural crack extending across the diameter and a second diameter line was intentionally scratched perpendicular to this crack. It is attributed to Neandertals.
taxon:	(plural *taxa*) a group of related organisms, such as a phylum, order, family, genus, or species.
temporal lobes:	the left and right temporal lobes lie inferior to the parietal lobes and anterior to the occipital lobes. They also enclose the hippocampus and the amygdala. The left temporal lobe appears to be critical to language comprehension, along with the right temporal lobe, which appears to interpret sounds and music.
thalamus:	(Greek; literally *inner room*) located at the top of the brain stem serves as a gateway to the cortex for sensory systems. It has reciprocal loops with all regions of the cortex, and it appears critical to attention.
theory of mind (ToM):	having an understanding of another's thoughts or beliefs.
therianthrope:	an artifact depicting a beast that is part animal, part human (e.g., a chimera). The most famous therianthrope is the Hohlenstein-Stadel figurine dating to about 32,000 years ago from southwestern Germany, which depicts a lion's head on a human body. A synonymous term is Löwenmensch (German for "lion-man").
theta rhythm:	a 6 Hz EEG wave identified in some non-human mammals that arises from the hippocampus and is often associated with specific functions such as exploratory behavior in cats and maze-learning in rats.
transhumance:	the seasonal migration of livestock and the people who tend them.

transverse temporal gyrus: an area within the superior temporal lobe which is responsible for hearing and basic sound processing. It receives input nearly directly from the cochlea (inner ear) and is considered primary auditory cortex.

trepanation: the process of intentionally boring a hole in the skull of a living human. There is evidence it was practiced over 10,000 years ago, although the reasons are unknown but suspected to be the alleviation of brain or behavioral problems.

trichromatic color vision: derived feature of anthropoid vision in which the retina has cones that detect three different frequencies of light, allowing the synthesis of all visible light colors.

Twin Rivers, Zambia: a site where there is evidence of pigment use dating to about 300,000 years ago and attributed to *Homo heidelbergensis*.

Upper Paleolithic: the final stage of the Paleolithic sequence, associated in Europe with anatomically modern humans, and characterized by ritualized burials, personal ornaments, cave art, figurines, and sophisticated bone and antler tools.

USO (underground storage organ): underground structures of certain plants that store moisture and nutrients that the plant uses during seasons of stress (roots, tubers, rhizomes, corms).

utilization behavior (environmental dependency syndrome): a term in neuropsychology to describe the tendency of patients with prefrontal-cortex damage to be highly dependent upon social and environmental cues for the selection of their behavior, regardless of the social inappropriateness of their behaviors.

ventricles: are spaces within the brain that conduct the flow of cerebrospinal fluid in order to nourish the brain's neurons.

visual field or visual half-field: also known as hemifield vision; the right half of each eye views only the left visual field, also referred to as the left visual half-field. It is a derived feature of primate vision.

visuospatial sketchpad: a subsystem of the working memory model for the temporary storage for the maintenance and manipulation of visual and spatial information. The visuospatial sketchpad is assumed to form an interface between the two sources of information. Visual information can also be integrated with other sensory information, perhaps, such as touch and smell; however, there are far fewer empirical studies of the visuospatial sketchpad compared to other components of the working memory model.

weed hypothesis: a metaphor created by Cachel and Harris to propose that *Homo erectus* was like a weed, spreading rapidly, surviving under varying and often hostile conditions, but never developing into large populations.

Wernicke's aphasia: a brain disorder where understanding is impaired but speech remains fluent.

Wernicke's area: an area of the superior gyrus of the temporal lobe that is responsible for the comprehension of speech.

white matter: refers to the color of brain tissue beneath the surface of the cortex. It appears white because of the strong presence of the white myelin sheath in these neurons.

working memory: a cognitive model proposed by experimental psychologist Alan Baddeley that contains a central executive, and two subsystems: phonological storage with an articulation processor, and a visuospatial sketchpad. An episodic buffer serves to integrate information from both subsystems and temporarily store this information for the central executive in order for it to be acted upon.

working memory span (working memory capacity): a measure of the amount of information one can hold and process in active attention in spite of interference.

References

Aboitiz, F., R. Garcia, C. Bosman, and E. Brunetti. 2006. Cortical memory mechanisms and language origins. *Brain and Language*, 98:40–56.

Adams, A.-M. and S. Gathercole. 2000. Limitations in working memory: Implications for language development. *International Journal of Language and Communication Disorders*, 35:95–116.

Adams, C. 2002. Practitioner review: The assessment of language pragmatics. *Journal of Child Psychology and Psychiatry*, 43:973–87.

Aiello, C. L. and P. Andrews. 2000. The australopithecines in review. *Human Evolution*, 15(1–2):17–38.

Aiello, L. and C. Key. 2002. Energetic consequences of being a *Homo erectus* female. *American Journal of Human Biology*, 14:551–65.

Aiello, L. C. and P. Wheeler. 1995. The expensive tissue hypothesis: the brain and digestive system in humans and primate evolution. *Current Anthropology*, 36:199–221.

Alexander, G. E., M. DeLong, and P. Strick. 1986. Parallel organization of functionally segregated circuits linking basal ganglia and cortex. *Annual Review of Neuroscience*, 9:357–81.

Allman, J. 2000. *Evolving Brains*. New York: Scientific American Library.

Ambrose, S. 2001. Paleolithic technology and human evolution. *Science*, 291:1748–53.

Anderson, D., A. Goudie, and A. Parker. 2007. *Global Environments through the Quaternary*. Oxford: Oxford University Press.

Anderson, J. 1998. Sleep, sleeping sites, and sleep-related activities: Awakening to their significance. *American Journal of Primatology*, 46:63–75.

Ando, J., Y. Ono, and M. Wright. 2001. Genetic structure of spatial and verbal working memory. *Behavior Genetics*, 31:615–24.

Anton, S. 2003. Natural history of *Homo erectus*. *Yearbook of Physical Anthropology*, 46:126–70.

Anton, S., W. Leonard, and M. Robertson. 2002. An ecomorphological model of the initial hominid dispersal from Africa. *Journal of Human Evolution*, 43:773–85.

Anton, S. and C. Swisher. 2004. Early dispersals of *Homo* from Africa. *Annual Review of Anthropology*, 33:271–96.

Antrobus, J., T. Kondo, and R. Reinsel. 1995. Dreaming in the late morning: Summation of REM and diurnal cortical activation. *Consciousness and Cognition*, 4:275–99.

Arsuaga, J. L. 2002. *The Neanderthal's Necklace: In Search of the First Thinkers*. Trans. A. Klat. New York: Four Walls Eight Windows.

Arsuaga, J. L. et al. 1999. The human cranial remains from Gran Dolina Lower Pleistocene site (Sierra de Atapuerca, Spain). *Journal of Human Evolution*, 37(3–4):431–57.

Aubrey, J. B., C. Smith, S. Tweed, and R. Nader. 1990. Cognitive and motor procedural tasks are dissociated in REM and stage two sleep. *Sleep Research Online*, 2:220.

Baddeley, A. D. 1993. Working memory or working attention?, in *Selection, Awareness, and Control: A Tribute to Donald Broadbent*. Edited by A. Baddeley and L. Weiskrantz. Oxford: Oxford University Press.

Baddeley, A. D. 2000. The episodic buffer: A new component of working memory? *Trends in Cognitive Science*, 4:417–23.

Baddeley, A. D. 2001. Is working memory still working? *American Psychologist*, 11:851–64.

Baddeley, A. D. 2007. *Working Memory, Thought, and Action*. Oxford: Oxford University Press.

Baddeley, A. and G. J. Hitch. 1974. Working memory, in *Recent Advances in Learning and Motivation*. Edited by G. A. Bower, pp. 47–90. New York: Academic Press.

Baddeley, A., S. Gathercole, and C. Papagno. 1998. The phonological loop as a language learning device. *Psychological Review*, 105:158–73.

Baddeley, A. and R. Logie. 1999. Working memory: The multi-component model, in *Models of Working Memory: Mechanisms of Active Maintenance and Executive Control*. Edited by A. Miyake and P. Shah. New York: Cambridge University Press.

Barham, L. 2002. Systematic pigment use in the Middle Pleistocene of South-Central Africa. *Current Anthropology*, 43:181–90.

Barker, G. et al. 2007. The "human revolution" in lowland tropical Southeast Asia: The antiquity and behaviour of anatomically modern humans at Niah Cave (Sarawak, Borneo). *Journal of Human Evolution*, 52:243–61.

Barkley, R. 2001. The executive functions and self-regulation: An evolutionary neuropsychological perspective. *Neuropsychology Review*, 11:1–29.

Barton, R. 2006. Primate brain evolution: Integrating comparative, neurophysiological, and ethological data. *Evolutionary Anthropology*, 15:224–36.

Barton, R. and R. Dunbar. 1997. Evolution of the social brain, in *Machiavellian Intelligence II*. Edited by A. Whiten and R. Byrne, pp. 240–63. Cambridge: Cambridge University Press.

Bar-Yosef, O. 2002. The Upper Paleolithic Revolution. *Annual Review of Anthropology*, 31:363–93.

Basaboe, A. and J. Yamagiwa. 2002. Factors affecting nesting site choice in chimpanzees at Tshibati, Kahuzi-Biega National Park: Influence of sympatric gorillas. *International Journal of Primatology*, 23:263–82.

Beatty, J. 1995. *Principles of Behavioral Neuroscience*. Madison: Brown & Benchmark.

Bechara, A., H. Damasio, A. Damasio, and G. Lee. 1999. Different contributions of the human amygdala and ventromedial prefrontal cortex to decision-making. *Journal of Neuroscience*, 19:5473–81.

Becker, J., D. MacAndrew, and J. Fiez. 1999. A comment on the functional localization of the phonological storage subsystem of working memory. *Brain and Cognition*, 41:27–38.

Bednarik, R. 1994. A taphonomy of palaeoart. *Antiquity*, 68:68–74.

Begun, D. 2004. Enhanced cognitive capacity as a contingent fact of hominid phylogeny, in *The Evolution of Thought: Evolutionary Origins of Great Ape Intelligence*. Edited by A. Russon and D. Begun, pp. 15–28. Cambridge: Cambridge University Press.

Begun, D. and L. Kordos. 2004. Cranial evidence of the evolution of intelligence in fossil apes, in *The Evolution of Thought: Evolutionary Origins of Great Ape Intelligence*. Edited by A. Russon and D. Begun, pp. 260–79. Cambridge: Cambridge University Press.

Begun, D. and A. Walker. 1993. The endocast, in A. Walker and R. Leakey (eds.), *The Nariokotome Homo erectus skeleton*, pp. 236–358. Cambridge, MA.: Harvard University Press.

Berger, T. D. and E. Trinkaus. 1995. Patterns of trauma among the Neandertals. *Journal of Archaeological Science*, 22:841–52.

Bickerton, D. 1990. *Language and Species*. Chicago, IL: University of Chicago Press.

Bird, A. 2007. Perceptions of epigenetics. *Nature*, 447:396–8.

Bjorkland, D. and J. Bering. 2003. Big brains, slow development, and social complexity: The developmental and evolutionary origins of social cognition, in *The Social Brain: Evolutionary Aspects of Development and Pathology*. Edited by M. Brune, pp. 113–51. New York: Wiley.

Blagrove, M. 1992. Dreams as the reflection of our waking concerns and abilities: A critique of the problem-solving paradigm in dream research. *Dreaming*, 2:205–20.

Blumenschine, R. 1987. Characteristics of an early hominid scavenging niche. *Current Anthropology*, 28:383–407.

Blumenschine, R. 1995. Percussion marks, tooth marks, and experimental determinations of timing of hominid and carnivore access to long bones at FLK Zinjanthropus, Olduvai Gorge, Tanzania. *Journal of Human Evolution*, 29:21–51.

Bocquet-Appel, J. 2006. Comment on "What's a mother to do: The division of labor among Neandertals and modern humans in Eurasia." *Current Anthropology*, 47:964–5.

Boë, L.-J., J.-L. Heim, K. Honda, and S. Maeda. 2002. The potential Neanderthal vowel space was as large as that of modern humans. *Journal of Phonetics*, 30:465–84.

Boëda, E. 1994. *Le Concept Levallois: Variabilité des Méthodes*. Paris: CNRS Editions.

Boëda, E., J.-M. Geneste, and L. Meignen. 1990. Identification de chaînes opératoires lithiques du Paléolithique ancien et moyen. *Paléo*, 2:43–80.

Bowler, J. and J. Magee. 2000. Redating Australia's oldest remains: A sceptic's view. *Journal of Human Evolution*, 38:719–26.

Boyer, P. 2001. *Religion Explained: The Evolutionary Origins of Religious Thought*. New York: Basic Books.

Brain, C. K. and A. Sillen. 1988. Evidence from the Swartkrans cave for the earliest use of fire. *Nature*, 336:464–6.

Bramble, D. and D. Lieberman. 2004. Endurance running and the evolution of *Homo*. *Nature*, 432:345–52.

Breasted, J. 1930/1991. *The Edwin Smith Surgical Papyrus: Hieroglyphic Transliteration Translation and Commentary (Vol. 1)*. Chicago, IL: University of Chicago Press.

Bruner, E. 2003. Fossil traces of the human thought: paleoneurology and the evolution of the genus *Homo*. *Rivista di Antropologia: Journal of Anthropological Sciences*, 81:29–56.

Bruner, E. 2004. Geometric morphometrics and paleoneurology: Brain shape evolution in the genus *Homo*. *Journal of Human Evolution*, 47:279–303.

Bruner, E., G. Manzi, and J. L. Arsuaga. 2003. Encephalization and allometric trajectories in the genus *Homo*: Evidence from the Neandertal and modern lineages. *Proceedings of the National Academy of Sciences*, 100:15335–40.

Bunn, H. and E. Kroll. 1986. Systematic butchery by Plio/Pleistocene hominids at Olduvai Gorge, Tanzania. *Current Anthropology*, 27:431–52.

Buss, D. 2003. *The Evolution of Desire: Strategies of Human Mating*. New York: Basic Books.

Byers, A. M. 1994. Symboling and the Middle–Upper Palaeolithic transition: A theoretical and methodological critique. *Current Anthropology*, 35:369–400.

Byrne, R. 2003. Tracing the evolutionary path of cognition, in *The Social Brain: Evolution and Pathology*. Edited by M. Brune, H. Ribbert, and W. Schiefenhovel, pp. 43–60. New York: Wiley.

Byrne, R. 2004. The manual skills and cognition that lie behind hominid tool use, in *The Evolution of Thought: Evolutionary Origins of Great Ape Intelligence*. Edited by A. Russon and D. Begun. Cambridge: Cambridge University Press.

Byrne, R. and A. Russon. 1998. Learning by imitation: A hierarchical approach. *Behavioral and Brain Sciences*, 21:667–721.

Byrne, R. and A. Whiten (eds.). 1988. *Machiavellian Intelligence: Social Expertise and the Evolution of Intellect in Monkeys, Apes, and Humans*. Oxford: Clarendon Press.

Cachel, S. and J. Harris. 1995. Ranging patterns, land-use and subsistence in *Homo erectus* from the perspective of evolutionary biology, in *Evolution and Ecology of Homo erectus*. Edited by J. Bower and S. Sartono, pp. 51–66. Leiden: Pithecanthropus Centennial Foundation.

Cachel, S. and J. Harris. 1998. The lifeways of *Homo erectus* inferred from archaeology and evolutionary ecology: a perspective from East Africa, in *Early Human Behaviour in Global Contexts: The Rise and Diversity of the Lower Palaeolithic Record*. Edited by M. Petraglia and R. Korisettar, pp. 108–32. New York: Routledge.

Calvin, W. 1993. The unitary hypothesis: A common neural circuitry for novel manipulations, language, plan-ahead, and throwing?, in *Tools, Language, and Cognition in Human Evolution*. Edited by K. Gibson and T. Ingold, pp. 230–50. Cambridge: Cambridge University Press.

Cantlon, J. F., E. M. Brannon, E. J. Carter, and K. A. Pelphrey. 2006. Functional imaging of numerical processing in adults and 4-year-old children. *PLOS Biology* 4:844–54.

Caplan, D. and G. S. Waters. 1995. On the nature of the phonological output planning processes involved in verbal rehearsal: Evidence from aphasia. *Brain and Language*. 48:191–220.

Carbonell, E. et al. 2005. An early Pleistocene hominin mandible from Atapuerca-TD6, Spain. *Proceedings of the National Academy of Sciences*, 106(16):5674–8.

Carruthers, P. 2002. The cognitive functions of language. *Behavioral and Brain Sciences*, 25:657–75.

Cartwright, R. and L. Lamberg. 1992. *Crisis Dreaming: Using Your Dreams to Solve Your Problems*. New York: Harper Collins.

Casson, E. 1981. *Language, Culture, and Cognition*. New York: Macmillan.

Chazan, M. 1997. Review of: *Le Concept Levallois: Variabilité des Méthodes*, by E. Boeda; *The Levallois Reduction Strategy* by P. van Peer; and *The Definition and Interpretation of Levallois Technology*, edited by H. Dibble and O. Bar Yosef. *Journal of Human Evolution*, 33:719–35.

Choi, J. and I. Silverman. 2003. Processes underlying sex differences in route-learning strategies in children and adolescents. *Personality and Individual Differences*, 34:1153–66.

Chow, T. and J. Cummings. 1999. Frontal-subcortical circuits, in *The Human Frontal Lobes*. Edited by B. Miller and J. Cummings, pp. 3–26.

Cicogna, P., V. Natale, M. Occhionero, and M. Bosinelli. 1998. A comparison of mental activity during sleep onset and morning awakening. *Sleep*, 21:462–70.

Clark, J. D. (ed.). 2001. *Kalambo Falls Prehistoric Site, Vol. III*. Cambridge: Cambridge University Press.

Collard, M. 2002. Grades and transitions in human evolution, in *The Speciation of Modern Homo sapiens*. Edited by T. Crow. Oxford: Oxford University Press.

Collete, F., and M. Van der Linden. 2002. Brain imaging of the central executive component of working memory. *Neuroscience and Biobehavioral Reviews*, 26:102–25.

Conard, N. J. and M. Bolus. 2003. Radiocarbon dating the appearance of the modern humans and timing of cultural innovations in Europe: New results and new challenges. *Journal of Human Evolution*, 44:331–71.

Coolidge, F. L. 1974. Memory consolidation as a function of sleep and the circadian rhythm. (Doctoral dissertation, University of Florida, 1974). *Dissertation Abstracts International*, 36B, 0934.

Coolidge, F. 2006. *Dream Interpretation as a Psychotherapeutic Technique*. London: Radcliffe.

Coolidge, F., L. Thede, and S. Young. 2000. Heritability and the comorbidity of ADHD with behavioral disorders and executive function deficits: a preliminary investigation. *Developmental Neuropsychology*, 11:273–87.

Coolidge, F. and T. Wynn. 2004. A cognitive and neuropsychological perspective on the Chatelperronian. *Journal of Anthropological Research*, 60:55–73.

Coolidge, F. and T. Wynn. 2005. Working memory, its executive functions, and the emergence of modern thinking. *Cambridge Archaeological Journal*, 15:5–26.

Corballis, M. C. 2002. *From Hand to Mouth: The Origins of Language*. Princeton, NJ: Princeton University Press; also in paperback, 2003.

Corballis, M. C. 2003. From hand to mouth: The gestural origins of language, in *Language Evolution: The States of the Art*. Edited by M. Christiansen and S. Kirby. Oxford: Oxford University Press.

Cosmides, L. 1989. The logic of social exchange: Has natural selection shaped how humans reason? Studies with the Wason selection task. *Cognition*, 31:187–276.

Cruse, D. 2000. *Meaning in Language: An Introduction to Semantics and Pragmatics*. Oxford: Oxford University Press.

Damasio, A. 1999. *The Feeling of What Happens: Body and Emotion in the Making of Consciousness*. New York: Harcourt and Company.

Daneman, M. and P. Carpenter. 1980. Individual differences in working memory and reading. *Journal of Verbal Learning and Verbal Behavior*, 19:450–66.

Daneman, M. and P. A. Carpenter. 1983. Individual differences in integrating information between and within sentences. *Journal of Experimental Psychology: Learning, Memory, and Cognition*, 9:561–84.

Daneman, M. and I. Green. 1986. Individual differences in comprehending and producing words in context. *Journal of Memory and Language*, 25:1–18.

Davidson, G., J. Neale, and A. Kring. 2004. *Abnormal Psychology*, 9th edn. Hoboken: Wiley.

Davidson, I. and W. Noble. 1992. Why the first colonisation of the Australian region is the earliest evidence of modern human behaviour. *Archaeology in Oceania*, 27:135–42.

Dawkins, R. 1989. *The Selfish Gene.* New York: Oxford University Press.

Deacon, H. 1993. Planting an idea: An archaeology of Stone Age gatherers in South Africa. *South African Archeological Journal,* 48:86–93.

Deacon, H. J. and J. Deacon. 1999. *Human Beginnings in South Africa: Uncovering the Secrets of the Stone Age.* Walnut Creek, CA: Altamira Press.

Dean, C. et al. 2001. Growth processes in teeth distinguish modern humans from *Homo erectus* and earlier hominins. *Nature,* 414:628–31.

de Castro, J. and M. Nicolas. 1997. Palaeodemography of the Atapuerca-SH Middle Pleistocene hominid sample. *Journal of Human Evolution,* 33:333–55.

DeGusta, D., W. Gilbert, and S. Turner. 1999. Hypoglossal canal size and hominid speech. *Proceedings of the National Academy of Sciences* 96:1800–4.

Delagnes, A. and H. Roche. 2005. Late Pliocene hominid knapping skills: The case of Lokalalei 2C, West Turkana, Kenya. *Journal of Human Evolution,* 48:435–72.

de la Torre, I. et al. 2003. The Oldowan industry of Peninj and its bearing on the reconstruction of the technological skill of Lower Pleistocene hominids. *Journal of Human Evolution,* 44:203–24.

Dement, W. 1972. *Some Must Watch While Some Must Sleep.* San Francisco: W. H. Freeman.

Dement, W. and C. Vaughn. 1999. *The Promise of Sleep: A Pioneer in Sleep Medicine Explores the Vital Connection between Health, Happiness, and a Good Night's Sleep.* New York: Delacorte Press.

Dennell, R. and W. Roebroeks. 1996. The earliest colonization of Europe: The short chronology revisited. *Antiquity,* 70:535–42.

d'Errico, F. and A. Nowell. 2000. A new look at the Berekhat Ram figurine: Implications for the origins of symbolism. *Cambridge Archaeological Journal,* 10:123–67.

d'Errico, F., C. Henshilwood, and P. Nilssen. 2001. An engraved bone fragment from *c.* 70,000-year-old Middle Stone Age levels at Blombos Cave, South Africa: Implications for the origin of symbolism and language. *Antiquity,* 75:309–18.

d'Errico, F. et al. 2003. Archaeological evidence for the emergence of language, symbolism, and music – an alternative multidisciplinary perspective. *Journal of World Prehistory,* 17:1–70.

d'Errico, F., C. Henshilwood, M. Vanhaeren, and K. van Niekerk. 2005. *Nassarius kraussianus* shell beads from Blombos Cave: Evidence for symbolic behaviour in the Middle Stone Age. *Journal of Human Evolution,* 48:3–24.

Domhoff, G. 1996. *Finding Meaning in Dreams: A Quantitative Approach.* New York: John Wiley & Sons.

Dominguez-Rodrigo, M. 2002. Hunting and scavenging by early humans: The state of the debate. *Journal of World Prehistory,* 16:1–54.

Dominguez-Rodrigo, M. and R. Barba. 2006. New estimates of tooth mark and percussion mark frequencies at the FLK Zinj site: The carnivore-hominid-carnivore hypothesis falsified. *Journal of Human Evolution,* 50:170–94.

Dominguez-Rodrigo, M. et al. 2001. Woodworking activities by early humans: A plant residue analysis on Acheulean stone tools from Peninj (Tanzania). *Journal of Human Evolution*, 40:289–99.

Donald, M. 1991. *Origins of the Modern Mind: Three Stages in the Evolution of Culture and Cognition*. Cambridge, MA.: Harvard University Press.

Dudai, Y. and P. Carruthers. 2005. The Janus face of Mnemosyne. *Nature*, 434.

Dunbar, R. 1993. Coevolution of neocortical size, group size and language in humans. *Behavioral and Brain Sciences*, 16:681–735.

Dunbar, R., L. Barrett, and J. Lycett. 2005. *Evolutionary Psychology: A Beginner's Guide*. Oxford: Oneworld.

Eals, M. and I. Silverman. 1994. The hunter-gatherer theory of spatial sex differences: Proximate factors mediating the female advantage in recall of object arrays. *Ethology and Sociobiology*, 15:95–105.

Ellman, S. and J. Antrobus. 1991. *The Mind in Sleep: Psychology and Psychophysiology*. New York: John Wiley & Sons.

Engle, R. and M. Kane. 2004. Executive attention, working memory capacity, and a two-factor theory of cognitive control, in *The Psychology of Learning and Motivation 44*. Edited by B. Ross, 145–99. New York: Elsevier.

Ericsson, K. and P. Delaney. 1999. Long-term working memory as an alternative to capacity models of working memory in everyday skilled performance, in *Models of Working Memory: Mechanisms of Active Maintenance and Executive Control*. Edited by A. Miyake and P. Shah, pp. 257–97. Cambridge: Cambridge University Press.

Ericsson, K. A. and W. Kintsch. 1995. Long-term working memory. *Psychological Review*, 102:211–45.

Evans, P. et al. 2005. *Microcephalin*, a gene regulating brain size, continues to evolve adaptively in humans. *Science*, 309:1717–20.

Everett, D. 2005. Cultural constraints on grammar and cognition in Piraha. *Current Anthropology*, 46:621–46.

Féblot-Augustins, J. 1999. Raw material transport patterns and settlement systems in the European Lower and Middle Palaeolithic: Continuity, change and variability, in *The Middle Palaeolithic Occupation of Europe*. Edited by W. Roebroeks and C. Gamble, pp. 193–214. Leiden: Leiden University.

Feldman Barrett, L., M. M. Tugade, and R. Engle. 2004. Individual differences in working memory capacity and dual-process theories of the mind. *Psychological Bulletin*, 130:553–73.

Fischer, S., M. Hallschmid, A. L. Elsner, and J. Born. 2002. Sleep forms memory for finger skills. *Proceedings of the National Academy of Sciences*, 99:11987–91.

Foley, R. and M. Lahr. 1997. Mode 3 technologies and the evolution of modern humans. *Cambridge Archaeological Journal*, 7:3–36.

Frankish, K. 1998a. A matter of opinion. *Philosophical Psychology*, 11:423–42.

Frankish, K. 1998b. Natural language and virtual belief, in *Language and Thought*. Edited by P. Carruthers and J. Boucher. Cambridge: Cambridge University Press.

Franklin, M. and M. Zyphur. 2005. The role of dreams in the evolution of the human mind. *Evolutionary Psychology*, 3:59–78.

Freud, S. 1900/1956. *The Interpretation of Dreams*. New York: Basic Books.

Fruth, B. and G. Hohman. 1996. Nest building behavior in the great apes: The great leap forward?, in *Great Ape Societies*. Edited by W. C. McGrew, L. Marchant, and T. Nishida. Cambridge: Cambridge University Press.

Fuster, J. M. 1997. *The Prefrontal Cortex: Anatomy, Physiology, and Neuropsychology of the Frontal Lobe*, 3rd edn. Philadelphia, PA: Lippincott-Raven.

Gabunia, L. et al. 2001. Dmanisi and dispersal. *Evolutionary Anthropology*, 10:158–70.

Gais, S., W. Plihal, U. Wagner, and J. Born. 2000. Early sleep triggers memory for early visual discrimination skills. *Nature Neuroscience*, 3:1335–9.

Gamble, C. 1999. *The Palaeolithic Societies of Europe*. Cambridge: Cambridge University Press.

Gangestad, S. 1997. Evolutionary psychology and genetic variation: Non-adaptive, fitness-related, and adaptive, in *Characterizing Human Psychological Adaptations, CIBA Foundation Symposium #208*. Edited by G. Bock and G. Cardew, pp. 212–30. New York: John Wiley & Sons.

Gannon, P., R. Holloway, D. Broadfield, and A. Braun. 1998. Asymmetry of chimpanzee planum temporale: Humanlike pattern of Wernicke's brain language area homolog. *Science*, 279:220–2.

Gargett, R. 1999. Middle Palaeolithic burial is not a dead issue: The view from Qafzeh, Saint-Cesaire, Kebara, Amud, and Dederiyeh. *Journal of Human Evolution*, 37:27–90.

Gatewood, J. 1985. Actions speak louder than words, in *Directions in Cognitive Anthropology*. Edited by J. Dougherty, pp. 199–220. Urbana, IL: University of Illinois Press.

Gathercole, S., S. Pickering, B. Ambridge, and H. Wearing. 2004. The structure of working memory from 4 to 15 years of age. *Developmental Psychology*, 40:177–90.

Gazzaniga, M., R. Ivry, and G. Mangun (eds.). 2002. *Cognitive Neuroscience*, 2nd edn. New York: W. W. Norton & Co.

Geneste, J.-M. 1988. Les industries de la Grotte Vaufrey: technologie du débitage, économie et circulation de la matiere première lithique, in *La Grotte Vaufrey a Cenac et Saint-Julien (Dordogne), Paléoenvironments, chronologie et activités humaines*. Edited by J. Rigaud, vol. 19, pp. 441–518. Paris: Mémoires de la Société Prehistorique Francaise.

Goldberg, E. 2002. *The Executive Brain: Frontal Lobes and the Civilized Mind*. London: Oxford University Press.

Goldman-Rakic, P. 1995. Architecture of the prefrontal cortex and the central executive. *Annals of the New York Academy of Sciences*, 769:71–84.

Golomb, C. 1992. *The Child's Creation of a Pictorial World*. Berkeley, CA: University of California Press.

Goren-Inbar, N., E. Werker, and C. S. Feibel. 2002. *The Acheulian Site of Gesher Benot Ya'aqov, Israel: The Wood Assemblage.* Oxford: Oxbow Books.

Gould, S. 2002. *The Structure of Evolutionary Theory.* Cambridge, MA: Belknap.

Gould, S. and E. Vrba. 1982. Exaptation – a missing term in the science of form. *Paleobiology,* 8:4–15.

Green, R. et al. 2006. Analysis of one million base pairs of Neanderthal DNA. *Nature,* 444:330–6.

Gregor, T. 1977. *The Mehinaku: The Dream of Daily Life in a Brazilian Indian Village.* Chicago, IL: University of Chicago Press.

Groves, C. and J. Sabater Pi. 1985. From ape's nest to human fix-point. *Man,* 20:22–47.

Haeusler, M. and H. McHenry. 2004. Body proportions of *Homo habilis* reviewed. *Journal of Human Evolution,* 46:433–65.

Hahn, J. 1986. *Kraft und Aggression: Die Botschaft der Eiszeitkunst in Aurignacien Süddeutschlands?* Vol. 7. Archaeological Venatoria. Tubingen.

Haidle, M. (in press). How to think a simple spear. In *New Contributions to Cognitive Archaeology.* Edited by S. de Baune, F. Coolidge, and T. Wynn Cambridge: Cambridge University Press.

Haldane, J. 1927. A mathematical theory of natural and artificial selection, part v: Selection and mutation. *Proceedings of the Cambridge Philosophical Society,* 23:838–44.

Halford, G. S., N. Cowan, and G. Andrews. 2007. Separating cognitive capacity from knowldge: A new hypothesis. *Trends in Cognitive Science,* 11:236–42.

Hallos, J. 2005. 15 minutes of Fame: Exploring the temporal dimension of Middle Pleistocene lithic technology. *Journal of Human Evolution,* 49:155–79.

Halpern, D. 1992. *Sex Differences in Cognitive Ability,* 2nd edn: L. Erlbaum.

Hamilton, A. F. and S. T. Grafton. 2006. Goal representation in human anterior intraparietal sulcus. *Journal of Neuroscience,* 26:1133–7.

Hansell, N. et al. 2001. Genetic influence on ERP slow wave measures of working memory. *Behavior Genetics,* 31:603–14.

Harlow, J. 1868. Recovery from the passage of an iron bar through the head. *Publications of the Massachusetts Medical Society,* 2:327–46.

Hart, D. and R. W. Sussman. 2005. *Man the Hunted.* Cambridge, MA: Westview Press.

Hartman, E. 1998. *Dreams and Nightmares: The New Theory on the Origin and Meaning of Dreams.* New York: Plenum.

Hauser, M., N. Chomsky, and W. Fitch. 2002. The faculty of language: What is it, who has it, and how did it evolve? *Science,* 298:1569–79.

Hayden, B. 1993. The cultural capacities of Neandertals: A review and re-evaluation. *Journal of Human Evolution,* 24:113–46.

Hazy, T., M. Frank, and R. O'Reilly. 2006. Banishing the homunculus: Making working memory work. *Neuroscience,* 139:105–18.

Henry, D. 1998. Intrasite spatial patterns and behavioral modernity: Indications from the late Levantine Mousterian rockshelter of Tor Faraj, southern Jordan, in *Neandertals and Modern Humans in Western Asia*. Edited by T. Azakawa, K. Aoki, and O. Bar-Yosef, pp. 127–42. New York: Plenum.

Henshilwood, C. and B. Dubreuil (in press). Reading the artefacts: Gleaning language skills from the Middle Stone Age in southern Africa, in *The Cradle of Language*. Edited by R. Botha. Stellenbosch, South Africa.

Henshilwood, C. and C. Marean. 2003. The origin of modern human behavior. *Current Anthropology*, 44:627–51.

Hermer-Velasquez, L. and E. Spelke. 1996. Modularity and development: The case of spatial reorientation. *Cognition*, 61:195–232.

Hermer-Velasquez, L., E. Spelke, and A. Katsnelson. 1999. Sources of flexibility in human cognition: Dual-task studies of space and language. *Cognitive Psychology* 39:3–36.

Hobson, J. 1988. *The Dreaming Brain*. New York: Basic Books.

Hobson, J. A., E. F. Pace-Schott, and R. Stickgold. 2000. Dreaming and the brain: Toward a cognitive neruoscience of conscious states. *Behavioral and Brain Sciences*, 23:793–842.

Hodgson, D. 2000. Art, perception and information processing: An evolutionary perspective. *Rock Art Research*, 17:3–34.

Hodgson, D. and P. Helvenston. 2006. The emergence of the representation of animals in palaeoart: Insights from evolution and the cognitive, limbic and visual systems of the human brain. *Rock Art Research*, 23:3–40.

Holloway, R. 1969. Culture: A human domain. *Current Anthropology*, 10:395–412.

Holloway, R. 1983. Human brain evolution: A search for units, models, and synthesis. *Canadian Journal of Anthropology*, 3:215–30.

Holloway, R. 1995. Toward a synthetic theory of human brain evolution, in *Origins of the Human Brain*. Edited by J.-P. Changeaux and J. Chavaillon. Oxford: Clarendon Press.

Holloway, R., D. Broadfield, and M. Yuan. 2004. *The Human Fossil Record Vol. 3: Brain Endocasts – The Paleoneurological Evidence*. New York: Wiley-Liss.

Hovers, E. 2006. Comment on "What's a mother to do: The division of labor among Neandertals and modern humans in Eurasia." *Current Anthropology*, 47:965–6.

Hublin, J. 1998. Climatic changes, paleogeography, and the evolution of the Neandertals, in *Neandertals and Modern Humans in Western Asia*. Edited by T. Azakawa, K. Aoki, and O. Bar-Yosef. New York: Plenum.

Hublin, J. 2007. What can Neanderthals tell us about modern human origins?, in *Rethinking the Human Revolution*. Edited by P. Mellars, K. Boyle, O. Bar Yosef, and C. B. Stringer, pp. 235–48. Cambridge: McDonald Institute for Archaeological Research.

Humphrey, N. 1976. The social function of intellect, in *Growing Points in Ethology*. Edited by P. Bateson and R. Hinde. Cambridge: Cambridge University Press.

Isaac, G. 1976. Stages of cultural elaboration in the Pleistocene: Possible archaeo-logical indicators of the development of language capabilities, in *Origins and Evolution of Language and Speech*. Edited by S. Harnad, H. Steklis, and J. Lancaster, pp. 275–88. New York: New York Academy of Science.

Jerison, H. 1973. *Evolution of Brain and Intelligence*. New York: Academic Press.

Johanson, D. 2004. Lucy, thirty years later: An expanded view of *Australopithecus afarensis*. *Journal of Anthropological Archaeology*, 60:465–86.

Jones, P. 1981. Experimental implement manufacture and use: A case study from Olduvai Gorge, Tanzania, in *The Emergence of Man*. Edited by J. Young, E. Jope, and K. Oakley, pp. 189–95. London: The Royal Society and the British Academy.

Joulian, F. 1996. Comparing chimpanzee and early hominid techniques: Some contributions to cultural and cognitive questions, in *Modelling the Early Human Mind*. Edited by P. Mellars and K. Gibson, pp. 173–19. Oxford: Oxbow.

Jouvet, M. 1980. Paradoxical sleep and the nature–nurture controversy. *Progress in Brain Research*, 53:331–46.

Kane, M. and R. Engle. 2002. The role of prefrontal cortex in working-memory capacity, executive attention, and general fluid intelligence: An individual-differences perspective. *Psychonomic Bulletin and Review*, 9:637–71.

Kappeler, P. 1998. Nests, tree holes, and the evolution of primate life histories. *American Journal of Primatology*, 46:7–33.

Kappelman, J. 1996. The evolution of body mass and relative brain size in fossil hominids. *Journal of Human Evolution*, 30:243–76.

Karni, A., D. Tanne, B. S. Rubenstein, J. J. Askenasy, and D. Sagi. 1994. Dependence on REM sleep of overnight improvement of a perceptual skill. *Science*, 265:679–82.

Kavanau, J. 2002. REM and NREM sleep as natural accompaniments of the evolution of warm-bloodedness. *Neuroscience and Biobehavioral Reviews*, 26:889–906.

Kawai, N. and T. Matsuzawa. 2000. Numerical memory span in a chimpanzee. *Nature*, 403:39–40.

Kay, R., M. Cartmill, and M. Balow. 1998. The hypoglossal canal and the origin of human vocal behavior. *Proceedings of the National Academy of Sciences*, 95:5417–19.

Keller, C. and J. Keller. 1996. *Cognition and Tool Use: The Blacksmith at Work*. Cambridge: Cambridge University Press.

Kimbel, W. et al. 1996. Late Pliocene *Homo* and Oldowan tools from the Hadar formation (Kadar Hadar Member), Ethiopia. *Journal of Human Evolution*, 31:549–61.

King, J. W. and M. A. Just. 1991. Individual differences in syntactic processing: The role of working memory. *Journal of Memory and Language*, 30:580–602.

Kirk, E. C. 2006. Visual influences on primate encephalization. *Journal of Human Evolution*, 51:76–90.

Klein, R. and K. Cruz-Uribe. 2000. Middle and Later Stone Age large mammal and tortoise remains from Die Kelders Cave 1, Western Cape Province, South Africa. *Journal of Human Evolution*, 38(1):169–95.

Klein, R. and B. Edgar. 2002. *The Dawn of Human Culture*. New York: Wiley & Sons.

Kleindienst, M. 1961. Variability within the Late Acheulian assemblage in East Africa. *South African Archeological Bulletin*, 16:35–52.

Knight, C. 2009. Language, ochre and the rule of law, in *The Cradle of Language Conference*. Edited by R. Botha and C. Knight. Stellenbosch, South Africa.

Knott, C. 2001. Female reproductive ecology of the apes: Implications for human evolution, in *Reproductive Ecology and Human Evolution*. P. Ellison, pp. 429–62. Aldine.

Kohn, M. and S. Mithen. 1999. Handaxes: Products of sexual selection? *Antiquity*, 73:518–26.

Koops, K., T. Humle, H. Sterck, and T. Matsuzawa. 2007. Ground nesting by the chimpanzees of the Nimba Mountains, Guinea: Environmentally or socially determined? *American Journal of Primatology*, 69:407–19.

Kosslyn, S. 1994. *Image and Brain: The Resolution of the Imagery Debate*. Cambridge, MA: MIT Press.

Krantz, G. 1980. Sapienzation and speech. *Current Anthropology*, 21:771–92.

Krippner, S. and W. Hughes. 1970. Genius at work. *Psychology Today*, June:40–3.

Kuhn, S. and M. Stiner. 2006. What's a mother to do: The division of labor among Neandertals and modern humans in Eurasia. *Current Anthropology*, 47:953–80.

Kyllonen, P. 1996. Is working memory capacity Spearman's g?, in *Human Abilities: Their Nature and Measurement*. Edited by I. Dennis and P. Tapsfield. Mahwah, NJ: Lawrence Erlbaum.

Kyllonen, P. and R. Crystal. 1990. Reasoning ability is (little more than) working–memory capacity? *Intelligence*, 14:389–433.

LaBerge, S. 1985. *Lucid Dreaming*. New York: Ballantine.

Laden, G. and R. W. Wrangham. 2005. The rise of hominids as an adaptive shift in fallback foods: Underground storage organs (USOs) and australopith origins. *Journal of Human Evolution*, 49:482–98.

Leakey, M. 1971. *Olduvai Gorge Vol. 3*. Cambridge: Cambridge University Press.

LeDoux, J. 1996. *The Emotional Brain: The Mysterious Underpinnings of Emotional Life*. New York: Touchstone.

Leigh, S. 2005. Brain ontogeny and life history in *Homo erectus*. *Journal of Human Evolution*, 50:104–8.

Levinson, S. 2000. *Pragmatics*. Cambridge: Cambridge University Press.

Levy, C. M., F. Coolidge, and L. C. Staab. 1972. Paired associated learning during EEG–defined sleep: A preliminary study. *Australian Journal of Psychology*, 24:219–25.

Lewis, H. 1982. Fire technology and resource management in aboriginal North America and Australia, in *Resource Managers: North American and Australian Hunter-gatherers*. Edited by N. Williams and E. Hunn, pp. 45–68. Washington, DC: American Association for the Advancement of Science.

Lezak, M. 1982. The problem of assessing executive functions. *International Journal of Psychology*, 17:281–97.

Lezak, M. 1995. *Neuropsychological Assessment*, 3rd edn. New York: Oxford University Press.

Lieberman, D. 1998. Neandertal and modern human mobility patterns: Comparing archaeological and anatomical evidence. In *Neandertals and Modern Humans in Western Asia*. Edited by T. Azakawa, K. Aoki and O. Bar-Yosef, pp. 263–76. New York: Plenum.

Lieberman, P. 1984. *The Biology and Evolution of Language*. Cambridge, MA: Harvard University Press.

Lieberman, P. 1989. The origins and some aspects of human language and cognition, in *The Human Revolution: Behavioural and Biological Perspectives in the Origins of Modern Humans*. Edited by P. Mellars and C. B. Stringer, pp. 391–41. Edinburgh: Edinburgh University Press.

Lima, S., N. Rattenborg, J. Lesku, and C. Amlaner. 2005. Sleeping under the risk of predation. *Animal Behavior*, 70:163–6.

Logie, R. 1995. *Visuo-Spatial Working Memory*. Hillsdale, NJ: Lawrence Erlbaum.

Lorenz, K. 1973. *Die Ruckseite des Spiegels*. Munich: R. Piper and Co.

Lou, H. et al. 2004. Parietal cortex and representation of the mental self. *Proceedings of the National Academy of Sciences*, 101:6827–32.

Lovejoy, O. 2005. The natural history of human gait and posture Part 1. Spine and pelvis. *Gait and Posture*, 21(1):95–112.

Luria, A. R. 1973. *The Working Brain: An Introduction to Neuropsychology*. New York: Basic Books.

MacAndrew, D. et al. 2002. The phonological similarity effect differentiates between two working memory tasks. *Psychological Science*, 13:465–8.

McBrearty, A. and A. Brooks. 2000. The revolution that wasn't: A new interpretation of the origin of modern human behavior. *Journal of Human Evolution*, 39:453–563.

McGrew, W. C. 1992. *Chimpanzee Material Culture*. Cambridge: Cambridge University Press.

McGrew, W. C. and L. Marchant. 1997. On the other hand: Current issues in and meta-analysis of the behavioral laterality of hand function in nonhuman primates. *Yearbook of Physical Anthropology*, 40:201–32.

McHenry, H. 1992a. Body size and proportions in early hominids. *American Journal of Physical Anthropology*, 87:407–31.

McHenry, H. 1992b. How big were early hominids? *Evolutionary Anthropology*, 1:15–20.

McHenry, H. and K. Coffing. 2000. *Australopithecus* to *Homo*: Transformation in body and mind. *Annual Review of Anthropology*, 29:125–46.

Machin, A., R. Hosfield, and S. Mithen. 2006. Why are some handaxes symmetrical? Testing the influence of handaxe morphology on butchery effectiveness. *Journal of Archaeological Science*, 34:883–93.

MacLarnon, A. 1993. The vertebral canal, in *The Nariokotome Homo erectus Skeleton*. Edited by A. Walker and R. Leakey, pp. 359–90. Cambridge, MA.: Harvard University Press.

MacLeod, C. 2004. What's in a brain: The question of a distinctive brain anatomy in great apes, in *The Evolution of Thought: Evolutionary Origins of Great Ape Intelligence*. Edited by A. Russon and D. Begun, pp. 105–21. Cambridge: Cambridge University Press.

McPherron, S. P. 2000. Handaxes as a measure of the mental abilities of early hominids. *Journal of Archaeological Science*, 27:655–63.

Malcolm-Smith, S. and M. Solms. 2004. Incidence of threat in dreams: A response to Revonsuo's threat simulation theory. *Dreaming*, 14:220–9.

Mandler, J. 2004. Thought before language. *Trends in Cognitive Science*, 8:508–13.

Mania, D. and U. Mania. 2005. The natural and socio-cultural environment of *Homo erectus* at Belzingsleben, Germany, in *The Hominid Individual in Context: Archaeological Investigations of Lower and Middle Palaeolithic Landscapes, Locales, and Artefacts*. Edited by C. Gamble and M. Porr, pp. 98–114. London: Routledge.

Maquet, P., S. Schwartz, R. Passingham, and C. Frith. 2003. Sleep-related consolidation of a visuomotor skill: Brain mechanisms as assessed by functional magnetic resonance imaging. *Journal of Neuroscience*, 23:1432–40.

Marshack, A. 1985. *Hierarchical Evolution of the Human Capacity: The Palaeolithic Evidence. James Arthur Lecture on "The Evolution of the Human Brain."* New York: American Museum of Natural History.

Marshack, A. 1997. The Berekhat Ram figurine: A late Acheulian carving from the Middle East. *Antiquity*, 71, 327–37.

Marshack, A. 2002. Okuzini: The complexity and variation of the symbolic imagery, in *Okuzini: Final Paleolithic Evolution in Southwest Anatolia*. Edited by I. Yalcinkaya, M. Otte, J. Kozlowski, and O. Bar-Yosef. Liege: University of Liege.

Martin, A. 2007. The representation of object concepts in the brain. *Annual Review of Psychology*, 58:25–45.

Martin, A., L. Ungerleider and J. Haxby. 2000. Category specificity and the brain: The sensory/motor model of semantic representations of objects, in *The New Cognitive Neurosciences*, 2nd edn. Edited by M. Gazzaniga, pp. 1023–36. Cambridge, MA: MIT Press.

Marzke, M. 1996. Evolution of the hand and bipedality, in *Handbook of Human Symbolic Evolution*. Edited by A. Lock and C. Peters. Oxford: Oxford University Press.

Mazza, P. et al. 2006. A new palaeolithic discovery: Tar-hafted stone tools in a European Mid-Pleistocene bone-bearing bed. *Journal of Archaeological Science*, 33:1310–18.

Medin, D. and S. Atran. 2004. The native mind: Biological categorization and reasoning in development and across cultures. *Psychological Review*, 111:960–83.

Mellars, P. 1996. *The Neanderthal Legacy: An Archaeological Perspective from Western Europe*. Princeton, NJ: Princeton University Press.

Middleton, F. and P. Strick. 2001. A revised neuroanatomy of frontal-subcortical circuits, in *Frontal-subcortical Circuits in Psychiatric and Neurological Disorders*. Edited by D. Lichter and J. Cummings. New York: Guilford Press.

Mithen, S. 1996. *The Prehistory of Mind*. London: Thames and Hudson.

Mithen, S. 2006. *The Singing Neanderthals: The Origins of Music, Language, Mind, and Body*. Cambridge, MA: Harvard University Press.

Miyake, A. and P. Shah (eds.). 1999. *Models of Working Memory: Mechanisms of Active Maintenance and Executive Control*. Cambridge: Cambridge University Press.

Miyake, A. et al. 2000. The unity and diversity of executive functions and their contributions to complex "frontal lobe" tasks: A latent variable analysis. *Cognitive Psychology*, 41:49–100.

Moore, A. M. T., G. C. Hillman, and A. J. Legge. 2000. *Village on the Euphrates: From Foraging to Farming at Abu Hureyra*. Oxford: Oxford University Press.

Mora, R. and I. De la Torre. 2005. Percussion tools in Olduvai Beds I and II (Tanzania): Implications for early human activities. *Journal of Anthropological Archaeology*, 24:179–92.

Morley, K. I. and G. W. Montgomery. 2001. The genetics of cognitive processes: Candidate genes in humans and animals. *Behaviour Genetics*, 31:511–31.

Morrison, A. 1983. A window on the sleeping brain. *Scientific American* 248:94–102.

Noble, W. and I. Davidson. 1996. *Human Evolution, Language, and Mind: A Psychological and Archaeological Inquiry*. Cambridge: Cambridge University Press.

Noonan, J. et al. 2006. Sequencing and analysis of Neanderthal genomic DNA. *Science*, 314:1113–18.

Norman, D. and T. Shallice. 1980. *Attention to Action: Willed and Automatic Control of Behaviour*. San Diego, CA: University of California.

Nowell, A. and F. d'Errico. 2007. The art of taphonomy and the taphonomy of art: Layer IV, Molodova, Ukraine. *Journal of Archaeological Method & Theory*, 14(1):1–26.

O'Brien, E. 1981. The projectile capabilities of an Acheulian handaxe from Olorgesailie. *Current Anthropology*, 22:76–9.

Oberauer, K., H.-M. Suss, O. Wilhelm, and W. Wittman. 2003. The multiple faces of working memory: Storage, processing, supervision, and coordination. *Intelligence*, 31:167–93.

O'Connell, J., K. Hawkes, and N. Burton Jones. 1999. Grandmothering and the evolution of *Homo erectus*. *Journal of Human Evolution*, 36:461–85.

Oppenheim, A. 1956. The interpretation of dreams in the ancient Near East, with a translation of an Assyrian Dream-Book. *Transactions of the American Philosophical Society*, 46:179–305.

Osaka, N., R. H. Logie, and M. D'Esposito (eds.). 2007. *The Cognitive Neuroscience of Working Memory.* Oxford: Oxford University Press.

Oswalt, W. 1976. *An Anthropological Analysis of Food-Getting Technology.* New York: John Wiley.

Parker, S. and K. Gibson. 1979. A developmental model for the evolution of language and intelligence in early hominids. *Behavioral and Brain Sciences*, 2:367–408.

Peigneux, P. S. et al. 2004. Are spatial memories strengthened in the human hipo-campus during slow wave sleep? *Neuron*, 44:535–45.

Pembrey, M. E. et al. and the ALSPAC Study Team. 2006. Sex-specific, male-line transgenerational responses in humans. *European Journal of Human Genetics*, 14:159–66.

Pennington, B. and S. Ozonoff. 1996. Executive functions and developmental psychopathology. *Journal of Child Psychology and Psychiatry*, 37:51–87.

Pinker, S. 1997a. *How the Mind Works.* New York: Norton.

Pinker, S. 1997b. Language as a psychological adaptation, in *Characterizing Human Psychological Adaptations, Ciba Foundation Symposia*, 208. Edited by G. Bock and G. Cardew, pp. 162–80. New York: John Wiley & Sons.

Plavcan, J. and C. van Schaik. 1997. Interpreting hominid behavior on the basis sexual dimorphism. *Journal of Human Evolution*, 32(4):345–74.

Pope, G. 1989. Bamboo and human evolution. *Natural History*, 10:48–57.

Pope, M. and M. A. Roberts. 2005. Observations on the relationship between Palaeolithic individuals and artefact scatters at the Middle Pleistocene site of Boxgrove, UK, in *The Hominid Individual in Context: Archaeological Investigations of Lower and Middle Palaeolithic Landscapes, Locales, and Artefacts.* London: Routledge.

Povenelli, D. and J. Cant. 1995. Arboreal clambering and the evolution of self-conception. *Quarterly Review of Biology*, 70:393–421.

Pye, D. 1964. *The Nature of Design.* London: Studio Vista.

Rabett, R. and G. Barker. 2007. Through the looking glass: New evidence on the presence and behaviour of Late Pleistocene humans at Niah Cave, Sarawak, Borneo, in *Rethinking the Human Revolution: New Behavioural and Biological Perspectives on the Origin and Dispersal of Modern Humans.* Edited by P. Mellars, K. Boyle, O. Bar-Yosef, and C. Stringer, pp. 411–24. Cambridge: McDonald Institute for Archaeological Research.

Reed, K. 1997. Early hominid evolution and ecological change through the African Plio-Pleistocene. *Journal of Human Evolution*, 32:289–322.

Reuland, E. 2005. On the evolution and genesis of language: The force of imagination. *Lingue e Linguaggio*, 4:81–110.

Revonsuo, A. 2000. The reinterpretation of dreams: An evolutionary hypothesis of the function of dreaming. *Behavioral and Brain Sciences*, 23:877–901.

Ribeiro, S., V. Goyal, C. V. Mello, and C. Pavlides. 1999. Brain gene expression during REM sleep depends on prior waking experience. *Learning & Memory*, 6:500–8.

Richmond, B. G., D. Begun, and D. Strait. 2001. Origin of human bipedalism: The knucklewalking hypothesis revisited. *Yearbook of Physical Anthropology*, 44:70–105.

Rightmire, G. 1981. Stasis in the evolution of *Homo erectus*. *Paleobiology*, 7:200–15.

Rightmire, G. 2001. Patterns of hominid evolution and dispersal in the Middle Pleistocene. *Quaternary International*, 75:77–84.

Rightmire, G. 2004. Brain size and encephalization in early to mid-Pleistocene *Homo*. *American Journal of Physical Anthropology*, 124:109–23.

Rightmire, G., D. Lordkipanidze, and A. Vekua. 2006. Anatomical descriptions, comparative studies and evolutionary significance of the hominin skulls from Dmanisi, Republic of Georgia. *Journal of Human Evolution*, 50:115–41.

Rijsdijk, F., P. Vernon, and D. Boomsma. 2002. Application of hierarchical genetic models to raven and WAIS subtests: A Dutch twin study. *Behavior Genetics*, 32:199–210.

Robbins, P. and F. Houshi. 1983. Some observations on recurrent dreams. *Bulletin of the Menninger Clinic*, 47:262–5.

Roberts, M. A. and S. A. Parfitt. 1999. *Boxgrove: A Middle Pleistocene Hominid Site at Eartham Quarry, Boxgrove, West Sussex*. London: English Heritage.

Rodman, P. and H. McHenry. 1980. Bioenergentics and the origin of hominid bipedalism. *American Journal of Physical Anthropology*, 52(1):103–6.

Roe, D. 1970. *Prehistory: An Introduction*. Berkeley, CA: University of California Press.

Roebroeks, W. 1988. *From Find Scatters to Early Hominid Behaviour: A Study of Middle Palaeolithic Riverside Settlements at Maastricht-Belvedere (The Netherlands)* Leiden: University of Leiden.

Roebroeks, W., N. Conard, and T. Kolfschoten. 1992. Dense forests, cold steppes, and the Palaeolithic settlement of northern Europe. *Current Anthropology*, 33(5):551–86.

Ross, C. 2004. Life histories and the evolution of large brain size in great apes, in *The Evolution of Thought: Evolutionary Origins of Great Ape Intelligence*. Edited by A. Russon and D. Begun, pp. 122–39. Cambridge: Cambridge University Press.

Rossano, M. 2006. The religious mind and the evolution of religion. *Review of General Psychology*, 10:346–64.

Rossano, M. 2007. Did meditating make us human? *Cambridge Archaeological Journal*, 17:47–58.

Roth, G. and U. Dicke. 2005. Evolution of the brain and intelligence. *Trends in Cognitive Science*, 9(5):251–7.

Russell, J. 1996. Development and evolution of the symbolic function: The role of working memory, in *Modelling the Early Human Mind*. Edited by P. Mellars and K. Gibson, pp. 159–77. Cambridge: McDonald Institute for Archaeological Research.

Sabater Pi, J., J. Vea, and J. Serrallonga. 1997. Did the first hominids build nests? *Current Anthropology*, 38:914–16.

Sagan, C. 1977. *The Dragons of Eden: Speculations on the Evolution of Human Intelligence*. New York: Random House.

Sandrine, C. et al. 2006. Les Pradelles (Marillac-le-Franc, France): A Mousterian reindeer hunting camp? *Journal of Anthropological Archaeology*, 25(4):466–84.

Sanz, C. and D. Morgan. 2007. Chimpanzee tool technology in the Goualougo Triangle, Republic of Congo. *Journal of Human Evolution*, 52:420–33.

Savage-Rumbaugh, D., S. Shanker, and T. Taylor. 1998. *Apes, Language, and the Human Mind*. New York: Oxford University Press.

Schacter, D. 2001. *The Seven Sins of Memory*. Boston: Houghton Mifflin.

Schacter, D. and D. Addis. 2007. The cognitive neuroscience of constructive memory: Remembering the past and imagining the future. *Phil. Trans. Soc. B.*, 362:773–86.

Schick, K. and N. Toth. 1993. *Making Silent Stones Speak: Human Evolution and the Dawn of Technology*. New York: Simon & Schuster.

Schick, K. et al. 1999. Continuing investigations into the stone tool-making capabilities of a Bonobo (*Pan paniscus*). *Journal of Archaeological Science*, 26:821–32.

Schlanger, N. 1996. Understanding Levallois: Lithic technology and cognitive archaeology. *Cambridge Archaeological Journal*, 6:231–54.

Schoenemann, P. 2006. Evolution of the size and functional areas of the human brain. *Annual Review of Anthropology*, 35:379–406.

Semaw, S. 2000. The world's oldest stone artefacts from Gona, Ethiopia: Their implications for understanding stone technology and patterns of human evolution between 2.6–1.5 million years ago. *Journal of Archaeological Science*, 27:1197–1214.

Semaw, S. et al. 2003. 2.6-million-year-old stone tools and associated bones from OGS-6 and OGS-7, Gona, Afar, Ethiopia. *Journal of Human Evolution*, 45:169–77.

Semendeferi, K. et al. 2001. Prefrontal cortex in humans and apes: a comparative study of area 10. *American Journal of Physical Anthropology*, 114:224–41.

Serre, D. A. et al. 2007. No evidence of Neandertal mtDNA contribution to early modern humans. *Public Library of Science Biology*, 2(3): e57; <www.doi:10.1371/journal.pbio.0020057>.

Sforza, E., J. Krieger, and C. Petiau. 1997. REM sleep behavior disorder: Clinical and physiopathological findings. *Sleep Medicine Revised*, 1:57–69.

Shah, P. and A. Miyake (eds.). 2005. *The Cambridge Handbook of Visuospatial Thinking*. Cambridge: Cambridge University Press.

Shea, J. 1993. Lithic use-wear evidence for hunting by Neandertals and early modern humans from the Levantine Mousterian, in *Hunting and Animal Exploitation in the Later Palaeolithic and Mesolithic of Eurasia*. Edited by G. Peterkin, H. Bricker, and P. Mellars, pp. 189–98. Washington, DC: American Anthropological Association.

Shea, J. 2006. Comment on "What's a mother to do: The division of labor among Neandertals and modern humans in Eurasia." *Current Anthropology*, 47:968.

Shea, J., J. Fleagle, and Z. Assefa. 2007. Context and chronology of early *Homo sapiens* fossils from the Omo Kibish, in *Rethinking the Human Revolution*. Edited by P. Mellars et al., pp. 153–64. Cambridge: McDonald Institute for Archaeological Research.

Shepard, R. 1997. The genetic basis of human scientific knowledge, in *Characterizing Human Psychological Adaptations*. Edited by G. Bock and G. Cardew, pp. 4–13. Chichester: Wiley & Sons.

Shostak, M. 1981. *Nisa: The Life and Words of !Kung Woman*. New York: Vintage Books.

Siegel, J. M. 2001. The REM sleep-memory consolidation hypothesis. *Science*, 294:1058–63.

Silverman, I. and M. Eals. 1992. Sex differences in spatial abilities: Evolutionary theory and data, in *The Adapted Mind: Evolutionary Psychology and the Generation of Culture*. Edited by J. Barkow, L. Cosmides, and J. Tooby, pp. 487–503. New York: Oxford University Press.

Silverman, I. et al. 2000. Evolved mechanisms underlying wayfinding: Further studies on the hunter-gatherer theory of spatial sex differences. *Evolution and Human Behavior*, 21:201–13.

Smith, C. and C. MacNeill. 1994. Impaired motor memory for a pursuit rotor task following Stage 2 sleep loss in college students. *Journal of Sleep Research*, 3:206–13.

Sockol, M., D. Raichlen, and H. Pontzer. 2007. Chimpanzee locomotor energetics and the origin of human bipedalism. *Proceedings of the National Academy of Sciences*, 104(30):12265–9.

Solms, M. 2000. Dreaming and REM sleep are controlled by different brain mechanisms. *Behavioral and Brain Sciences*, 23:843–50.

Speth, J. 2006. Housekeeping, Neandertal-style: Hearth placement and midden formation in Kebara Cave (Israel), in *Transitions Before the Transition: Evolution and Stability in the Middle Paleolithic and Middle Stone Age*. Edited by E. Hovers and S. Kuhn, pp. 171–88. New York: Springer.

Stanley, S. 1992. An ecological theory for the origin of *Homo*. *Paleobiology*, 18:237–57.

Stanovich, K. 1999. *Who is Rational? Studies of Individual Differences in Reasoning*. Hillsdale, NJ: Erlbaum.

Stickgold, R., L. James, and A. Hobson. 2000. Visual discrimination learning requires sleep after training. *Nature Neuroscience*, 2:1237–8.

Stout, D. 2002. Skill and cognition in stone tool production. *Current Anthropology*, 43:693–722.

Stout, D. et al. 2000. Stone tool-making and brain activation: Positron emission tomography (PET) studies. *Journal of Archaeological Science*, 27:1215–23.

Straus, L. G. 1996. The archaeology of the Pleistocene-Holocene transition in southwest Europe, in *Humans at the End of the Ice Age: The Archaeology of the Pleistocene-Holocene transition*. Edited by L. G. Straus, B. V. Eriksen, J. Erlandson, and D. Yesner. New York: Plenum Press.

Stringer, C. B. 2007. The origin and dispersal of *Homo sapiens*: Our current state of knowledge, in *Rethinking the Human Revolution*. Edited by P. Mellars, K. Boyle, O. Bar-Yosef, and C. B. Stringer, pp. 15–20. Cambridge: McDonald Institute for Archaeological Research.

Suddendorf, T. and M. Corballis. 2007. The evolution of foresight: What is mental time travel, and is it unique to humans? *Behavioral and Brain Sciences*, 30:299–313.

Teaford, M., P. Ungar, and F. Grine. 2002. Paleontological evidence for the diets of African Plio-Pleistocene hominins with special reference to early *Homo*, in *Human Diet: Its Origin and Evolution*. Edited by P. Ungar and M. Teaford, pp. 143–66. Westport, CT: Bergin and Garvey.

Thieme, H. 1997. Lower Palaeolithic hunting spears from Germany. *Nature*, 385:807–10.

Thieme, H. 2005. The Lower Palaeolithic art of hunting: The case of Schoningen 13 II–4, Lower Saxony, Germany, in *The Hominid Individual in Context: Archaeological Investigations of Lower and Middle Palaeolitic Landscapes, Locales, and Artefacts*. Edited by C. Gamble and M. Porr, pp. 115–32. New York: Routledge.

Thorne, A. et al. 1999. Australia's oldest human remains: age of the Lake Mungo 3 skeleton. *Journal of Human Evolution*, 36:591–612.

Tobias, P. 1987. The brain of *Homo habilis*: A new level of organization in cerebral evolution. *Journal of Human Evolution*, 16:741–61.

Tomasello, M. and J. Call. 1997. *Primate Cognition*. New York: Oxford University Press.

Toth, N. 1985. Archaeological evidence for preferential right-handedness in the Lower and Middle Pleistocene, and its possible implications. *Journal of Human Evolution*, 14:607–14.

Toth, N. et al. 1993. Pan the tool-maker: Investigations into the stone tool-making and tool-using capabilties of a bonobo (*Pan paniscus*). *Journal of Archaeological Science*, 20:81–91.

Trinkaus, E. 2006. Modern human versus Neandertal evolutionary distinctiveness. *Current Anthropology*, 47:597–622.

Tulving, E. 2002. Episodic memory: From mind to brain. *Annual Review of Psychology*, 53:1–25.

Turkheimer, E. 2000. Three laws of behavior genetics and what they mean. *Current Directions in Psychological Science*, 9:160–4.

Ungar, P., F. Grine, M. Teaford, and S. Zaatari. 2006. Dental microwear and diets of African early *Homo*. *Journal of Human Evolution*, 50:78–95.

Uomini, N. 2006. Where are the left–handed knappers?, in *XVth Congress of the International Union for Prehistoric and Protohistoric Research*. Lisbon, Portugal.

Valli, K. et al. 2005. The threat simulation theory of the evolutionary function of dreaming: Evidence from dreams of traumatized children. *Consciousness and Cognition*, 14:188–218.

Van de Castle, R. 1983. Animal figures in fantasy and dreams, in *New Perspectives on Our Lives with Companion Animals*. Edited by A. Kacher and A. Beck, pp. 148–73. Philadelphia, PA: University of Pennsylvania Press.

Van de Castle, R. 1994. *Our Dreaming Mind: A Sweeping Exploration of the Role that Dreams Have Played in Politics, Art, Religion, and Psychology, from Ancient Civilizations to the Present Day*. New York: Ballantine Books.

Vertes, R. P. and K. E. Eastman. 2000. The case against memory consolidation in REM sleep. *Behavioral and Brain Sciences*, 23:867–76.

Villa, P. 1983. *Terra Amata and the Middle Pleistocene Archaeological Record of Southern France*. Berkeley, CA: University of California Press.

Vincent, J. et al. 2007. Intrinsic functional architecture in the anaesthetized monkey brain. *Nature*, 447:83–6.

Wadley, L., B. Williamson, and M. Lombard. 2004. Ochre in hafting Middle Stone Age southern Africa: A practical role. *Antiquity*, 78(301):661–75.

Wagner, U., S. Gais, and J. Born. 2001. Emotional memory formation is enhanced across sleep intervals with high amounts of rapid eye movement sleep. *Learning & Memory*, 8:112–19.

Wagner, U. et al. 2004. Sleep inspires insight. *Nature*, 427:352–5.

Walker, A. and R. Leakey (eds.). 1993. *The Nariokotome Homo erectus Skeleton*. Cambridge, MA: Harvard University Press.

Walker, A. and C. Ruff. 1993. The reconstruction of the pelvis, in *The Nariokotome Homo erectus Skeleton*. Edited by A. Walker and R. Leakey. Cambridge, MA: Harvard University Press.

Walker, M. 2005. A refined model of sleep and the time course of memory formation. *Behavioral and Brain Sciences*, 28:51–104.

Walker, M. and R. Stickgold. 2004. Sleep-dependent learning and memory consolidation. *Neuron*, 44:121–33.

Walker, M. P. et al. 2002. Practice with sleep makes perfect: Sleep dependent motor skill learning. *Neuron*, 35:205–11.

Walker, M. P. et al. 2003. Sleep and the time course of motor skill learning. *Learning & Memory*, 4:275–84.

Weaver, A. H. 2005. Reciprocal evolution of the cerebellum and neocortex in fossil humans. *Proceedings of the National Academy of Sciences*, 102:3576–80.

Wells, C. and J. Stock. 2007. The biology of the colonizing ape. *Yearbook of Physical Anthropology*, 50:191–222.

Welsh, M. and B. Pennington. 1988. Assessing frontal lobe functioning in children: Views from developmental psychology. *Developmental Neuropsychology*, 4:199–230.

Westway, K. et al. 2007. Age and biostratigraphic significance of the Punung Rainforest fauna, East Java, Indonesia, and implications for *Pongo* and *Homo*. *Journal of Human Evolution*, 53(6):709–17.

White, M. and N. Ashton. 2003. Lower Palaeolithic core technology and the origins of the Levallois method in North-Western Europe. *Current Anthropology*, 44:598–609.

White, R. 2001. Personal ornaments from the Grotte du Renne at Arcy-sur-Cure. *Athena Review*, 2:41–6.

White, T., B. Asfaw, and D. DeGusta. 2003. Pleistocene *Homo sapiens* from Middle Awash, Ethiopia. *Nature*, 423:742–7.

Wing, Y. K., S. T. Lee, and C. N. Chen. 1994. Sleep paralysis in Chinese: Ghost Oppression Phenomenon in Hong Kong. *Sleep*, 7(7):609–13.

Winson, J. 1990. The meaning of dreams. *Scientific American*, 263:89–96.

Wolpoff, M. et al. 2004. Why *not* Neandertals? *World Archaeology*, 36(4):527–46.

Wood, B. A. and M. Collard. 1999. The human genus. *Science*, 284:65–72.

Wrangham, R. W. et al. 1999. The raw and the stolen: Cooking and the ecology of human origins. *Current Anthropology*, 40:567–94.

Wynn, T. 1989. *The Evolution of Spatial Competence*. Urbana, IL: University of Illinois Press.

Wynn, T. 1991. Tools, grammar, and the archaeology of cognition. *Cambridge Archaeological Journal*, 1:191–206.

Wynn, T. 2002. Archaeology and cognitive evolution. *Behavioral and Brain Sciences*, 25:389–438.

Wynn, T. and F. Coolidge. 2004. The expert Neandertal mind. *Journal of Human Evolution*, 46:467–87.

Wynn, T., F. Tierson, and C. Palmer, 1996. Evolution of sex differences in spatial cognition. *Yearbook of Physical Anthropology*, 39:11–42.

Yamakoshi, G. 2004. Evolution of complex feeding techniques in primates: Is this the origin of great ape intelligence?, in *The Evolution of Thought: Evolutionary Origins of Great Ape Intelligence*. Edited by A. Russon and D. Begun. Cambridge Cambridge University Press.

Zachos, J. et al. 2001. Trends, rhythms, and aberrations in global climate 65 MA to present. *Science*, 292(5517):686–93.

Zeveloff, S. and M. Boyce. 1982. Why human neonates are so altricial. *American Naturalist*, 120:537–42.

Index